MORAL EDUCATION

SECULAR AND RELIGIOUS

MORAL
EDUCATION

SECULAR AND RELIGIOUS

John L. Elias
Fordham University

ROBERT E. KRIEGER PUBLISHING COMPANY
MALABAR, FLORIDA
1989

Original Edition 1989

Printed and Published by
ROBERT E. KRIEGER PUBLISHING CO., INC.
KRIEGER DRIVE
MALABAR, FLORIDA 32950

Library of Congress Cataloging-in-Publication Data

Elias, John L., 1933-
    Moral Education

    Bibliography: p.
    Includes index.
    1. Moral Education--United States. 2. Social values.
I. Title.
LC311.E45 1989   370.11'4   87-29715
ISBN 0-89464-260-X

10   9   8   7   6   5   4   3   2

TABLE OF CONTENTS

PREFACE

This book is a labor of love. It has taken many years of hard work to put its various parts together and to bring it to completion. For twelve years I have read and gathered material, discussed the various chapters with students and colleagues both in the United States and in Britain, and taken the painful effort to revise the material on many occasions. Though I have written other books during this time, this is the work that has most engaged my thoughts and my energies. I am relieved that the labor is now over.

Thinking back over the years I remember not only the labor but also the love that has come into my life during this time. I remember fondly the many students and colleagues with whom I have worked with this material at Trenton State College, LaSalle University, Fordham University, the University of Birmingham, England, St. Mary's College, Strawberry Hill, England, and most recently at Union Theological Seminary, New York City. In England I benefited greatly from conversations about the book with John Hull, Michael Grimmitt, and Donal O'Leary. In this country I have been enriched at Fordham University by collaboration with Gloria Durka, a keen and loving colleague and critic.

I am very grateful to Christina Rodriquez Battista, my editor at Krieger Publishing Co., for her many helpful suggestions.

The writing of this book has benefited from my labor of love in attempting to influence the moral character of my two daughters, Rachel and Rebecca.

I dedicate this book to my wife Eleanor Flanigan who has patiently waited for this book these many years and whose love has made my labor less strenuous and more rewarding.

John Elias
Fordham University

INTRODUCTION

MORAL EDUCATION: AN OVERVIEW

In the most recent criticisms of the public schools and colleges of this country politicians, educators, and ordinary citizens have called upon the schools to involve themselves in moral education or education in values. This call has come from both liberals and conservatives. President Reagan, Secretary of Education William Bennett, Governor Mario Cuomo and many others have focused attention on the need for schools to move beyond basic knowledge and skills in order to deal with questions of moral choice. The calls for moral education also include appeals for greater family involvement, continued church and synagogue participation, and the support of all institutions of society.

These recent calls for more moral education need to be brought into contact with renewed scholarly interest in this field during the past two decades. Scholarly and popular journals have published numerous articles on these topics. This new interest in moral and values education questions the conventional wisdom and practice of many countries. According to conventional wisdom religion and morals are exclusively the province of religious bodies and the family while schools and other institutions are responsible for education in basic skills, academic learning and career or job training. Concern for the role of moral education on the part of many institutions is a dimension of this new interest. Particular interest has arisen with regard to the role of all forms of schooling in the teaching of moral values. The increase in the teaching of ethics in colleges, universities, and professional schools is an aspect of this recent phenomenon (Callahan and Bok 1980). Though it focuses primarily on the young, the interest in moral education also includes adults of all ages. The work of developmental psychologists now extends to the study of maturation in moral reasoning throughout the entire life span (Kohlberg 1984).

The present concern with moral education is not unprecedented in educational history. Moral education has long been associated with schooling as well as with the responsibilities of families and religious bodies. In most countries the first schools were established under religious auspices in order to provide religious training and to aid in the formation of good moral character. The Protestant ethic or moral system was for many years an explicit part of the curriculum in schools in the United States. England and European countries have traditionally included programs to promote the values of good citizenship and to encourage moral standards in society. Private and religious schools in England and Europe, as well as in the United States, have been even more explicit than public or state schools about the moral values which they attempt to inculcate in their students.

Public schools in the United States and elsewhere have in the course of time given less explicit attention to moral education. With the rise of cultural and religious pluralism, scientific objectivity, and sensitivity to the rights of all persons, moral education as distinct from civic education is no longer considered the province of public schools. In recent times teachers in public schools have avoided serious inquiry into the realm of moral values, especially on controversial topics. In higher education, however, this has not always been the case. Ethics courses have always been a part of the curriculum of many colleges (Sloan 1980).

Today moral education again engages educators in the United States and elsewhere. Attitude changes and the events of the past two decades have raised moral questions for society in general and for schools in particular. Such issues as nuclear war, poverty, violence, abortion, sexual freedom, and medical experimentation are matters of public debate in many societies. Moral issues have been raised in the United States relating to the Watergate scandals, CIA activities, the Iran-Contra scandals, capital punishment, over-consumption of food, the pollution of the environment, attacks by terrorists, and the depletion of natural resources. There are a multitude of issues pertaining to both individual and social life where ethical decisions must be made and where education can play at least a modest role in the decision-making process.

A concern for moral education is manifest in the writings of past and present educators. In the United States, such educators as Horace Mann and William T. Harris clearly stated that a major task of the public school was the moral education of children and youth (Perkinson 1977). At the heart of John Dewey's (1916) progressive theory of education was a pervading concern for moral instruction. The religious philosopher Jacques Maritain (1943) argued during World War II for a liberal education which included training in values as an essential part. Charles Silberman (1970), a critic of American education in the early 1970s, contended that the problem with American education at that time was the lack of attention to the moral purposes of education. The Latin American educator, Paulo Freire (1970) has criticized all forms of education that purport to be neutral in the values which they foster. In more recent times Neil Postman (1979) has argued for a more conservative curriculum which would emphasize moral education through literature, history, religion, and social studies. A strong plea for attention to both moral and religious education is also found in Harold Bloom's (1987) critique of American education. Educational philosphers in the United Kingdom, notably Peters (1966), Wilson (1967), and Hirst (1974) have presented analyses of moral education and even offered concrete programs for its implementation.

It must be clearly noted that these proponents of moral education are in the liberal tradition and have strenuously argued against all forms of moral guidance which are not consonant with the principles of human freedom. Proposals for a renewed moral education have also come from conservative forces, religious and nonreligious, and often do not show adequate sensitivity to the demands of human freedom and the conditions of a democratic society. Their suggestions often espouse forms of indoctrination which attempt to induce others to accept particular moral stances. Since many of these proposals are often made in the name of religion, one of the aims of this book is to show that a religiously based moral education need not offend sound educational theory and practice.

MORAL EDUCATION: AN INTERDISCIPLINARY STUDY

My interest in the study of moral education began with a seminar that I taught in the 1970s on the teaching of moral values. What I learned from this seminar was that moral education is a far more complex matter than I had thought. My initial feeling was that armed with the knowledge of Lawrence Kohlberg's theory of moral development and education as well as with the strategies of the values clarification approach, teachers were in a position to do a credible job of educating the young in moral values. This book is an argument against this simplistic position.

Moral education is an interdisciplinary field of study. To approach this field through one discipline only is both limited and dangerous. Educators must give attention to theories and research which come from a number of disciplines and which contribute to our understanding of the complex processes of moral education. In this book I have attempted to bring together what I consider the most promising work in this field.

First it is necessary to know the history of past efforts in moral education, many of which involved the activities of religious bodies to socialize their young members. Such efforts reveal interesting connections between religious beliefs and moral behaviors. Religious institutions attempted to balance moral education for life in this world with education for eternal life. Religious educators advocated both soft and hard forms of pedagogy. The most relevant part of this history is the issue of the development of various approaches to a secular moral education with the work of Durkheim, Piaget, and Dewey. Much of the present debate about moral education must be seen in relationship to the work of these men. Even present proposals for a religiously based moral education must attend to the theories developed in secular spheres.

Moral education has always received extensive coverage by philosophers of all schools of thought. Plato and Aristotle produced the first systematic treatises in moral education—Plato's *Republic* and *Laws*, and Aristotle's *Ethics* and *Politics*. Medieval philosophy was greatly engaged in issues of the nature and acquisition of virtue. All systems of modern philosophy have devoted attention to moral education. Existentialists have focused on issues of human freedom. Analytic philosophers have discussed the concepts and arguments used in moral education. Pragmatic thought, following Dewey's work, has concentrated on educational theory and strategies in this area. In their concern to define the good life, the good society, and the good person, all philosophers have entered in some way the domain of moral education.

In recent years the discipline of psychology has perhaps made the most significant contribution to the theory and practice of moral education. While the basic thrust of psychology in the United States has been behavioristic, a growing number of psychologists have focused on the formation of internal attitudes. Lawrence Kohlberg's work is foremost in this area, with his carefully researched theory of moral stages. Yet the full contribution of psychology is not appreciated unless works from other moral psychologists are also examined. Among the significant theories in this area are a psycho-analytic approach (Erikson 1964), a social learning theory (Bandura 1977), and a humanistic approach (Allport 1955; Rogers, 1969; Maslow 1968). There is also an effort to integrate these various psychological theories for developing a theory of moral leadership (Burns 1978).

The study of values and their transmission has always been of concern to social scientists, especially social psychologists, sociologists, and anthropologists. Social scientists take on the perspectives of groups, institutions, and culture and the influence of these in transmitting values, including moral values. A behavioristic approach is found in Milton Rokeach's (1973) analysis of values and attitudes. The discipline of sociology of knowledge probes at a theoretical level the acquisition and formation of values. A classic work in the functionalist tradition of sociology is Durkheim's *Moral Education* (1961) which argues for the essential role of the schools for forming moral persons. Important issues in empirical social science studies include the influence of families, peer groups, schools, religious bodies, media, the world of work, and the general community on the development of moral values. A cross cultural perspective is presented in the classical works of anthropologists such as Ruth Benedict (1956), Clyde Kluckholn (1962), Margaret Mead (1970), and Clifford Geertz (1973).

Considering the attention paid to moral education by scholars in the previously mentioned disciplines, it is surprising to find that theologians and religious scholars have not paid much attention to the educational dimensions of morality. The field of religious ethics or moral theology is an extensive one but most of this kind of work takes the confessional, the pulpit, the lecture hall, and counseling situation as the point of reference and application. Religious educators have of course written extensively in this area, but most often their work is not grounded in strong theological principles. C. E. Nelson (1967) and Craig Dykstra (1981) have written important works on religious education that address moral instruction. One of the main purposes of this book is to examine more closely the relationship of theology, religious ethics, and education.

As might be expected educationists have given the most attention to moral education. No clear distinction can be made between this group and previous groups because educationists usually view issues from the perspective of the academic disciplines of history, philosophy, psychology, and the social sciences. The uniqueness of the educationists' contribution lies, however, in their concern for curricular theory and development, the design of methods for teaching and learning, and the evaluation of processes of moral education. Several distinctive approaches to moral or values education have appeared in the field of education: values clarification, moral reasoning, problem solving, behavioral modification as well as such social learning processes as modeling, internalization, and imitation. Each of these theories will receive exposition, analysis, and criticism in chapter six.

The interdisciplinary approach to moral education has the advantage of including many different perspectives. Yet the approach may be a bit bewildering if there are not some central issues which are common to the various disciplines and which serve as unifying focuses. My major unifying focus will be the attempt to bring religion into dialogue with other disciplines. I will discuss this in the next section. There are, however, other themes which I will discuss from chapter to chapter, the presentation of which will be less systematic. A mention of these themes will alert the reader to other issues which I consider of paramount importance.

First, moral education must deal with the tension between serving individual purposes and social purposes. As educators we may experience tension in attempting to educate both good individuals and good citizens. Secondly, moral educators must make decisions on the existence and importance of moral principles, as well as their justification and application. Thirdly, the relative merits of reason and affect must be weighed as elements in moral education. Fourthly, moral educators must grapple with the content and form that moral education should take in its actual practice.

Underlying all of these issues is a question: how does one describe the morally educated person? I have asked this question in several chapters to organize various theories. In describing how the moral person is educated attention must be paid to the promotion of freedom and the avoidance of indoctrination. Chazan (1985) has analyzed theories around such principles as I have enunciated. The one issue which has not engaged him in his important work is the role of religion. The possible role that religion plays is the distinctive contribution that this work may bring to the study and practice of moral education.

RELIGION AND MORAL EDUCATION

My purpose in this book is to develop an approach to moral education based on sound principles of religious faith and secular learning. To do this I will have to treat both secular and religious theories. My book attempts to integrate religious faith with contemporary understandings of persons, communities, and societies. My judgment is that moral education in religious bodies, and especially in religious schools, is not profoundly religious if it ignores either religious traditions or contemporary scientific theories and research. I also think that moral education in secular contexts can benefit from an analysis of the contribution that religion can make to moral education.

I have not written this book because of a belief that a secular moral education is either impossible or undesirable. Actually, I believe that the development of a secular approach should be an important goal for all schools. The excellent systems of moral education that are based on purely educational grounds needs more attention from policy makers and teachers in public schools. Efforts in moral education appear much stronger in the United Kingdom than in the United States, because religious education is a compulsory subject for schools in Britain.

It is my belief that educators in public or state schools may benefit from a knowledge of the possible contributions of religion to moral education. There is an extremely close connection between the religious and the moral both at a theoretical level and in the everyday lives of individuals. Teachers cannot realistically ignore their own religious convictions and those of their students in classroom teaching. Great care must be exercised in this area, as a discussion of the topic in later chapter will show. Secular educators have come to this realization, especially in Britain but also in the United States. Writing on the inadequacy of a completely secular and cognitive approach to moral education, Oliver and Bane noted that:

Educators, philosophers, and psychologists should join with theologians and sensitive youth in a search for the kind of powerful metaphor with which our Christian heritage once provided us. We somehow need to create myths and celebrations by which we can project the common joys, sorrows and compassion that we share simply by the fact that we are human (1971, ch. 9).

Though I heartily agree with these sentiments, it is my belief that we need to extend our search beyond the Christian heritage to include the insights of all religious faiths on moral education.

CHAPTER 1

HISTORICAL PERSPECTIVES ON MORAL EDUCATION

Moral education has a long and interesting history which cannot be retold in this relatively short chapter. A historical perspective, however, is essential since what happens in moral education today is related in many ways to how previous generations attempted to produce good and moral persons. It must be noted that forms of moral education from the past might appear to be more appropriately called moral or character training, for they were directed more at controlling the activities and behaviors of persons than at appealing to their reason and judgment. Earlier forms, however, are still interesting and important because it is clear that they still exist today, especially in the education of young children.

My intention in this chapter is to present some of the highlights of theory and practice in moral education. In the earlier sections of the chapter greater attention is given to forms of moral education which are inspired by religious principles. The Renaissance and Enlightment periods were times in which more secular approaches to moral education began to appear. Twentieth century developments include secular and religious approaches. The reader will be surprised to learn that what are often presented as new ideas resemble ideas of ancient times. My major source for the earlier sections of this chapter is Castle's classic work *Educating the Good Man: Moral Education in* ✓ *Christian Times* (1958).

Other than in the first part of this chapter my historical survey will include mainly Christian writers on moral education. In chapter five I will treat orthodox and modern forms of Jewish moral education.

JUDAISM AND EARLY CHRISTIAN TIMES

In moral education, as in other areas of life, the early Christians drew on the moral and religious training practiced in Judaism. The lives of the patriarchs, the sermons of the prophets, and the advice found in the writings of the sages were important sources for early Christians. Christians also continued a number of practices found in Judaism. In Judaism and Christianity the crucial institution for moral training was the family. In the home the father was both teacher and priest. His primary religious duties were found in the *Shema*, the daily prayer of the Jews for the past two thousand years. It was the father's responsibility to recite and teach the highest moral formula in both Judaism and Christianity:

> Hear, O Israel: The Lord our God is one Lord; and you shall love the Lord your God with all your heart, and with all your soul, and with all your might. And these words which I command you this day shall be upon your heart; and you shall teach them diligently to your children, and shall talk of them when you sit in your house, and when you walk by the way, and when you lie down, and when you rise (Deuteronomy 6:4–7 Revised Standard Version).

The responsibility of Jewish parents was to teach the law of God through example and through brief ceremonies which were intended to provoke questions from children. Formal moral education consisted in teaching, studying, and obeying the Torah—the written law of the Pentateuch and the moral tradition concerning moral behavior. At four children were taught the *Shema*; at thirteen they were taken to the synagogue to become responsible for observing the entire law, a law which included the commandments of Moses, the prescriptions of the Torah, and regulations added by rabbis and Jewish leaders.

To supplement the work of the family some schools were established in the later Hellenistic period. In these schools pupils learned the sacred writings by constant repetition and mnemonic devices. The Book of Proverbs apparently supplied the educational philosophy for these schools. Punishment and learning were close allies in the educational process. There were also more pleasant inducements to learning, such as a handful of nuts and a taste of honey. The work of the family and of these schools was reinforced by a closely knit community that carefully supervised the activities of the young.

Besides following the practices of Judaism, early Christians were also influenced by Greek and Roman forms of education. In the early years Christians did not set up their own schools, but rather sent their young to Greek and Roman schools. Many Christian leaders had misgivings about this practice because they perceived a fundamental conflict between the Christian scriptures and the pagan literature that included the values of Greece and Rome. Some Christians attempted to gather sound values from such secular writings without being corrupted by the errors they found there. Thus the practice of censoring certain objectionable passages in pagan writings began early in the history of the Christian Church.

In the early centuries Christian moral education drew mainly on the four Gospels and on the Epistles of Paul. The actions, sermons, and parables of Jesus expressed the highest ideals of the community. These contained both moral demands and exhortations. Jesus acted in accordance with the rabbinic tradition when he assumed the role of teacher of the law and teller of stories that contained moral messages. His example and message were the primary sources used in preaching to and teaching the adult members of the community. In later centuries his message was adapted for the education of young Christians to such an extent that moral education became identified with education of children. The adult-centeredness of education in Christian living which is emphasized today is a recovery of an original posture of the Christian Church.

There are numerous teachings and exhortations in the Epistles of Paul which stressed the need for moral and religious conversion. His message, like that of Jesus, was addressed primarily to adult members of the community. In Paul's letter to the Ephesians, however, there is an example of moral education relating to children:

Children, obey your parents in the Lord, for this is right. "Honor your father and mother" (This is the first commandment with a promise), "that it may be well with you, and that you may live a long life on earth." Fathers, do not provoke your children to anger, but bring them up in the discipline and instruction of the Lord (Ephesians 6:1–4, RSV).

The moral education proposed both explicitly and implicitly in Christian scriptures can be briefly grouped around a number of themes (O'Connell 1976, pp. 20–29). Through baptism Christians enter into a moral *covenant* with God by virtue of which they believe that God will be faithful to them if they keep his commandments. Moral life has the purpose of fostering the coming of the *reign of God*, God's power over all creation. The Gospel call is in the form of a summons to *repentance*, a change of mind and heart involving a personal moral revolution. All Christians are called to *discipleship*, a life of learning from and about Jesus. As one of its major elements this discipleship includes the following of the *law* which Jesus proclaimed, a law which puts less emphasis on external rituals and more on interior attitudes. Nowhere is this interiority stressed more than in the law of *love* which Jesus proclaimed as the essential characteristic of the Christian community. Finally, moral demands are expressed in the demanding *beatitudes*, which promised blessedness for qualities and deeds which go counter to what is ordinarily expected of individuals.

The Christian community by attempting to live up to these high ideals was itself a force for moral education, as was the Jewish community. The Book of the Acts of the Apostles present us with a picture of a community which held all things in common and which was concerned with breaches of moral law. An essential purpose for the ministry of teaching was to establish moral control over the community. There were also regular meetings of Christians for the supervision of members and correction of deviations from acceptable standards by community members. In small communities these deviations were well known and steps had to be taken lest bad example and scandal be given to other members of the community.

Early writings of the Christian community placed a great stress on the necessity of proper moral formation. The *Didache* described two ways, the way of virtue and the way of evil. Christian writers such as Clement of Alexandria and Jerome of Jerusalem attempted to balance a moral optimism which looked favorably on secular values with a moral pessimism which emphasized dangerous and sinful elements of the culture. In the writings of Basil of Caesarea is found the suggestion that parents and teachers should balance love, sympathy, and humanity with correction and punishment. The task of the teacher of the young is to correct their sins with fatherly compassion by applying appropriate sanctions to each offender (Castle 1958, pp. 22–25).

Though many of the early Christian writers wrote on moral training, it is John Chrysostom who presented the most complete treatise on the subject. In his address *On Vainglory and the Right Way for Parents to Bring up their Children* he spoke of moral training as molding the plastic material of childhood into a shape approved by God. In his view the task of parents is to provide and uphold laws that inspire fear and that are firm. Chrysostom recommended using some of the more fearful tales of divine retribution found in the Bible: Cain, Esau, and Sodom. He gave a dubious bit of advice when he recommended that parents and older children should test a child's advancement in self control by provoking the child to anger (Castle 1958, p. 26).

Some of the wisest advice on moral education in the early church is found in the writings of Augustine, Bishop of Hippo, a man recognized as a moral rigorist. In his theory of education he emphasized the "indwelling" capacity of the pupil to learn with encouragement and love. Augustine presented a strikingly modern approach to the development of ethical insight in his emphasis on internal dynamics, introspection, and induction. Furthermore, he counseled teachers to begin their instructions with an awareness of the concrete situation of each child. For Augustine learning derived from a response of the students to the teacher's confidence in their capacity to respond correctly. Moral education, like all education, is possible because of the capacity of one person to dwell within another and because of the sympathetic disposition that affects both teachers and pupils.

The early Christian Church's interest in moral formation showed itself in the institution of the catechumenate (Dujarier 1979). Those who wished to join the community had to undergo a period of training and testing with special care by members of the community and under the direction of the bishop. Candidates for membership were expected to establish their moral character as a prerequisite for initiation into the community. Alongside instruction in the doctrines and beliefs of the church the catechumens also received instruction in the moral responsibilities of Christians living in a non-Christian society. When the practice of infant baptism became wide-spread, the catechumenate for adults was abandoned. In the past two decades there has been in the Roman Catholic Church an attempt to restore the adult catechumenate.

Another insight into the moral formation of adults is found in the Penitential books which appeared in the sixth century. Confession of sins, publicly and privately, was viewed as a powerful method of moral and religious development. Penitential books contained lists of typical sins and appropriate penances for them. These books were used by priest-confessors, first in Ireland and then in other areas. For many persons this practice had the effect of reducing the Christian life to a minimal practice, focusing as it did on the avoidance of specific sins. Yet the entire institution of repentance which included confession, absolution, and penance has remained in many Christian churches a powerful force for moral insight and development.

In summary then, the earliest teaching on Jewish and Christian moral education included several methods: example, obedience, exhortation, punishment, development of habits, the study of religious literature and censored secular literature, correction, the use of fear, the provocation of temptations, and the loving approach in Augustine's teaching on personal indwelling. Many of these forms will appear again in the later history of moral education.

MIDDLE AGES

An essential aspect of medieval thinking in religious circles was a concentration on attaining a place in the next world. Other-wordly piety thus became the great concern of religious and moral education. This attitude was manifested in the religious life of parishes and monasteries but particularly in the newly founded schools in the Empire. The educational theory of these new schools was also largely shaped by ideas and practices of the earlier period of Christian education.

The accounts of education in the schools of this period give little in the way of the moral content of education or the methods of discipline used. Grammar, liberal arts, and the Scriptures made up the curriculum of the medieval school. Secular knowledge went hand and hand with religious knowledge. Flogging and the use of the rod appeared to be major instruments in the moral education of the young in medieval schools, although there are some examples of more kindly efforts.

One of the great medieval schoolmasters was Alcuin (d. 804). His major accomplishment was the development of education during Charlemagne's reign, especially at the palace of the Emperor. In his educational theory he added the seven gifts of the Holy Spirit (wisdom, understanding, fortitude, counsel, knowledge, piety, understanding, and fear of the Lord) to the seven liberal arts in keeping with his devotion to the Christian Church and its task of elevating moral life in society. Alcuin's interest in educating adults for literacy was subordinated to religious and moral purposes. Moral virtues were to be the by-product of reading and writing. For him secular knowledge was the handmaiden of divine wisdom and the steps of grammatical and philosophical discipline were to lead to the summit of evangelical perfection (Duckett in Castle 1958, p. 33). A critical commentary on Alcuin's efforts to educate persons whom he considered barbarians points out that his desire was to draw persons nearer to the Divine truth through a better understanding of religious literature. His method of training for virtue was based on the view that:

> The road to virtue being religion, and the road to religion being religious knowledge, the educational enterprise acquired a character and tone which made it more than remedial literacy or a royal hobby (Broudy and Palmer 1965, p. 58).

Among the educators of this time, Anselm of Canterbury (d.1109) was a strong voice for kind treatment of the young. He opposed beatings as a way to correct them. He advised that: "The weak must be treated with gentleness and won with love; you must invite a soul to virtue with cheerfulness and charitably bear with its defects" (Anselm in Castle 1958, p. 38).

Although many monastic institutions did not always heed Anselm's advice on the gentle invitation to virtue, one person who did listen was the eminent chancellor of the University of Paris, John Gerson (d. 1429). His writings on the moral education of children emphasized the importance of smiles, play, and praise in leading children to Christ. Gerson advised special concern in dealing with children in the confession of sins.

Unfortunately, Anselm and Gerson represented exceptions to the general educational systems of this period (Castle 1958, p. 41). Both recognized that the practice of incessant flogging was contrary to the example of Jesus in the Gospels and the advice of the Apostle Paul. The practice of "developing character" through flogging and beatings is one with a long history in moral training. Even in our time there are periodic arguments and debates over the educational and reformist value of such punishments.

A different form of moral education took place in the schools for chivalry where middle class boys were prepared for professional careers. In these schools the attempt was made to join military and Christian ideals. The ideals stressed in chivalric education included courage in battle, loyalty to comrades, and mercy to the vanquished. To these were added some ideals of a more religious and moral nature: faithfulness to the Church, protection of the weak, charity to the poor, fidelity to the pledged word, and courtesy to all persons (Castle 1958 p. 43).

A number of methods were used in schools of chivalry to achieve these lofty moral ideals. Discipline was to be learned by obedience to material things (e.g., horses and weapons), obedience to persons (master and mistress), and obedience to the ideals of the Christian religion. To this method of discipline was added emulation, which consisted of education through example. Younger boys were therefore encouraged to learn from their elders.

Any assessment of chivalric education, however, must balance its high ideals with its major weakness, its connection with one particular class in society. This education eventually became reduced to ceremonies at court and thus lost its moral characteristics. Chivalric education at its best, however, fostered valuable ideals which were later incorporated into the humanism of the Renaissance.

Education in morality was also a concern of theologians at the great medieval universities. As theological study became systematized, summaries of Christian thought were compiled which gave explicit attention to the moral life of Christians. A brilliant synthesis of theology and morality is found in the work of the Franciscan priest, Bonaventure. In his view the purpose of theological education was to make persons holy by encouraging them to use the power of their wills to decide and choose to live a moral life. Bonaventure was in the tradition of Augustine when he emphasized the power of God within persons, a power which enables them to ascend to God through the practices of various virtues.

The greatest of the medieval *summas*, however, was written by the Dominican, Thomas of Aquinas. Within his thought is found a moral theology of virtues which is indebted to the philosophy of Aristotle and the theology of Augustine. The primary thrust in Aquinas' ethical system is the emphasis on human reason and intellect. A knowledge of what is good must precede the doing of what is good. A modern interpreter of Aquinas states that he "would say that no child should be made to do a thing without understanding why he is doing it" (Beck 1964, p. 118). Following in the Augustinian tradition Aquinas argued that the living principle of knowledge and education is within the pupil. The teacher's role is secondary in contributing judgment, intellectual skill, and understanding. In the next chapter the work of Jacques Maritain, a Thomistic philosopher, will be examined to show the continuing influence of this view.

RENAISSANCE HUMANISM

The Renaissance with its goal of the development of the whole person who could be competent in many spheres of life brought about a number of particular emphases in the conduct of moral education. Inspired by humanist principles educators called for a marriage between the claims of Christian faith and the emphasis on the glorious and recently rediscovered potential of the human being. The Renaissance ideal was that of *l'uomo universale*, a soldier and a person of action, a many sided individual, noble in bearing, courtly in speech, a connoisseur of the fine arts, and a loyal subject of the Christian Church.

While the middle ages witnessed little speculation on education, the Renaissance ushered in a period of intense discussion of all aspects of education, with a special interest in moral education. The influence of such ancient educators as Quintilian and Plutarch is evident in the educational writings of this period in which the importance of home training by parental example was stressed. Parents were advised to be aware of the innate potentialities of their children and to educate them toward wholeness. A stress was placed on physical, literary, and religious education. Also, the young were to be kept from harmful companions, literature, and art.

Of the many humanists who wrote on moral education perhaps the most noteworthy were Erasmus, Sadoletto, and Roger Asham. Erasmus of Rotterdam (d. 1536) discoursed on the elements of a complete education: Christian piety, scholarship, the conduct of moral life, and preparation for civic life. He held to a belief in the innate capacity of the child to learn moral values. Like all humanists, he placed great stress on parental example, direct moral and religious instruction, and the natural associations between old and young. He advocated not a religion of outward observance but an intimate personal religion including dependence upon the Creator. Erasmus criticized the schools of his time for using the rod and the fear of punishment as their principal methods of moral education. Like Gerson he appealed to the example of Christ in proclaiming that teaching by beating was not a liberal education.

Erasmus's educational theory is found primarily in a work designed to be used by a tutor for princes (Erasmus 1936). The tutor must possess a fine character, observe high moral principles, maintain purity of life, and converse in an affable manner. One who is to tutor princes must take the middle road between severity and indulgence by scolding without railing, praising without flattering, and controlling without breaking. This work of Erasmus was influential in Renaissance discussions on the education of princes and their subjects.

Cardinal Sadoletto (d. 1547), a friend of Erasmus, was also deeply concerned with the moral education of the young. He believed in the importance of the necessity of a healthy moral environment for the young. He opposed moralizing because of his faith in the ability of the young to sense the moral quality of the people around them. Sadoletto argued that the development of habits came not from efforts external to the person but from the rational efforts of persons. He also counseled that the development of sentiments of fear and shame in children were important attitudes in moral education. Thus in a real sense Sadoletto advocated conscience building and formation. He suggested that children be kept from forming morbid or sin ridden consciences by the development of internal mechanisms for approving and disapproving their actions.

This same type of humane approach to education is found in the Roger Ascham's *The Scholemaster* (1900). In this work the tutor to Elizabeth I, the future Queen of England, presented both ethics and methods in moral education. He recognized that the work of tutors could only build on the positive example and instructions of parents. The schoolmaster is urged to employ love rather than fear, gentleness rather than beatings. In dealing with students, he is urged to use encouragement and not punishment, admonitions rather than rebukes. It is clear that for Ascham education in the classics was subordinated to the moral purposes of education.

The final example of the humanist's ideas is found in the writings of Thomas More. More's *Utopia* is considered the greatest educational work of the English Renaissance (Cremin 1970, p. 85). More believed that individuals should live the virtuous life and apply their learning to the benefit of their community. True learning included being aware of one's limitations.

The tradition of Renaissance humanism was a high point in the history of moral education. The ideals of Renaissance humanism were a simple piety, a civility of manners, and a love for learning. These ideals helped to shape education in Europe, the British Empire, and the New World. The writings of these humanists were read and debated by educators in the American Colonies and formed the educational philosophy of the institutions of higher education in the United States (Cremin 1970).

MORAL EDUCATION IN THE REFORMATION PERIOD

The ideals of Renaissance humanism influenced educational theory in the periods of the Protestant Reformation and the Catholic Reformation. All of the reformers made education a central concern in their efforts at renewing Christian faith. The emphasis placed on education attempted to correct abuses of superstition in the medieval church.

Martin Luther (d. 1546) continued the tradition of Renaissance humanism in his insistence that classical learning be used to foster moral character and spiritual growth. Under his influence schools became open to persons of various social classes. This was possible now that the right of secular authorities to establish schools was made clear. Luther admonished parents to balance love and fear in their treatment of children's moral lapses. He laid the ruin of children at the door of parents who failed either from undue softness or unbending severity.

As could be expected, Luther wanted the fear of God's punishment for sin to be so implanted in the young that it would last throughout their entire lives. The young were to be introduced to the Scriptural teaching about the terrors of God's judgment on sinful lives. Luther, however, recommended that punishment in the schools be mixed with gentle admonition and emulation. A fair appraisal of Luther's view on moral education is given by Castle who asserts that throughout his writings Luther maintained that:

> Only on the solid foundation of education, especially moral and religious education, can the new Church and the reforming States hope to generate a new type of Christian citizen. His admonitions to adults are couched in terms far more harsh than those he used when writing on the needs of children, for whom he has always a loving concern, seldom untouched with severity, but never repressive or unmindful of their immaturity (Castle 1958, pp. 74–75).

John Calvin's interest in education was nearly as strong as Luther's. The rules he detailed for the academy at Geneva describe a school with a regimen of regularity, order, strict supervision, unbreakable routine, and complete suppression of individuality. While Calvin warned teachers and parents against any deliberate harshness, he did urge that corporal punishment be administered at set times for purposes of moral training. Prayer in the schools was also important and the teachings of religion, especially in Sunday sermons, were to be valuable moral influences in the lives of both adults and the young.

The religious emphasis on morality had a strong place in one of the most influential works in all of education, *The Ratio Studiorum* of Ignatius of Loyola (1933 edition). The founder of the Society of Jesus systematized every aspect of schooling: motivation, presentation, practice, and teaching. A prefect of studies was to see to the religious practices of students: Mass, repetition of doctrine, daily prayers, examination of conscience, confession of sins, meditation, the reading of the lives of the saints, and the avoidance of dangerous books. Spiritual direction was provided through private conversations designed to strengthen religious convictions and aid students in difficulties. It was the conviction among the early Jesuit educators that a single private talk was more powerful for building moral character than many lectures and sermons.

Within the *Ratio Studiorum* moral rules were detailed for the schools, (e.g., don't come to school with knives or daggers, be constructively occupied in school, and avoid public spectacles and comedies). Teachers were to use praise to reinforce every desirable response and to show disapproval of undesirable actions. Discipline was to be strict but never harsh. Punishment of students was to be left to an official who was not a member of the Jesuits. This was done in order to preserve the teacher and pupil relationship from all elements of personal antipathy.

An assessment of Jesuit education must include both its positive and negative aspects. On the positive side one can commend the notion that boys should be taught by men of the highest character and culture, the rational approach to discipline, and the concern with virtuous living rather than with sinful deeds. Jesuit education, on the other hand, so stressed the classical and the literary that for a long time it was unable to assimilate the scientific and the technological (Broudy and Palmer 1965, p. 62). The major weakness of this system was the apparent rigidity in not attending to individual differences or to differences in moral capacities.

The efforts of the Jesuits were matched by those of the Puritans of the early Protestant movement. Johann Amos Comenius (d. 1670) was especially interested in character formation through what he termed "the guarded life or education": censorship of books, protection from the world's corrupting ways, and full and continuous employment in work or play. In his book *The Great Didactic* (1896) Comenius advocated education which relied on nature as the teacher. Adult example, the natural workings of the child's spirit, and the power of reason should be relied on as far as possible. Comenius recognized the limitations of this approach in his advocacy of punishment as a last resort. The Puritan emphasis on moral training played a large part in the history of education in the United States as a later section of this chapter will bring out.

Similarities to the guarded education of the Puritans are found in schools established by Roman Catholic religious orders in the seventeenth and eighteenth centuries. While the Jesuits primarily educated the Catholic elite, such teaching orders as the Christian Brothers of John Baptiste de la Salle (d. 1719) attempted to train the children of the lower classes. Silence and strictness were high priorities in the de la Salle technique. Stern discipline was insisted upon, especially because of the large number of boys that the brothers instructed. Moral education came through the learning of moral precepts in catechisms, the recitations of such prayers as the Rosary, and the example of teachers.

In seventeenth century France increasing attention was paid to the education of girls. Religious orders of women established convent schools for the education of young women. As might be expected, these religious orders developed a rather controlled and protective form of moral training. Francois Fenelon wrote an influential book *On the Education of Girls* (1920 ed.) in which he emphasized the child's developing powers of reason, natural curiosity, the importance of play, and the notion that industry should have a happy atmosphere. Fenelon proposed that attraction and not compulsion should be the primary principle of all education. He urged that a mild system of disciplinary correction should prevail in order to win the child's confidence. Threats might be used but an appeal should be made to the naturally developing sense of shame. This appeal to natural capacities was a forerunner of educational theory developed by several influential Enlightenment educators.

MORAL EDUCATION
IN ENLIGHTENMENT EDUCATIONAL THEORY

The period of the Enlightenment in European history had major repercussions in the field of education. Educators now tended to place less emphasis on tradition and authority in education (especially religious tradition and authority) and more emphasis on the natural capacities of individuals. An example of this shift is found in John Locke's (d. 1702) proposal for discipline through understanding (Locke 1968 ed.). In this classic work Locke proposed four great goals of education: *virtue* as the moral life based on belief in Christ; *wisdom* as the competent management of one's worldly affairs; *breeding* as the ability to think favorably of oneself and others; and *learning* as a plentiful supply of useful knowledge. The formation of the virtuous character received most attention among these ends. In keeping with his rational approach to Christianity, Locke advised that religious precepts should be invoked only in so far as they could be shown to be reasonable. According to Locke, virtue was to be nurtured in the household. He seldom referred to schools and churches in his educational writings. Locke emphasized teaching of virtue when he advised that:

> The great business of all is virtue and wisdom . . . . Teach him to get a mastery over his inclinations, and submit his appetite to reason. This being obtained, and by constant practice settled into habit, the hardest part of the task is over (Locke, 1968, pp. 313–314).

Education in virtue for Locke should include exposing children to the prayers and Scriptures of the Christian faith for he considered the Bible the foundation of all morality. Yet Locke also believed that virtue should be taught more by practical experience than by learning rules from a book. For the earlier years of childhood he recommended the deliberate use of praise and shame as techniques of reinforcement. For the later years of childhood, there should be systematic encouragement of efforts at self control.

The strongest critic of the severity of previous methods of moral education is without a doubt John Jacques Rousseau (d. 1778). In his *Emile* (1956 edition) he proposed a "natural education" wherein the spontaneous development of the child's powers is central to education. In this work Rousseau raised important educational issues: society and the individual, authority and freedom, adult and child, as well as home and school. In the ordinary course of living, especially in play, the child learns by observing the various things in his environment and by responding to and using these things in a natural or untaught manner. Instead of the traditional obedience to persons and their commands as the basis of education, Rousseau argued for obedience to things of the natural order. He stipulated, however, that the physical environment should be so controlled by others that children would feel that they were free in what they were doing. Moral guidance was also to come from the example of adults and teachers.

Rousseau contradicted the Calvinism of his time in his assertion that individuals are naturally good and are made bad by society. Calvinism held that individuals are naturally bad and are made good through life in society. In Rousseau's view, if persons are not led into vice by others, they will come to the right adaptation to the social world, and thus to virtue. Rousseau's theory is called a romantic one and has found favor among many radicals and reformers in education.

Rousseau was especially attentive to moral growth during adolescence. According to him, adolescents should develop morally through a study of history and society where they would discover the noble and ignoble passions of men and women. He recommended that teachers should not use preaching or drill methods in teaching adolescents. He also insisted on an open and natural sex education. On this matter his advise was: "If you cannot keep Emile ignorant until he is sixteen, tell him everything before he is ten." It was also his view that only in adolescence could teachers make appeals to the rational powers of adolescents for purposes of moral education.

Rousseau's influence, especially in moral education, has been strong in the twentieth century in the United States and in Europe. The progressive movement drew on many of the ideas of Rousseau for its principles of naturalism and child-centeredness. John Dewey's early writings were considerably influenced by the liberating ideas of Rousseau's *Emile*. The educational reform movement of the 1960s was termed a new romanticism since it echoed criticism originally made by Rousseau, the great romantic in education. A. S. Neil's (1960) experiment at Summerhill reintroduced a system which is rather close to the natural education of Rousseau.

Rousseau was not without his critics in his own lifetime. Madame Necker de Saussure (d. 1841) was a foremost critic of Rousseau both from a religious orientation and from within his native country. What Madame de Saussure found most objectionable about Rousseau's educational philosophy was his neglect of religion in the moral formation of children. In her view parents and teachers should not only remove bad examples from children but should also gently move them in a desirable direction. She recommended that the obedience expected of children be placed within the context of genuine affection. For her it was not the freedom that Rousseau proposed but rather a firm security which was the basic need of children. This insight has found support among contemporary psychologists, including Erik Erikson. Like Erikson, Madame de Saussure placed the origins of religion in the awakening of affections between mother and child (Castle 1958, pp. 146–148).

The issue of balancing the needs of freedom and obedience was a major concern of the German philosopher, Emmanuel Kant (d. 1804). In his book, *Education* (1960 edition) he devoted considerable attention to moral training. While recognizing the child's capacity for goodness, he stressed a moral training that would use discipline to educate children to use their powers of freedom wisely. Kant's program called for submission and positive obedience in early childhood and the gradual introduction of freedom of action, accompanied by the teaching of definite rules.

For balancing freedom and obedience, Kant offered a number of suggestions: freedom is to be permitted so long as children do not interfere with the freedom of others; one can attain one's goals only if others attain theirs; discipline is necessary so that freedom may be used wisely. According to Kant, children will learn to balance freedom and obedience if they are taught moral maxims or practical rules for life in the home, school, and society. Kant even suggested the use of a catechism of right conduct for inculcating correct behavior. For him the major goal of moral education is to teach youth to understand the meaning of duty and to realize that obedience is the product of a rational call of duty.

Kant's idea of a reasoned approach to religion was opposed to the rote learning of the Bible and the traditional catechism used by Christian educators. His treatment of moral education is philosophical in that it stressed goals and principles rather than the translation of these into everyday life. But his advice is practical and sound when he proposed that children:

> Must learn to substitute . . . the fear of their own conscience, for the fear of man and divine punishment; self-respect and inward dignity, for the

opinions of men; the inner value of actions, for works and mere impulses; understanding for feeling; and joyousness and piety with good humor, for a remorseful, timid, and gloomy devotion (1960, p. 109).

While Kant was mainly concerned with the theory of moral education, the Swiss educator Johann Heinrich Pestalozzi (d. 1827) dedicated his life to developing practices for humanizing the processes of educating children. He discussed three types of education: of the head (intellectual), of the heart (moral), and of the hand (practical). For him, however, moral and practical education had priority. The major thrust of Pestalozzi's educational effort, one that corrects the overly rational approach of Kant, is that good parenting and schooling are founded on love. He emphasized that affection and confidence must be present before obedience can be demanded and that fear was destructive in the lives of children. Pestalozzi advised teachers to rely more on sympathy and encouragement in moral training (Pestalozzi 1896).

Pestalozzi's experimental schools were not administrative successes. Yet those who visited them from many parts of the world marvelled at what he was able to accomplish with many poor children. In his pietist Christian faith he believed that love for the child would enkindle love in the child. This love would broaden from love of mother to love of family, mankind, and God. In his life he combined the idealism, the love of children, and the enthusiasm found in many great educational reformers.

While Pestalozzi's concerns centered on the moral education of children, the German philosopher Georg Hegel (d. 1831) devoted attention to older children and young adults. For Hegel, education is:

> the art of making man moral: it regards man as one with nature and points the way in which he may be born again, in which his first nature may be changed into a second—a spiritual nature—in such a way that the spiritual nature may become habitual to him (In Castle 1958, p. 203).

Hegel recognized the importance of the formation of good moral habits in childhood. He argued that moral education of a more intellectual nature be given in later years. Hegel's proposals amounted to a course in college ethics which utilized a direct presentation of ideas and ideals. The course of study included notions of right and justice, freedom of the individual, the rights of family and state, the meaning of law and government, and religious concepts of conscience, faith, the nature of sin, and God (MacKenzie 1909).

The purpose of Hegel's course in ethics was to acquaint the conscious mind with moral ends and to promote reflection upon them. To Hegel the individual and the school became subordinate to the community and the state. Teachers became civil servants whose task was to promote moral education as a social duty. This approach made less of innate capacities than did other enlightenment theories, but more of social needs and responsibilities. Hegel's subordination of individuality has gained him the criticisms of educational reformers in the past century. Yet his educational theory makes us aware of strong social motives and functions of education.

While Hegel focused on the young adult's moral education, Johann Friedrich Herbart (d. 1841) was concerned with the moral pedagogy of the young. In his book, *Science of Education* (1893), he argued that fundamentally the purpose of education was the formation of moral persons. The moral person is to be judged by the degree of inner freedom the person exercises, the efficiency of the will in doing the good, and the degree of benevolence, justice, and equity manifested in one's actions.

Herbart devoted much of his efforts to developing an educational method that could be used in all areas of life and schooling. His method is concerned with the relationship between encouraging interests in individuals and influencing their will to act according to these interests. Because he believed in a close connection between desires, interests, and choices, the important task of education is to present correct interests to children. Herbart proposed a five-step method which became widely used in the education of teachers: *preparation* of the students; *presentation* of ideas; *association* of new ideas with previously learned ideas; a *systematization* of new and old ideas; and an *application* of these ideas to problems in life.

In his treatises on education Herbert devoted attention to a number of important issues. He discussed the relationship between discipline and instruction. While instruction had as its purpose the formation of character, discipline was to clear the way for such instruction. Herbart did not view discipline as restraint but rather as the creation of attitudes that would make instruction fruitful. Herbart defined discipline as the establishment of a mutual trust between teachers and pupils. This trust would theoretically create an authority within the person that was more powerful than any external controls.

Herbart's influence on educators was world wide and even in the United States there was a Herbartian Society for many years. He is noted for his emphasis on the power of discipline, school atmosphere, and direct instruction in forming moral character in children. His unique contribution was his insistence that school instruction and the right use of knowledge were rational means of achieving moral purposes (Castle 1958, p. 213).

The German educator who presented the most explicitly religious vision of moral education was Frederich Froebel (d. 1852), the father of the kindergarten. In his book, *The Education of Man* (1911 ed.), he stated that the purpose of education was to accelerate the process of growth in tune with the Creator's purposes. The teacher must recognize that God is at work within children guiding their growth. Children are like plants that develop from within and whose development requires skillful gardening. In moral training Froebel contended that example and precept are good but they do not go far enough: they must be part of the wholeness of family and school life which includes play, shared activities, encouragements, and shared sorrows, as well as burdens and joys. Though Froebel attended to the smallest details of the kindergarten education, his greatest contribution to education was his emphasis on the wholeness of the educational process and his recognition that children are individuals with their own identities and needs.

Froebel attempted to find a middle ground between education by teacher command and education by reliance on pupil impulse. He put emphasis on a third element to which both pupils and teachers were to submit. This element was the correct and the best thing inherent in each situation. In each situation there was the best thing to be done and teachers and pupils alike were to strive to determine what this was. This essential goodness inherent in each situation was to be obeyed by both teachers and pupils. Good actions are not determined by what teachers command or by what pupils want to do but by an examination of the very nature of each human activity. Froebel's "naturalism" moves him close to recognizing a natural law, or a quasi law rooted in each human situation. In his view:

The child, the pupil, has a very keen feeling, a very clear apprehension, and rarely fails to distinguish whether what the educator, the teacher, or the father says or requests is personal or arbitrary, or whether it is expressed by him as a general law and necessity (1911 edition, p. 15).

Thus far in this section I have reviewed the ideas and practices of English, French, German, and Swiss educators. Before moving to the history of moral education in the United States, I will present a sampling of nineteenth century British educators. The British system of schooling at this time consisted of rigid structures in which moral education was connected with religious education. To this religious education in the British system are added components of moral education.

The most comprehensive approach to moral education in nineteenth century England is found in Thomas Wyse's book, *Education Reform* (1836). Wyse recognized the interrelatedness of feeling, reason, will, and character in moral education. Of these, feeling was of utmost importance for him. Wyse was aware that children often have a moral sense before they act as moral persons. He believed religion must be included because the purposes of morality and religion are the same: the formation of the good moral character by strengthening the will through training, direction, and good habits.

Wyse focused attention on the critical role of the school in moral education. The school should develop a number of important sentiments: a feeling for order, a sense of justice, and a spirit of benevolence and generosity. The school will be able to provide moral education if it provides a community where standards of conduct are acquired indirectly and not through force or punishments. Wyse rejected a system of emulation that depends on prizes and medals because of the vanity which it promotes. He preferred that children compete with themselves and find satisfaction in their own growth. Though Wyse does not often find a place in ordinary histories of education, he deserves one. In Castle's assessment "there is, indeed, a wholeness and civilized ring about Wyse's programme for a better schooling: nothing so comprehensive appears in writings of his time" (1958, pp. 229–230).

A narrower focus on moral training in the home is found in William Newnham's book, *The Principles of Physical, Intellectual, Moral and Religious Education* (1827). This comprehensive 1200 page work treats many aspects of childhood and the role of parents. In Newnham's view moral education entails instilling obedience in children by creating in them a fear of offending their parents or the law of God. Children who disobey are to be reasoned with and told that their conduct is offensive to God and parents and is rejected by people in society.

An Englishman who receives a place in all histories of education is Herbart Spencer (d. 1903). In his classic work in educational theory, *Education: Intellectual, Moral and Physical* (1963 ed.) he presented an extensive discussion of educational issues. One of the main contributions of the work was the emphasis placed on the rights of children as distinct from their needs. This work was also important in giving natural science a prominent place in the school curriculum. Spencer insisted on the superiority of self-acquired and self-verified knowledge over knowledge accepted on the basis of tradition or authority. Spencer also opposed the rigid methods of instruction and discipline practiced in English schools as well as the coercive methods of child-rearing used by parents.

For moral training Spencer recommended the discipline of natural consequences, first proposed by Rousseau, as the most productive method. He does, however, see value in warning children of the painful consequences of foolish conduct. Spencer explicitly excluded the religious element from his consideration of moral education, not because he rejects it, but from a desire to provide the broadest possible basis for his approach which emphasizes natural consequences. He leaves it to others to supplement his work with considerations of a religious or transcendental kind.

In the long history of schooling in England, one theme is dominant: the idea of the school as a community of persons who have moral responsibilities to one another. English writers stress the powerful influence of principal or head and staff in creating a school community which can be a strong instrument in the moral growth of individuals.

In summary, several trends are found in Enlightenment educational theory. There is less emphasis on a moral education based exclusively on religious grounds. A rational or intellectual approach which appeals to reason is often presented. At times the appeal in moral education is made to individual freedom while at other times the appeal is made to the needs of society and the state. The importance of feeling as a force in moral education is stressed by some theorists. Moral education through encountering the natural consequences of one's actions has the support of a number of educators. Educators also give attention to the similarities between human growth and natural processes. In several ways the Enlightenment has raised many important issues for today's moral educators. These issues reappear in later theories of moral education.

TWENTIETH CENTURY EUROPEAN DEVELOPMENTS

Some of the theories and practices introduced in the remaining sections of this chapter will be covered in more detail in later chapters. Their treatment in this historical chapter serves the purpose of presenting them in their historical contexts. Twentieth century developments in moral education in both Europe and the United States bear the influence of the newly developed social and psychological sciences.

One of the major achievements in Europe at the beginning of the twentieth century was the development of a secular moral education for state schools that appealed not to revealed religion (based on the Bible viewed as God's word) but to the power of human reason. This was precisely the task that Emile Durkheim set out to accomplish in his book, *Moral Education: A Study in the Theory and Application of the Sociology of Education* (1961). Durkheim's ideas will receive a brief treatment here since they will be reported at greater length in chapter four.

Durkheim is one of the founders of sociology. His work on moral education has to be seen in the context of his scholarly task. In his view society after various European revolutions was in danger of becoming lawless because of the decreased influence of religion in maintaining social control in society through its system of rewards and punishments both in this world and in the next. In searching for a new way in which society could be ordered he focused upon the school as the instrument of socialization and control.

For Durkheim, moral education, like all education, is primarily a social means to a social end: to guarantee the survival of a civilized society. Durkheim argued that a socially relevant moral education could only take place in schools. An effective moral education for social purposes could not take place in the family because the ethos of affection within the family is not suitable for the stern demands of social morality. This education could not be deferred until adulthood or entrusted to agencies encountered in adulthood since this would come too late. This moral education would take place through the discipline of the school, its use of rewards and punishments, the attachment the school promotes to social groups, the school environment, the teaching of such subjects as history and literature, and the development of autonomy in students.

Durkheim's stress on the social or collective purposes of moral education goes against the more individualistically oriented approaches advocated by some educators during the Enlightenment. It is similar, however, to the ideas of Hegel on this subject. Both of these educators were sensitive to the role of schools in fostering the virtues and values needed in a nation state.

At the other extreme of Durkheim's approach was the philosophy entailed in the short lived experiment of Leo Tolstoy (d. 1910), who conducted a school based on his belief that children were naturally good. Though Tolstoy's experimental school was established in the middle of the nineteenth century, its philosophy is more akin to that of the new education which emerged in the earlier part of the twentieth century. Tolstoy's educational philosophy sprung from his romantic view of life, according to which utmost importance is attached to the individual's free human spirit nourished by God and directed by interest, emotion, and desire. Tolstoy decried the:

> Strange psychological condition which I call the "school state of mind", and which . . . consists in all the higher capacities, imagination, creative power and reflection, yielding to a semi-animal capacity to produce words without imagination or reflection (In Castle 1958, p. 336).

Tolstoy attempted to combat this school state of mind by advocating a classroom free of compulsion and a teacher who loved both subject and pupil. Teachers were not to compel obedience or even to ask for it. Tolstoy did not want his teachers to move into the moral domain. He argued that:

> The school must have one aim—the transmission of information, of knowledge, without attempting to pass over into the moral territory of convictions, belief and character; its aim is to be nothing but science, and not the results of its influence upon human personality (Tolstoy 1967 ed., p. 146).

Teachers were moral educators through their moral convictions and the artistry of their teaching. Disorder was permitted in the classroom. Tolstoy believed that if only teachers would be patient, the disorder would appear as creative energy. Given this extreme approach to nonintervention, it is not surprising that the experiment at Yasno Polyana lasted only two years.

A more moderate form of nonintervention in the life of the child is found in Maria Montessori's (d. 1952) approach to character education. Montessori began her work with poor and abandoned youth. It was her conviction that in a controlled environment normal children should be left free to educate themselves. In her view character developed spontaneously from the gradual development of an internal order. For Montessori character training in school came down to obedience, an obedience developed not by direct commands but by methodical exercises. Rewards and punishments were not advocated in this approach.

For older children and adolescents Montessori advocated moral training through an organized group in order to take advantage of the herd instinct of children. The organized group was to take the form of "a moral union of children who have consented to form part of a society which has a moral aim, and which requires its members to live up to a certain moral level (In Standing 1957, p. 357). It was important to Montessori that children freely consent to belong to such a group. She found such moral unions in the organizations of boy scouts and girl scouts.

The approach to moral education in twentieth century Europe was to a degree influenced by the theories of psychoanalysts. By the end of the First World War the theories of Freud and Adler began to influence some classrooms. Freud's contention that adult neuroses had their origins in childhood and Adler's attribution of children's behavior difficulties to the frustration of self-assertive impulses gave impetus to approaches to moral education in which teachers were advised not to interfere in child development. Schools organized according to these principles stressed that schools were to take on the ethos of family life, that the stern commands of religion were eliminated, and that the discipline of authority was to give way to self-discipline and control.

In England this theory of advocating the nonintervention of teachers in moral education was connected with the theory of the right of children to self-government. Homer Lane started a school called the Little Commonwealth in Dorset in 1913. Boys and girls became members of a self-supporting farm community in which they had a significant role in establishing rules. Love, freedom, and self-government were the chief regulations for this community school. Adults were not to use compulsion in their dealings with children. In Lane's view badness as such did not exist in children; what appeared as badness was merely misdirected goodness. Lane's insight that moral training is the process of assisting children to adopt creative ideals as their own and to discard futile and false ideas is a valuable ideal for all moral education.

A. S. Neil, a well known British educator, has acknowledged his dependence on Homer Lane in the establishment of his world famous experimental school at Summerhill. Neil was also influenced by Freud's contention that many adult neuroses had their origins in moral and religious training in childhood. Moral development, in Neil's view, should follow the principle of allowing children to be from all forms of repressive discipline as well as from the strong influences of teachers. Since children are considered by him to be intrinsically good, they must be given the opportunity to express themselves freely. The task of moral education is to produce not the disciplined child but the self-regulated one. To put this into practice, Neil's Summerhill was under the self-government of both teachers and pupils. Neil did not consider a school truly progressive unless it allowed self-government.

Neil's rather extreme approach to freedom is seen in his rejection of moral rules and religious codes for his school:

> We imposed no standard of behavior or dress or manners or language. All ancient taboos about sex were dismissed, and no religion was brought into the school (1953, p. 30).

Only in this way, Neil believed, would children be able to develop into mature adults without guilt obsessions, especially about sex.

Neil's premises and methods have received considerable criticisms over the years. Even he recognized the perennial problems of the individual versus the community that his approach raised. His freedom principle and educational experiment attracted the attention of school critics in the United States in the 1960s with the publication of his book *Summerhill* (1960). The founders of many free schools which arose as alternatives to public schools in the 1960s appealed explicitly to Neil's philosophy. The challenge of this experiment and philosophy was that it brought to the fore in moral education the important issues of freedom and self-government.

Neil's appeal to psychoanalysis as one of the bases for his approach to moral education is indicative of a significant change concerning moral education in this century. Moral education was no longer the sole province of theologians and philosophers. The new sciences of psychology, sociology, and anthropology began to present theories and research related to moral education. The tension that exists between these disciplines and traditional theology is also found in the field of moral education. In chapters three and five these tensions will be explored more fully.

In Europe the most significant psychological research relating to moral education was done by Jean Piaget (1965), the celebrated Swiss psychologist. Piaget and his collaborators presented extensive research on how children distinguish right from wrong. Piaget's focus has been on cognitive moral reasoning and various stages of development within this reasoning. This work inspired a great deal of research both in Europe and in North America and it will receive additional treatment in chapter three.

In England a serious attempt to study moral education on an interdisciplinary basis is found in the work of Wilson, Williams, and Sugarman (1967) which reports the results of research at the Farmingham Trust Research Unit at Oxford. Utilizing scholarly work in the disciplines of philosophy, psychology, and sociology, this study attempts to describe the morally educated person and the processes that produce such a person. This work has given the impetus to further research in England which is reported in the British *Journal of Moral Education* and other educational journals.

Moral education exists as a specific school subject in England and other European countries. In England there are some connections between moral education and religious education, although the subject is very often taught without reference to religious training. The same situation is found in the state schools in European countries.

MORAL EDUCATION IN THE UNITED STATES

In the early period of education in the United States forms of moral education were greatly influenced by English theories and practices. Many agencies, both formal and informal contributed to the education of citizens (Cremin 1970). Families, churches, schools, youth groups, and libraries were among the agencies that fostered piety, advanced learning, and promoted civility. Moral and religious purposes were powerful forces in establishing and influencing all of these agencies in the colonial period. Though schools were the major educational agencies, they must be seen in their relationships to other agencies of education.

In the United States schooling has always been connected with moral purposes. Moral education has been considered central to the formation of a democratic society. Democracy is so defined that it demands persons of good character and virtue. Again and again, the schools have been asked to educate children in particular moral values which are viewed as essential to the maintenance of a democratic government. This viewpoint goes back to the beginnings of the republic as is attested in an ideal presented in a July 4th oration in 1798:

It is highly important that every order and class of citizens exert themselves in the cultivation of those sentiments and principles on which rest our political happiness and national existence. Knowledge and religion are the supports of a republican government. The means of education, and moral and religious instruction, ought therefore to engage our serious and vigorous attention (Thomas Sparhawk in Hersh, Miller, and Fielding 1980, p. 15).

The public school as we know it today began to take shape in the early years of the nineteenth century. Within this shape was included a strong emphasis on moral education. Advocates of a common school challenged the explicitly religious and denominational character of the nation's schools. Horace Mann led the effort in New England to remove the schools from sectarian control and to establish the principle of community control of schools which persons of all religions could attend. Religious and moral education continued to take place in the schools but not according to the beliefs of any particular religious denomination. This training consisted of prayers in schools, the reading of the Bible, moral stories in such readers as McGuffey's, and the presentation of historical events as moral examples.

Many reports on schools in the nineteenth century complained about severe discipline problems which were usually met with corporal punishment. Many believed that the secular nature of the school promoted this breakdown of discipline. One solution to this problem was a stress on the teacher's role as moral educator. Various ways were advanced for accomplishing this role: explicit religious and moral education; the educative value of certain subjects such as manual work, natural sciences, and physical training; and an improvement of the physical conditions of the school.

In general terms, two approaches to moral education were proposed at this time. The first approach saw the secularization of the school as the major problem and decried the decline of religion in the schools. For the advocates of this view there was an indissoluble connection between religion and morality. All moral education was to be based on the honor and respect due to the Creator. Without this basic respect for God and his law, it was impossible to have an effective moral education since morality is fundamentally a matter of duty and obedience to the will of God. In this viewpoint moral education was a form of religious education and social problems were thought of in moral terms (Kaestle 1973, p. 113).

A second view gradually developed by the middle of the nineteenth century. It attempted to create education for citizenship, especially for the children of immigrants who had recently come to the United States. In this position the schools should not enter into religious education, the domain of the churches. The theory's foremost proponent, William T. Harris (d. 1909) was greatly influenced by Hegel's view of the state and the role of education in preserving the values of the state. The 1888 report of the Committee on Moral Education of the National Council of Education contained the heart of Harris's opinions:

> The so called discipline of the school is its primordial condition, and is itself a training in habits essential to life in a social whole, and hence is itself moral training. . . . A whole family of virtues are taught the student

and taught him so thoroughly that they become fixed in character . . . obedience, punctuality, regularity, silence, and industry. Moral education must begin in merely mechanical obedience and develop gradually out of this stage toward that of individual responsibility (In Castle 1958, p. 319).

Harris was a commanding figure in educational history in the nineteenth century since he held the office of the first United States commissioner of education. The purpose of schooling for this religious reformer was to adjust children to the social order by inculcating in them social virtues. The schools were to directly train children's wills in the habits of virtue. Education for older children was to bring them to the point of freely and voluntarily accepting all lawful authority. This was to be done by engaging the older children in a rational discussion of the values of the society. In this view the essence of moral education is to provide insight into the reasonableness of moral commands. What the schools should avoid is developing unreasoning obedience to a demagogue or a leader in crime (Cremin 1961; Perkinson 1977).

Although Harris's ideas were influential throughout the latter part of the nineteenth century, by the end of the century a major weakness had been identified: the failure to attend to the emotional factors in children's behavior. This weakness was rectified by the emphasis on child study in early progressive education and the work of the psychologists within the progressive movement.

Child Study Movement

The scientific knowledge that was missing in the views of earlier educators began to develop among the first experimental psychologists in the United States. G. S. Hall (d. 1924), believing in the natural potential for goodness in the child, set out to discover the content of children's minds at various stages of growth. In Hall's view a great deal of anti-social behavior is to be expected of children because they must in their short times recapitulate the entire history of the human race. This behavior purges children of behavior that would be destructive in adult life. Hall's study of adolescence led him to condemn methods of repression and to stress the need for freedom of expression as well as the educative value of play and group activity. Ideas of right and wrong were developed through the social experience of give and take. The task of the teacher in this enterprise was to enable children to recognize reasons for their conduct, no matter how inadequate or crude.

Hall considered moral education more important than industrial training. He attempted to inculcate certain key virtues: respect for property and honesty, a sense of honor, and the more important virtue of justice. As means of education in justice and other virtues, Hall proposed religious instruction and history. Religion was necessary for giving a supernatural sanction to rights. History would teach the differences between right and wrong as these forces worked themselves out in practice. Also, Hall was in favor of sex instruction, to be given separately to adolescent boys and girls (Curti 1959, pp. 419–420).

Some contemporary historians of early progressive education have pointed out a number of contradictions in Hall's theories. They argue that he was actually elitist and reactionary in wanting to restrict an intellectual education to the genetically gifted, while consigning others to training in parenthood, industry, and citizenship. They also question his commitment to producing persons with true freedom and responsibility (Strictland and Burgess 1965, pp. 22–24). Notwithstanding these criticisms, Hall's proposals for more attention to child study began an important trend in education in the United States.

The experimental ideas of psychology practiced by Hall found support in the individual psychology of William James (d. 1910). James's writings cover psychology, philosophy, and religion. One of his major contributions to the progressive method was his treatment of the role of habits in education. In his view, persons have certain instinctive tendencies to react. As a result of the repetition of actions, habits emerge. A central task of education is the inculcation of as many good and useful habits as possible. Character training for James can simply be reduced to an education for behavior and habits of behavior. Among his maxims for teachers he includes this piece of advice:

> Don't preach too much to your students or abound in good talk in the abstract. Lie in wait rather for the practical opportunities, be prompt to seize those as they pass, and thus at one operation get your pupils both to think, to feel, and to do. The strokes of behavior are what give the new set to the character, and work the good habits into its organic tissue. Preaching and talking too soon become an intellectual bore (James 1958, pp. 60–61).

The ideas of progressive educators received their strongest intellectual exposition in the theories of John Dewey (d. 1952). Since his ideas will receive full treatment in the next chapter, I will indicate only the general thrust of his work.

Dewey's belief that there are no moral absolutes led him to the conclusion that morality is subject to changing social needs. For him morality was a process of solving social problems rather than a set of ideas or even habits. Moral education consisted in reflection and not in character training or preaching. Children are to acquire a working morality from practical experiences of living at home and school. Thus children learn morality in the same way they learn everything else: by involvement in practical situations of life. What Dewey opposed most in moral education was reducing it to "some kind of catechetical instruction or lessons about morals" (1916, p. 411).

Dewey's concepts have been influential in many contemporary approaches to moral education, although his ideas were less influential in the period after the Second World War because of the emphasis on academic training at the expense of such softer areas as moral or values education. Dewey's influence in the resurgence of interest in moral education is strong at the present time. Many theories and approaches draw on his philosophy for important principles.

Dewey also influenced the circle of religious educators, even though many religionists were strongly opposed to elements of his educational philosophy. George Coe showed his dependence on Dewey's social-cultural approach to moral education when he wrote:

Religious and moral education, accordingly, cannot be anything less than the progressive attainment of freedom; and its method can be nothing less than placing the child in a series of concrete situations as shall reveal him to himself as really interested in good and self-enlisted on its side. This involves a growing knowledge of good and evil, a developing spiritual appreciation, and training of the will (Coe 1904, p. 133).

Character Education in Religious Education

A prominent form of moral education popular in religious groups was character education, which has received careful historical analysis by William Chapman (1977). This movement deserves special attention because of its attempt to place moral education within the context of religious education. The focus on this approach was on a three fold development: individual, socio-cultural, and religious. For Hugh Hartshorne, a student of Coe's, "there is only a step from morality to religion. . . . The Christian character is one that is organized consciously around the will of the Christian God" (1915, p. 1–2).

Those concerned with character education recognized that there were many agencies of moral education. Many advocates gave extensive attention to the home and family. Even though the public school received less attention in this movement, many educators in these schools struggled with modes of character education. A committee on character formation gave a report to the U.S. National Educational Association in 1924 in which it stated that:

Love of God and fellow men includes belief in moral standards, in the intrinsic value of the moral life and of personality, compared with which all other values are but relative. Acceptance of this standard does not involve the public schools in religious sectarianism. There should be no reference to differences in creeds nor to absence of creed. Whatever conceptions patrons of the public schools may have of God, they generally agree that there is in the universe a power that makes for righteousness, or at least they agree to a moral ideal and regard this ideal as a real power that guarantees the values of the moral life (In Chapman 1977, p. 46).

Many religious educators at this time saw the churches as agencies of moral education, though some qualified this insight with criticisms of churches as often mechanized, conventional, and repressive. Worship within the churches especially was seen to have potential for moral education. Character educationists also saw the potential of youth groups for moral education.

The major research that came out of the character education movement was reported by Hugh Hartshorne and Mark May in three volumes entitled *Studies in the Nature of Character* (1926; 1929; 1930). Volume I contained research on deceit and honesty, drawing on a sample of more than 10,000 youths between the ages of eight and sixteen. In a brilliant bit of summarization the authors drew together their twenty-four conclusions into one terse statement:

Our conclusion, then, is that an individual's honesty or dishonesty consists of a series of acts and attitudes to which these descriptive terms apply. The consistency with which he is honest or dishonest is a function of the situations in which he is placed in so far as (1) these situations have common elements, (2) he has learned to be honest or dishonest in them, and (3) he has become aware of their honest or dishonest implications or consequences (1926, p. 379).

Hartshorne and May saw a number of implications for moral education in this research: people are not honest or dishonest by nature; the mere urging or discussion of standards has little effect on behavior; more attention must be paid to the situation in which the child is placed and the personal relations involved. They also urged that educators should consider social background, physical conditions of the home, companions, and personal limitations in order to understand children's behavior (1926, pp. 412–414).

Volume II of the research study reported findings on service and self-control. Hartshorne and May observed from this study additional implications for educators: experience is crucial for learning; children must be allowed to pursue their interests and learn specific conduct; the established practice and code of the group is a powerful hindrance or assistance to acquiring desirable responses; moral standards and ideals should function as tools for moral learning and not as objects of study; the achievement of specific standards, attitudes, and modes of conduct does not imply their integration, for integration of these is a specific achievement (1929, p. 454).

The conclusion of the 1929 study was reinforced in Volume III which stated that a person's character traits and moral conduct lacked any consistent pattern of integration. Thus high achievement in honesty does not imply high achievement in other virtues. Among the ideas found in this study was one that fitted perfectly with Dewey's educational philosophy.

The moral unit for character formation is the group or small community, which provides cooperative discussion . . . and the moral support required for the adventurous and effective use of ideals in the conduct of affairs (1930, p. 379).

The research of Hartshorne and May served in its time to dash the hopes of many religious educators who made exaggerated claims for the relationship between religious education and moral behavior. No discernible differences were found between those who received religious education and those who received little or no religious education. A similar conclusion has been reached by Lawrence Kohlberg (1967) in his study of moral development. This matter is highly controversial and will receive attention in chapters two, three, and five.

Religious Reaction to Character Education

Not all religious educators embraced the approach to character building that fostered moral development through social experiences. Many religious educators viewed this approach as fundamentally irreligious because of its rejection of absolute moral values. These persons argued that moral education should proceed either from biblical teaching or from authoritative church teachings.

A strong condemnation came from Roman Catholic educators and their criticisms are found in an encyclical letter by Pope Pius XI on *The Christian Education of Youth* (1936). The Pope objected to systems of moral education that relied on the power of nature alone and took no account of original sin or divine grace. Also rejected were those:

> Modern theories which . . . agree in regarding it as fundamental in all forms of education that children be allowed to mold their own character completely at their own will and discretion, rejecting all advice from teachers or elders and taking no account of any law or assistance, human or divine (In Castle 1958, p. 330).

A reading of the encyclical indicates a rejection not only of the moral education fostered by progressive educators but also a rejection of the whole trend toward freedom favored by many European and American educators.

The Catholic philosopher, Jacques Maritain, criticized attempts on the part of the schools to directly shape character and develop moral virtues, tasks which he considered more appropriate for families and churches. The school's role in moral education, according to Maritain, was the indirect formation of the will through intellectual enlightenment, utilizing a study of history and literature (Maritain 1962, p. 113). For Maritain moral education must have a religious component because of the close connection between the moral and the religious. His concept of a religiously oriented moral education will receive fuller treatment in the next chapter.

Since character education was closely allied with progressive education and liberal theology, its fortunes took a fall when the neo-orthodoxy of Reinhold Niebuhr and Paul Tillich challenged liberalism in theology and education. Moral education in Protestantism then became more biblically oriented as will become clear in chapter five.

Moral Education in the Past Two Decades

Moral education in public schools declined considerably in the years after the Second World War because of a greater concentration on academic studies and because of Supreme Court decisions prohibiting teaching religion and recitation of prayers in schools. In removing these practices from schools the Court seemed to many to have also outlawed moral education.

Notwithstanding these legal decisions, the past two decades have demonstrated a resurgence of interest in moral education. As suggested in the introductory chapter, events in the 1960s raised serious moral questions which could not be ignored by educators. Schools themselves were criticized for failing to raise the moral consciousness of students about national and international issues such as the war in Vietnam and the civil rights struggle. In this new context books and articles about moral education began to appear. The influential educational journal *Phi Delta Kappan* devoted its June 1975 issue to moral education with contributions by eminent philosophers, theologians, psychologists, and educationists. In one article a survey of teachers revealed a consensus on the need for greater involvement of the schools in moral education. Articles on moral education abound in educational journals at this time.

In the United States the two major systems to moral education in the past two decades have been values clarification (Raths, Harmin, and Simon 1966) and the moral development theory of Lawrence Kohlberg (1981; 1984). Public school educators and religious educators have debated over these ideas, which receive extended treatment in later chapters.

The resurgence of moral education programs in schools has been matched by an increased interest in the teaching of ethics and moral philosophy at college and professional levels. Many books and collections of articles have appeared on this subject. New topical journals have emerged: *The Journal of Moral Education, Philosophy and Public Affairs*, and the *Journal of Medicine and Philosophy*. Scholars of many disciplines have begun to address the issues of moral education and the teaching of ethics.

The 1980s have witnessed another public debate on teaching values in public schools. Politicians and educators expressed positive interest in values education. The former secretary of education, William Bennett, became a strong advocate for encouraging the schools not to avoid issues relating to morality. Conservatives and liberals are on record as favoring the teaching of values in public schools, while some interest groups promote particular moral positions. The debate at this time in American history recalls to mind similar arguments in the past. Fortunately there are now sound theories and research upon which to base discussions and policies on moral education.

As this chapter as made clear there are no easy answers to the many problems of moral education. In presenting the goals of moral education an educator must make a stand on the very nature of the society in which we live. Moral education includes handing on the values which maintain a society in existence and providing the tools for criticizing that society's values. In a pluralistic society there are many competing value systems among families, churches, communities, schools, and other institutions. Frequently public debates are deeply concerned with issues of values. In the remaining chapters we will examine what thoughtful scholars have written about these issues in order to learn about the possibilities and limits of moral education in our society.

CHAPTER 2

PHILOSOPHIES OF
MORAL EDUCATION

As a group, philosophers have been very interested in moral education. In fact all educational classics from Plato's *Republic* to Skinner's *Walden II* are deeply concerned with educating individuals and societies in moral values. The previous chapter presented in brief form the philosophical teachings of a number of philosophers, including Rousseau, Kant, Hegel, and Dewey. This chapter examines in greater depth and in a more systematic fashion four different philosophical efforts to deal with moral education.

Four theories were chosen because the dominant philosophical tradition in the English speaking world in recent years has been that of various forms of analytic philosophy or philosophy of language. Philosophers in this tradition from Great Britain, the United States, and Canada have carefully examined the entire area of moral education. The philosophical analyses of Richard Peters (1966), John Wilson (1967), Clive Beck (1971), and James McClellan (1976) are notable for careful analysis of the use of language and for arguments used in moral education.

In the present chapter my intention is to go beyond this particular tradition to include the work in other philosophical traditions. The four philosophies to be examined are: Neo-Thomistic or Neo-Rationalist, Pragmatic or Experimental, Existential-Phenomenological, and Analytic. Though work in the non-analytic philosophies is not abundant nor of recent vintage, these theories contain important insights into and valuable recommendations for moral education. These non-analytic approaches often provide a better understanding of the actual practice of moral education than do the purely analytic ones since they go beyond questions of analysis of concepts to describe and propose programs for moral education.

In keeping with one of the major aims of this book—to explore the religious dimensions of moral education—special attention is given to the more religiously oriented versions of the particular philosophies, where this is possible. The religious dimension is strongest in Neo-Thomism; yet it is also present in the other theories, at least in so far as they have implications for a religiously oriented moral education.

As a framework for my analysis I shall employ Frankena's (1970) schema for analyzing normative philosophies of education. This analysis will include a study of: 1) the dispositions of the persons to be fostered by the educational theory, (i.e., its view of the morally educated person); 2) the rationale for advocating such dispositions (e.g., philosophic positions, theological premises, or empirical factors); 3) any recommendations about methods for developing the morally educated person; 4) rationales for the recommendations about method (e.g., factual premises or normative arguments). I must add that it is not my view that a particular philosophic position logically entails a specific approach to moral education. Thus a neo-Thomist may favor many of the educational recommendations of the pragmatist. Yet some loose connection usually exists between general philosophical positions and educational practices.

NEO-THOMISM: MORAL EDUCATION
AS INTELLECTUAL ENLIGHTENMENT

The philosophy of Neo-Thomism has had a long history in Western thought. Neo-Thomists take their name from Thomas Aquinas, the great medieval philosopher and theologian, who established an impressive synthesis of Greek philosophy and Christian theology. Contemporary philosophers in this tradition have attempted to update his thought by bringing it into contact with modern philosophy and science.

The foremost neo-Thomist of our time was Jacques Maritain, the French philosopher who lectured frequently in this country. Maritain's writings range over a wide area: theory of knowledge, metaphysics, social and political philosophy, and philosophy of education. His philosophy of moral education will be discussed in this chapter because it is the most extensive and representative of this position. The other notable neo-Thomist in our time was Etienne Gilson, Director of the Pontifical Institute of Medieval Studies, Toronto. Gilson, however, did not develop a specific philosophy of education along Thomistic lines and thus has had less impact in this field.

Prominent neo-Thomists who have developed philosophies of education include Robert Henle (1965), William McGucken (1942), and George Beck (1964). Neo-Thomism as a philosophy of education has been closely connected with Catholic education. The authoritative encyclical of Pope Pius XI on *The Christian Education of Youth* (1936) and the Vatican II *Declaration on Christian Education* (Abbott, 1966) have given special authority to neo-Thomistic principles.

Neo-Thomism's dominance in Catholic philosophy and theology has waned in the past two decades as Catholic scholars have espoused other philosophical positions such as existentialism, pragmatism, process philosophy, analytic philosophy, and even Marxism. However, a group of influential Catholic scholars have attempted to develop a philosophy of transcendental Thomism that endeavors to join Thomistic philosophy with modern thought, especially the philosophy of Kant and phenomenology. The chief exponents of this view are the Jesuit theologians, Bernard Lonergan and Karl Rahner. Little effort has been made to relate this approach specifically to philosophy of education, although this would probably be a fruitful enterprise.

Closely related to neo-Thomism as a religious philosophy is what has been termed neo-rationalism. Prominent neo-rationalists include Mortimer Adler (1940), Robert Hutchins (1968), Mark Van Doren (1959), and A. Whitney Griswold (1959). A more recent example of this form of philosophy is found in the position paper *Paideia* (Adler 1982) written by Adler and subscribed to by a number of prominent educators. The neo-rationalists draw in varying degrees on Greek philosophers and Thomas Aquinas, though they do not usually accept the theological teachings of Aquinas. However, their basic educational principles are similar to those of Aquinas: the development of the intellectual, moral, and spiritual powers of persons through a rigorous intellectual education in the humanities or liberal arts.

Maritain's Philosophy of Moral Education

Maritain's philosophical writings include *Education at the Crossroads* (1943), his Terry Lectures at Yale University, and *The Educated Man* (1962), an edited collection of articles and talks written over a period of time. Though Maritain's teaching was at the university level, he addressed his philosophy of education to all levels. In this analysis of his ideas I will use the following categories: 1) the morally educated person and the rationale for his description of this person and, 2) the means suggested for educating this person and the rationale for the recommended means.

The Morally Educated Person   In Maritain's writings there is an intimate connection between his description of the morally educated person and the rationale for this description. The primary aim of education, for him, is the formation of a whole person. Maritain distinguished this aim from such secondary goals as transmitting a culture, preparing a person for life and citizenship, and equipping a person for a career or role in life. His indebtedness to Greek, Jewish, and Christian sources is indicated in this description of the whole person:

Man as an animal endowed with reason, whose supreme dignity is in the intellect; and man as a free individual in personal relation with God, whose supreme righteousness consists in voluntarily obeying the law of God; and man as a sinful and wounded creature called to divine life and the freedom of grace, whose supreme perfection consists in love (1943, p. 7).

The objective of education for Maritain must be related to the nature of the human person. Since the ultimate destiny of persons is life with God after this earthly life, education must be directed to both earthly life and eternal life. Morally educated people are those who have learned to love God and neighbor in such a way that they merit eternal life with God. The existence of the human soul or spirit that transcends earthly existence is thus the primary principle upon which his entire educational philosophy depends.

Maritain establishes a clear hierarchy of values in his philosophy of education. He contends that "knowledge and love of what is above time are superior to, and embrace and quicken knowledge and love of what is within time" (1962, p. 52). Following Aristotle and Aquinas, Maritain holds that "education in its final and highest achievement, tends to develop the contemplative capacity of the human mind" (1962, p. 54). The creative power of work in the world and service to others comes from this properly developed contemplative capacity.

Maritain presents a rationale for his view of the morally educated person, drawing primarily on the perennial principles of theology and philosophy. These inform us of the nature of persons, their place and value in the world, and their ultimate destiny. Though Maritain admits that the human being evolves in history, he recognizes no essential changes in the nature, value, dignity, rights, and destiny of persons. What may change is our knowledge of what humans are. Maritain expresses an openness to what scientific or empirical studies may reveal about people, but he does not admit the possibility of an incompatibility between this knowledge and his philosophic position. If empirical knowledge is correct, it will complement the truth of perennial philosophy.

For Maritain formation in moral life and virtues—the powers or abilities that comprise this life—is the most important part or primary aim of education. What is most distinctive about his view is his assertion that the moral life is necessarily linked with religious belief and experience. He contends that:

If the existence of the One who is Absolute Being and the Absolute Good is not recognized and believed in, no certitude in the unconditional and obligatory nature of the moral law and ethical standards can be validly established and efficaciously adhered to (Maritain 1962, p. 76).

Maritain does not believe that non-religious persons are necessarily bad or that religious persons necessarily good. His opinion is that "with regard to the average behavior of mankind, morality without religion undermines morality, and is able to sustain human life for but a few generations" (1962, p. 117).

Maritain presented a detailed description of the virtues of a morally educated person. With regard to the individual, education has as its objective personal development and liberation. Five dispositions must be fostered to achieve this liberation: the love of truth, the love of good and justice, a simplicity and openness with regard to existence, the sense of a job well done, and a sense of cooperation (1943, p. 36–38).

Educational Method   The lofty dispositions that Maritain sets for the morally educated person require an equally exalted methodology. Before examining his specific recommendations, it may be helpful to look at his general norms for the dynamics of education. Teachers are to recognize that their chief task is the liberation of the mind. Great emphasis should be placed on the inner depths of the personality and the spiritual dimension of the individual. Educators should attempt to foster the internal unity especially by imparting wisdom from knowledge of the basic principles of moral life. Finally, teaching should promote the mastery of reason over things learned (1943, pp. 39–49).

As to the specific area of moral education, Maritain makes an important distinction between the *direct formation of the will* which is the task of the family and the church and the *indirect moral formation* (intellectual enlightenment) which is the task of the school. The family educates morally through the force of mutual love, the example of parents, prescribed rules of conduct, religious habits, and inspiration. Family life thus educates through common experiences, trials, efforts, sufferings, hopes, daily labor, affection, and punishment. Maritain recognizes that the example set by parents is not always beneficial nor is the work of education always well directed in families. Yet he believes that:

Even at its mediocre average level, nature at play in family life has its own spontaneous ways of compensating after a fashion for its own failures, its own spontaneous processes of self-regulation, which nothing can replace, and provides the child with a moral formation and an experience of mutual love, however deficient it may be, which nothing can replace (1943, pp. 119–120).

Maritain's treatment of the church's role in moral education is brief. He points out that the church educates through its teaching, precepts, sacraments, liturgy, spiritual training, guidance, and organizations. Like the family, the church educates through the law of love proper to the family of God, which especially manifests itself in the purification of mutual love that enables everyone to become a neighbor.

Maritain devotes most of his attention to the role of the school in moral education. With regard to direct influence on the will the school is involved in *premoral training*, which takes place through school policies, common life, and discipline. Premoral training is not involved with morality but rather with the preparation of the person for moral education.

The role of the school which most interests Maritain is its *indirect action on the will by means of intellectual enlightenment*. The school's task is to bring students to a knowledge of good and evil. It must recognize its limitations in this area since knowledge of the good is of itself insufficient for doing good. Maritain opposes efforts of schools to educate the will directly or to engage in direct programs of character-building. The school should restrict itself to imparting knowledge about morality. Maritain's insistence on this limited role of the school is based on his philosophical theory of the relationship between knowledge and morality and on his criticisms of efforts in wartime Germany and other European countries to engage in a direct training of the will which bypassed intellectual understanding.

According to Maritain, to be truly effective in moral education the school must teach two types of morality, natural and supernatural. *Natural morality* is contained in the natural law and lofty ethical ideals taught in the humanities or liberal arts, especially literature, poetry, fine arts, and history. These writings contain the moral experience of mankind and give a knowledge of piety, the distinction between good and evil, honor, the dignity of the person, and the greatness of human destiny.

Maritain argues that the school must also teach a *supernatural morality*, one based on the life of faith and religion. Moral teaching should be accompanied with religious inspiration. Care should be taken, however, to show that the moral rules of religion have the backing of reason. In arguing for a religiously based moral education, Maritain recognized that he was going against conventions of contemporary education. But for him God had as much right to be in the schools as Euclid or John Dewey, and children had the right to formal religious knowledge. Maritain suggested that this religiously based moral education be given by various teachers who belonged to the different religious creeds to which the students ascribed. Those students who nurture a bias against theology could be released from such classes and be "allowed to remain incomplete in wisdom at their own pleasure" (1943, p. 75).

Evaluation Maritain must be examined at two levels: as a philosopher of Catholic or religious schools and as a philosopher of moral education in secular schools. Indeed Maritain has presented the classic philosophy for Catholic schools with high ideals and a suitable methodology. A number of questions, however, can be raised about his educational philosophy. His basic distinction between the natural and supernatural has been rejected or at least modified by many contemporary theologians and philosophers who espouse a more integrated view of the human person. His view of the human person as constituted of different faculties of the soul (e.g., senses, intellect, and will) now appears a rather inappropriate way to describe human psychology.

Maritain wrote out of a conception of the Catholic Church as the infallible interpreter of faith and morals. Modern religious philosophers and theologians have demonstrated that the religious certainty proposed by Maritain cannot be justified even on purely religious grounds. The Christian Scriptures are open to various interpretations. Church doctrine has been developed over the centuries. Maritain's appeal to universal truths and moral absolutes fails to take into account both development and errors in religious teachings.

These somewhat negative criticisms, however, must be balanced by values in Maritain's educational philosophy which offer a corrective to modern educational practices. One of his greatest strengths is his emphasis on the intellectual in moral education. Maritain's warnings make one suspicious of any effort in moral or religious education which attempts to change attitudes or behavior without first appealing to reasoned thought. Though Maritain may be accused of an exaggerated rationalism in his educational proposals, his warnings against anti-intellectualism and voluntarism in education are as important today as when he first uttered them.

Perhaps the most disputable aspect of Maritain's philosophy is his argument for a moral education based on religious principles even for public or state schools. While what he proposes may be possible in some countries, the laws and traditions of many countries, including the United States, go contrary to such a form of moral education. Developments in the United States in the decades since he made his proposal have made his suggestions even more unfeasible. The controversy over prayer in schools shows the strong opposition to any form of religion or religious education in schools.

Though it is true that the religious pluralism of many countries prevents an approach to moral education based on religious principles, the whole issue of religion in public or state schools demands more careful study. Some educators in the United States have espoused a teaching *about* religion (e.g., a course in the Bible as literature or a course in comparative religions) which they feel is consonant with national traditions and law (Engel 1974; Byrnes 1975). In England and Canada there appear to be more possibilities for a moral education that draws at least in part on religious teaching and traditions (Taylor 1975; Beck 1976, 1981).

While Maritain's arguments are doubtful with regard to public schools, they need to be seriously considered in the case of moral education in families, religious bodies, and religious schools. The advantage of his position is that he attempts to steer a middle road between authoritarian indoctrination and neutralism, or between imposition and free expression (Hill 1973, p. 246). What Maritain offers us, I believe, is not so much a valid description of a morally educated person and recommendations for forming this person but rather a mode of utilizing philosophy and theology in developing a religious approach to moral education. Maritain placed himself in dialogue with the human sciences of his time. From a Christian standpoint he grappled with the pragmatic and positivistic thrust in education. In this he is an excellent model for the educator who wants to be faithful both to religious tradition and to contemporary culture.

That the tradition represented by Maritain is not a dead one is indicated by the arguments put forward by Bloom (1987) for the introduction of a more serious liberal education into our schools and universities. Bloom also decries the fact that religion and morality do not play a large role in the education of the young. He contends that:

The other element of fundamental learning that has disappeared is religion. . . . Attending church or syngagogue, praying at table were a way of life, inseparable from the moral education that was supposed to be the family's special responsibility in this democracy. Actually, the moral teaching was the religious teaching (Bloom 1987, pp. 56–7).

All education should have a moral purpose, deal with such issues as, what is the human person, what moral values should permeate our lives, and what is human destiny. This education takes place by opening students to the moral, intellectual, and spiritual values contained in the great books of our civilization.

MORAL EDUCATION AS SCIENTIFIC INQUIRY: JOHN DEWEY

While Jacques Maritain based his philosophy of moral education on the principles of a metaphysical philosophy and a supernaturalist theology, the American philsopher John Dewey developed a theory of moral education which relied on a naturalistic philosophy and empirical science. Dewey's writings have been influential in many of the approaches to moral education that have emerged in recent years (Hersh, Miller, and Fielding 1980, p. 25). Values clarification, the cognitive developmental approach of Kohlberg, social action models, and valuing analysis all appeal in some way to the seminal ideas of John Dewey. Even religious educators have attempted to adapt his naturalist philosophy for the purposes of education in religion.

The philosophical position underlying Dewey's concept of moral education is pragmatism or instrumentalism. Looked at broadly, one can find in pragmatic thought six major dimensions: adherence to the scientific method for discovering knowledge; a pluralist world view; an emphasis on subjectivity at the expense of an unreachable objectivity; a concern for social action; acceptance of consequences of actions as constitutive of truth and morality; and a careful analysis of language and ideas. Each of these dimensions plays a key role in Dewey's philosophy.

The Morally Educated Person   John Dewey rejected any approach to morals that viewed the moral dimension of the person as distinct from other aspects. Thus the moral is in continuity with the intellectual, biological, and social. In his view:

> Morals concern nothing less than the whole character, and the whole character is identical with man in all his concrete make-up and manifestation. To possess virtue does not signify to have cultivated a few nameable and exclusive traits; it means to be fully and adequately what one is capable of becoming through associations with others in all the offices of life (1916, p. 358).

Dewey not only envisioned a unity of the moral aspect with all aspects of the person but also identified the moral dimension with the social life of individuals.

The aim of moral education in Dewey's theory can be clarified from a consideration of his view of the human person. Dewey's naturalist view of the person is opposed to theological or metaphysical views such as proposed by Maritain. His theory of the human person comes from biology, psychology, and the social sciences. The human person develops by interactive adaptation to the environment. While the environment shapes people, their intelligence adapts the environment to their needs. Human nature is thus manifested in the formation of habits which result from the degree to which intelligence has controlled and shaped the impulses of emotion.

One of the distinctive features of Dewey's philosophy of the person is his opposition to the dualisms of traditional philosophy: body and soul, physical and spiritual, character and actions, and motives and consequences. He also opposed the accepted resulting dualisms in education: child and society, interest and discipline, vocation and culture, and knowledge and action. Dewey saw these dualisms as favoring the aristocracy of past knowledge and tradition, where one set of values was considered superior to another, over an openness to new knowledge and understandings. Though he admitted distinctions among the various aspects of human nature, he was more interested in showing the unity and the continuity among all aspects of the person.

There is little room in Dewey's philosophy of the person for what is described in religious teachings as original sin, that is, innate evil propensities in individuals. Neither, as time went on, did he accept the romantic view that people are predisposed toward the good. Persons, according to him, are neither predisposed to evil nor to good but are rather full of potentialities which can be directed either to destructive or constructive ends. The natural tendencies, impulses, and emotions of persons are capable of being nurtured and developed through an educational process and an educational environment which can simplify, order, purify, and idealize these dispositions as well as create situations wherein they can be developed (1916, p. 22).

In a true sense it is not possible to state precisely what Dewey's view of the morally educated person is since Dewey considered growth the only proper aim of education. The final end of growth cannot be determined beforehand; its ends are not fixed. Thus the chief ends of education for Dewey are processes rather than static stages. He spoke of the promotion of reflective behavior as well as the promotion of growth and health. Education was for him its own end. Thus in his view the morally educated person would be one who had developed skill in processes of inquiry, understanding, and continuing commitment to seek proper moral attitudes. All of these characteristics must be developed within the context of a social group or community.

While Dewey spoke of the objectives of education in terms of growth, he also clearly stated that education is to fulfill certain social ends or goals. In fact social goals loom large in his philosophy because of his concern for social reform. It appears that there exists in his philosophy a subordination of individual goals to societal goals. This will be a point of discussion in evaluating Dewey's philosophy of moral education.

Educational Method in Moral Education   The importance that Dewey attached to moral education can be seen in his classic pamphlet *My Pedagogic Creed* (1964) published in 1897. In this short work Dewey introduced themes which appeared again and again in his later writings. Dewey recognized that all persons are involved in an *unconscious education* (now called socialization) in which the intellectual and moral resources of human history were assimilated. He called conscious education *formal* or *technical education*. This was described as "the stimulation of the child's powers by the demands of the social situation in which he finds himself" (1964, p. 427). All education thus has two sides: a psychological side that includes the child's instincts and powers and a sociological side that includes the social conditions in which these instincts and powers develop. Though education begins with the psychological, it is more important as a social activity where the child's powers can be of service to society (1964, p. 430).

In Dewey's view the school is primarily a social community or institution where children are socialized into the values of society through interactive learning activities. Dewey considered it the task of the school to deepen and extend the moral training and sense of values which were learned in the home. The moral education which Dewey proposed for the school is one that centers on:

> The school as a mode of social life [where] the best and deepest moral training is precisely that which one gets through having to enter into proper social relations with others in a unity of work and thought (1964, p. 431).

The role of the teacher in this type of school is not to impose ideas or to form certain habits but rather to be a member of the community in selecting the influences that will bear upon the child and to assist the child to respond properly to these influences. Dewey thus stressed the social responsibility of the teacher's role. The teacher was to be an example and an advocate of the highest values of society.

Dewey recognized that moral education also has an individualist purpose in that it is also directed at the formation of a certain character which is needed as a foundation for right living. He stresses a rather socialistic aspect of moral education which:

> Recognizes that this right character is not to be formed by merely individual precept, example, or exhortation, but rather by the influence of a certain form of institutional or community life upon the individual, and that the social organism through the school, as its organ, may determine ethical results (1964, p. 437).

It is clear that for Dewey a progressive moral education was closely connected with the school's fundamental purpose of social progress and reform.

The themes which Dewey introduced in his pedagogic creed found their way into other writings on moral education. One of his early statements, written in 1903, is found in "Logical Conditions of a Scientific Treatment on Morality" (1964). Dewey here adjudged that the approach to moral education that taught particular virtues was narrow, formal, external, and pathological. He suggested an approach to moral education that used the scientific method: one begins with felt needs or real doubts; isolates and clarifies problems; develops hypotheses; projects and rehearses solutions and consequences in the imagination; and creatively considers ideas in a new configuration. According to Dewey, this scientific method will ensure objectivity in moral judgment and provide the necessary public justification.

In this same article Dewey gave careful attention to the formation of a moral character that possessed a sense of social responsibility. One who had this moral character possessed a "power of social agency, an organized capacity of social functioning." This power also included "social insight or intelligence, social executive power, and social interest or responsiveness" (1964, p. 133).

This formation of character, according to Dewey, demanded not only having good intentions but also developing force and efficiency in action. The teacher does this by finding the native potential of the child and organizing it into definite modes of action-habits. Dewey, however, did not recommend brute force for bringing this about but rather encouraged the development of the power of judgment and emotional responsiveness trained by actual experiences with concrete problems. Thus moral education in the school must proceed from a willingness to allow children to express their impulses and potential. The power of judgment will be developed only if children have the opportunity to select for themselves and put their selections into action. Emotional responsiveness is promoted by the aesthetic environment of the school and the contact of children with the best in literature, history, and the arts.

Dewey did not completely reject moral principles, laws, and rules but considered them of little value unless they were stated in psychological and social terms as well as translated "into the actual conditions and working habits which make up the doing of the individual" (1964, p. 138). What more metaphysically oriented theorists termed absolute moral principles Dewey considered significant historical and social statements which have been developed through common human experience and which may be important for judging cases today. One moral principle that Dewey came close to recognizing as an absolute is democracy.

Dewey's approach to moral education is exemplified in the undergraduate textbook *Ethics* (1978) which he published in 1908 with James Tufts. This book, which went through twenty-five printings before it was revised in 1932, covered the history of ethics, the theory of ethics, and the world of action in which ethical principles were applied to concrete social problems. The aim of this book was to give students a sense of how moral conduct is connected to solving personal and social problems in a social setting. In this approach to ethics an integral and inseparable relationship exists between knowledge, and action, research and its consequences, science and ethics, the natural world and human values.

In his theories Dewey was true to his basic principles for organizing a curriculum. The unity of the curriculum is found, according to him, not in classical works, metaphysical principles, or religious truth but in the solution of concrete life problems through the use of the methods of science. This emphasis on morality for solving social problems is in keeping with Dewey's basic view of the moral which he expressed in these terms:

Ultimate moral motives and forces are nothing more or less than social intelligence—the power of observing and comprehending social situations—and social power—trained capacities of control—at work in the service of social interests and aims (Dewey 1964, p. 130).

Evaluation of Dewey's Philosophy of Moral Education   John Dewey's influence on moral philosophy and moral education has been considerable. He has been praised for his introduction of a more serious consideration of moral principles in the educational process and maintaining the union of the intellectual and the moral (Beck et al. 1971, p. 4). His integration of social psychology and moral philosophy has received praise and endorsement (Kohlberg 1971, p. 24). Kohlberg also contends that his own cognitive developmental theory is rooted in Dewey's view that moral education should begin with the stimulation of the natural development of the child (1971, p. 71). Advocates of values clarification assert that their theory is built upon Dewey's moral theory (Raths, Harmin, and Simon 1968, p. 7). Finally, in a probing analysis of contemporary theories Dewey is presented as a "chairman" for a discussion of key theories (Chazan 1985).

Notwithstanding Dewey's great influence, his ethical theory can be criticized for a number of reasons. While many agree with his rejection of metaphysical and ethical absolutes, his grounding of ethics in empirical facts rather than in moral principles or values is considered a serious weakness. In his philosophy Dewey almost obliterated the distinctions between fact and value, between empirical statements and value statements, as well as between what is and what ought to be. A distinction must be drawn between what one values and what one recognizes as a fact. To say that one values something is to indicate one's approval of the action, an implied prescription that others would be wise to do the same thing and an implied standard for making such a judgment.

Dewey may or may not be correct in his rejection of an absolute good such as a *summum bonum* or an absolute standard by which everything is to be judged. Yet he goes too far in the limited value he gives to principles in his ethical theory and in the stress that he places on consequences. Hierarchies of values do exist: for example, life is more valuable than property and truth is more valuable than pleasure. Also, one can believe in a relativity of values and still admit the importance of general principles and standards.

Two contradictory criticisms have been made of Dewey's ethical theory. While some have criticized him for advocating an extreme individualism, others contend that in his moral philosophy the individual is dissolved into social functions (Maritain, 1943; Hollins, 1964). These criticisms go to heart of the essential ambiguity in progressive education. One strand of progressivism—the child centered emphasis—led to a stress on the needs of the child. Another strand emphasized the adjustment of the child to society. Dewey addressed this problem in his later educational work *Experience and Education* (1938), where he rejected both positions in favor of a middle way.

My reading of Dewey leads me to the conclusion that he valiantly struggled with this fundamental problem in his moral theory. When he first began writing on education, his opponents were the advocates of absolute and universal moral principles. Dewey criticized them for appearing to be insensitive to interests and impulses in children and the power of children to shape their individual selves. In this context Dewey minimized the harmful inclinations of individuals and the possibly negative influences of certain cultures. He put greater stress on social values and minimized the need of individuals for a great deal of self-direction. At this time in his life he was still under the influence of Hegel's idealism which stressed social values over individual values.

Later in Dewey's career he became aware of extreme forms of individualism to which many were led by the application of his theory of education. Thus in *Experience and Education* (1938) he attempted to deal with the excesses of an overly individualistic morality and education by arguing for a more influential role to be exercised by teachers, society, and cultures. By this time he was also aware of the dangers of indoctrination which are inherent in any form of moral education that attempts to use education for purposes of social progress and reform. Dewey in this work distanced himself from some left-wing socialist educators who urged teachers to indoctrinate children in the principles of economic and political socialism.

While there are problems at the heart of Dewey's ethical theory, it has made several extremely important contributions to the field of moral education. The greatest of these may be the emphasis on developing critical intelligence in the young and the recognition that moral values are not immutable. Dewey's method of moral education stressed the need for children to learn about values in a practical context as well as the need for them to make choices of their own after a study of consequences. Dewey was also sensitive to the fact that the age and intelligence of children must be seriously weighed in moral education. His stress on the learning of values in cooperation with others is an important dimension in many contemporary forms of moral education. What Dewey leaves unresolved are the important issues of the hierarchies of values and the limits that should be placed on the free inquiry of the young into the very bases of society.

Dewey and Religion Education   While Maritain's theory of moral education is deeply rooted in religious faith, Dewey's theory contains a certain anti-religious dimension, which reflects his abandonment of traditional religious faith in favor of a common faith of humanity. His denial of moral absolutes made his ethical theory unacceptable to many religious contemporaries. It should be noted, however, that Dewey's opposition to *religions* did not extend to the *religious* dimension of life. A recent appraisal of Dewey suggests that his attitude towards the religious in education needs more careful consideration today (Burnett 1979).

Now that many theologians have softened their position on absolute moral values and have also admitted the validity of empirical facts in helping to determine moral values, there is a greater openness among religious educators to the philosophy Dewey advocated. Dewey's ideas have always found acceptance among religious educators who have espoused a liberal theological approach to both religion and education (Coe 1917; Elliot 1940; Fahs 1952). This particular system of moral and religious education has been termed the social-cultural approach (Burgess 1975).

Moral education in this theory does not relate moral character primarily to such religious practices as Bible reading and church attendance but is more importantly the education of persons for social responsibility. Moral education has as its purpose the promotion of social welfare, social justice and a world society (Coe 1917, pp. 57–59). In this theory limited use is made of specifically religious sources in moral education. Though the theory tended to identify the religious with the social, it has made a significant thrust in awakening religious persons to the this-worldly character of all religious faiths. Contemporary religious educators attempt to utilize the resources of religious faith and social interaction in developing approaches to moral education.

EXISTENTIALISM AND MORAL EDUCATION: MARTIN BUBER

Existential philosophy developed in France and Germany between the two World Wars as part of a broad cultural movement which shaped not only philosophy but also psychology, psychotherapy, religion, and the arts. Though there are many differences among existentialist thinkers, what they have in common is an emphasis on the personal, dramatic, and emotional elements of human existence rather than on the rational, abstract, and objective elements. Existentialists are fearful of such developments in modern society as technology and powerful nation states that weaken human freedom and individuality. Within existentialism one finds a strong opposition to any form of behaviorism or determinism. All existentialists attempt to come to grips with limit or crisis situations such as suffering, consciousness, freedom, alienation, human relationships, faith, and death.

Among existentialists one can find both optimistic and pessimistic thinkers on the human condition, though the pessimistic thinkers tend to predominate. While many existentialists reject religious faith, a number of influential existentialists propose a radical religious faith. The differences as to religious faith are manifest in two twentieth century precursors of existentialism. Soren Kierkegaard (d. 1955) analyzed the dread of human freedom which people experience in their attempt to break out of oppressive political and ecclesiastical systems. The tragedy of life in his view could only be managed by a leap of faith which brought a person to a dependence on God (Kierkegaard, 1941). For Frederick Nietzsche (d. 1900) the denial of religious faith in God opens the way for persons to create their own values and to live fully and dreadfully responsible to themselves (Nietzsche 1966).

Twentieth century existentialist philosophers include such diverse thinkers as Jean Paul Sartre, Albert Camus, Gabriel Marcel, Martin Heidegger, and Martin Buber. Of these only Buber has written explicitly on education, though he presents insights into education rather than a systematic educational theory. His existentially based character education will be the main focus of this section.

Before examining the moral education based on existential thought, I will first describe in brief form some themes of existentialism that have some bearing on moral education. Because of the wide range of views among existentialists, it is difficult to generalize these themes to all thinkers in the same way.

Existentialism is a philosophy of revolt. It contains an emotional revolt against the limits placed on human existence. It calls into question the contemporary scientific world view and opposes efforts to explain the world in rational terms. Bureaucracy and technology are forms of social life that they find most destructive. Existentialists also reject the depersonalization, dehumanization, and destructive potential of modern social structures. Finally, existentialists, even those who favor religion such as Buber, Marcel, and Jaspers, are in revolt against institutionalized religious faiths.

A second basic theme in existentialism is the priority of human existence over any preconceived nature or essence of human beings. Existentialists have no prototypes of the human such as the classical view of persons as rational animals. There is in persons a peculiar freedom that enables them to fashion their own essences. The ethical thrust of this belief is that persons use their freedom to make themselves, their history, and their destinies. Humans are viewed not abstractly but rather as unique individuals who are able to shape themselves through free choices.

The uniqueness of each individual is related to the contingency of human existence, the realization that everything could have been otherwise. Sartre expresses this contingency in his play *Nausea*: "Every existing thing is born without reason, prolongs itself out of weakness and dies by chance" (1949, p. 180). This principle is in opposition to a rigid natural law or determinist view of the world. For religious existentialists such as Paul Tillich (1951), this awareness of contingency gives rise to a belief in a Ground of Being that undergirds all of life.

The awareness of the contingency of human existence has led some existentialists to a belief in the absurdity or irrationality of human existence. In this view no rational explanation can be given for the present state of affairs in the world. Camus' *Myth of Sisyphus* (1955) is a dramatic attempt to dialogue with the absurdity of human existence. Camus contends that it is human destiny to live with awareness in an absurd and meaningless world. The leap of faith that religious existentialists propose in such a situation is no less demanding an option than atheism, for it entails living in a world without a firm and objective anchor in God.

All existentialists are agreed on the important fact that persons must exercise freedom and bear responsibility for their choices. Existential freedom is affirmed even in the face of strong scientific evidence for determinism. For Sartre freedom is absolute in the sense that neither science, nor morality, nor God, nor reason have any power over human freedom. Freedom for him is actually a great burden because persons must bear ultimate responsibility for the effect that their choices have on others (Sartre 1956, p. 554). This radical freedom is a prerequisite for morality. Other existentialists such as Tillich and Buber stress human freedom and responsibility but also recognize some of the limitations placed on it.

A final theme that is found in all existentialists is the importance of personal relationships. Martin Buber in his classic *I and Thou* (1958) analyzed two possible relationships: "I and It", a subject-object relationship in which one person uses other persons or things without allowing them to exist for themselves in their uniqueness; "I and Thou", a relationship of openness, directness, mutuality, and presence. It is this relationship which opens a person to a relationship with the Eternal Thou. Buber's views are echoed by Marcel's (1967) notion of the unique personal presence that is felt in deep human relationships.

At the other end of the spectrum from Buber's positive and inspiring view is Sartre's view of human life as the inevitable clash of persons in which freedom and dignity become diminished. He believes most human relationships are inauthentic because either one person seeks to dominate another (sadistic relationship) or to be dominated by another (masochistic relationship). Sartre unfortunately does not consider the possibility of authentic existence wherein one does not act, pose, or posture for another but chooses a path that is one's own and thereby maintains freedom. In *No Exit* (1948) Sartre showed how other persons are threats to freedom and human existence. In his well known expression "Other people are hell" he expressed his fear that others have the potential to annihilate our personal freedom and authentic existence.

Paralleling the developments in existentialism has been the philosophical movement of phenomenology. Edmund Husserl, the father of phenomenology, attempted to present a rigorous description of the elements of human consciousness, (e.g., what it means to know, be free, love, think, and feel). The hybrid, existential phenomenology, coming from a combination of existential and phenomenological analysis, attempts to investigate the conditions of human existence in systematic ways. A few philosophers of education have utilized this approach in dealing with educational issues, notably Freire (1970; 1973) and Vanderberg (1971), but no approach to moral education distinct from existentialism has yet appeared employing this form of analysis. An excellent review of developments in phenomenology of education is found in Vanderberg (1979).

Education for Character According to Martin Buber

The religious existentialism of the Jewish philosopher Martin Buber has influenced several academic areas: philosophy, theology, psychology, and education. Although Buber did not publish a book devoted exclusively to education, he did address educational issues in various articles, speeches, and letters. His most detailed treatment of education is found in two chapters of his *Between Man and Man* (1965).

Buber is best interpreted as a philosopher of the human person (i.e., a philosophical anthropologist). The object of his lifelong study was the concrete, self-conscious individual. Major themes in his philosophy include the I-Thou and I-It relationships, the centrality of dialogue in human life, a stress on human freedom, an openness to a relationship with God, and a preference for the small community over the large collective. All of these central themes are brought to bear on issues concerning the nature and methods of moral education.

The Morally Educated Person   In describing what he considers the person of great character Buber rejects what he considers are two well known views: the natural law emphasis on absolute values and the pragmatic emphasis on habits. In rejecting the idea that persons possess great ethical character if they obey absolute values, maxims, or principles, Buber is in disagreement with the natural law ethics of Maritain and other metaphysical thinkers. Buber accepts the fact that there is widespread denial of the absoluteness of moral norms and that the arguments to establish absolute values are useless. Yet at other times he does not totally reject the usefulness of absolute or eternal values, since he does state that norms play a role in morality as guides or commands to be considered in a particular situation.

Buber explicitly rejects the pragmatic view which he somewhat mistakenly associates with John Dewey's opinion that the great moral character possesses a system of habits gained through life experiences. His argument against Dewey is that habits do not often prepare us for the particular ethical choices we face in life. Buber admits the value of habits but contends that they are limited and are not at the heart of the ethical character. Habits do not prepare us for what is unique in the moral situation.

Buber describes the morally educated person:

> I call a great character one who by his actions and attitudes satisfies the claim of situations out of deep readiness to respond with his whole life, and in such a way that the sum of his actions and attitudes expresses at the same time the unity of his being in its willingness to accept responsibility (1965, p. 114).

In this description of the great moral character Buber stresses two key existential concepts: a free response to a particular situation and the acceptance of responsibility for one's responses and actions. Yet Buber's interpretation of these concepts differs considerably from interpretation of other existentialists, such as Sartre or Camus, since he grounds his theory in a religious view of life.

Buber's moral theory is founded on religious faith and the relationship between the I and the Absolute Thou. When he asked himself a question about the ultimate aim of education, he rejected such images as the Christian, the gentleman, and the citizen. For him the ultimate aim of education is:

> Nothing but the image of God. That is the indefinable, only factual direction of the responsible modern educator. . . . When all directions fail there arises in the darkness over the abyss the one true direction of man, toward the creative Spirit. . . . Man, the creature, who forms and transforms the creation, cannot create. But he, each man, can expose himself and others to the creative Spirit. And he can call upon the Creator and perfect his image (1965, pp. 102–103).

Buber's analysis of the relationship between religion and morality is profound. God is at the basis of morality since God reveals self in human relationships. The way to God is opened up and made clear in a relationship of person to person, and person to the world. Neither God nor moral values are known as transcendent realities which are knowable in themselves apart from dialogue with others or the world.

Buber's grounding of his moral theory in religion does not, however, give him the certitude which other systems of religious ethics often assume on the basis of a special revelation. Buber used the expressive metaphor of the "narrow ridge" to describe his religious standpoint to his friends. By this expression he meant that he:

> Did not rest on the broad upland of a system that includes a series of sure statements about the absolute, but on a narrow rocky ridge between the gulfs where there is no sureness of expressible knowledge but the uncertainty of meaning that remains undisclosed (1965, p. 184).

This lack of certainty in the moral sphere comes from Buber's realization that the knowledge of God is intimately linked with the knowledge of persons. His experience of Jewish mysticism during the First World War gave him "the thought of the realization of God through man." Humans appeared to him as the beings "through whose existence the Absolute, resting in its truth, can gain the character of reality (1965, p. 185).

Buber's Educational Method Buber's great interest in moral education is shown by his attention to methods. His purpose in proposing three main methods was to suggest a moral education which did not have to confront established dogmatic creed with another dogma (Cohen 1979, p. 757).

The first method which Buber proposed was a reading by students and teacher of spiritual documents in the Jewish tradition. These readings enabled learners to assimilate works of the human spirit that deal with ethics and values. Buber's second method was to lead students to recognize the limits of science, move to the boundaries of reason, and ask questions that were accessible only through prayer.

For Buber, however, the main method of moral education lay in the example of the teacher made manifest in the dialogical relationships with students. Moral characters are formed not by moral geniuses but by persons who are wholly alive and able to communicate with fellow human beings. To be effective, moral educators need the humility to recognize that they are only one element in the lives of their students. They must be aware of their responsibility in selecting the reality they make manifest to students. Finally, and most important, teachers need to develop the confidence of students in them that comes from participation in students' lives.

Though Buber, with other existentialists, emphasized the freedom of individuals, he recognized that in the educational process teachers must have a strong directive role. Educators are responsible for selecting and arranging the world of values which they present to students. This selection and arrangement should not be done in an arbitrary manner but should proceed from a deep penetration of the life of students and of the world. Educators, according to Buber, must "include" the life of students.

The concept of "inclusion" is an important one for Buber. An inclusion relationship exists between two persons who experience a common event in which at least one person actively participates. In this relationship:

One person without forfeiting anything of the felt reality of his activity, at the same time lives through the common event from the standpoint of another. . . . I call it experiencing the other side (Buber 1965, p. 97).

Through this concept Buber was able to maintain the dialogical relationship in education, but still recognize that there cannot be the total mutuality that characterizes the relationship of friendship.

One further dimension of Buber's moral education needs to be developed, his concept of social education. With the rise of Nazism in Germany during the 1920s and 1930s, Buber vehemently opposed the educational goals being set by the collective society. In this situation Buber proposed that educators bring values to the attention of their students, lead discussions on the meaning of values, propose alternative value systems, submit all value systems to critical investigation, and describe examples of personal truth in action. Buber cautioned against involvement in social movements which used methods of compulsion rather than methods of freedom. The form of social education which he proposed:

Seeks to arouse and to develop in the minds of its pupils the spontaneity of fellowship which is innate in all unravaged human souls and which harmonizes very well with the development of personal existence and human thought (Buber 1957, p. 176).

Thus throughout his life Buber was consistent in his philosophy of values and his views on moral education. These are founded on personal consciousness, freedom, responsibility, dialogue, community, and relationship with the Absolute Thou.

Evaluation of Buber's Philosophy of Moral Education   Buber's philosophy of moral education has found limited acceptance among educators in North America. The same can be said in general about existential philosophy of education. Carl Rogers (1969), Reuel Howe (1963) and Wayne Rood (1970) have responded in a positive manner to his ideas. More recently, assessments on religious education (Gordon 1977a, 1977b; Goodman 1978) have indicated the enduring strengths of Buber's philosophy of education.

Buber's attempted to avoid the two extremes of imposition of values by society or collectives and an abandonment of persons to choosing their own values without outside assistance and direction. Buber seemed to avoid these extremes both in his religious and philosophical writings. He proposed the use of Hasidic stories and Bible stories for bringing students into contact with a religious heritage. Yet the heart of his teaching is the reality of the dialogical relations which enables persons to respond to other persons, works of art, the Bible and God. In this way Buber is able to balance the demands of tradition and culture with those of freedom and responsibility.

In reading Buber's description of the teacher-student relationship in character education one can sense the demand being made on the teacher. More than with other philosophers of education one gets the impression that Buber's philosophy arises out of his own practice. The ideals which Buber presents are both lofty and expressed in poetic language. These ideals would make most teachers feel rather inadequate. Gordon (1977b) shows an awareness of this difficulty when he remarks that while educators have his books on their shelves "discussions on how to live as Buber indicated are scarce" (p. 581).

Besides his teaching on dialogue, the most significant issue in Buber's philosophy is the relationship between religion and morality. There is an apparent contradiction in Buber's refusal to recognize a traditional creed of received values and his assertion that all ethical values have their source in God alone and that divine revelation brings us into relationship with God. Ordinarily believers in God and in divine revelation appeal to universal principles and rules. Buber's resolution of this apparent contradiction is profound. God's revelation is found in the Bible. But this revelation does not impose values on human persons for God neither dictates nor fixes the confines within which persons are constrained to act. Persons are free to choose and act. This immanentist approach to God's action in the world and God's relationship to man's moral activity has influenced theological ethics.

What Buber's theory leaves unclear is what makes actions morally good or morally evil, if personal freedom is the ultimate determinant of moral values. Also, though Buber scholars (e.g. Cohen 1979, p. 747), contend that Buber's position differs radically from that of Sartre who reduced morality to absolute existential freedom, just how this is so is not made clear. Buber's response to this problem is in terms of the inherent risk involved in moral decision making.

Buber grappled for his entire life with the problem of evil. He came to believe that no person is irretrievably bad and that radical evil is impossible in relations of person to person. Yet he also recognized the evils in Germany during the Nazi regime. His attitude toward evil needs closer analytic study (Hill 1973, p. 194).

Notwithstanding these critical issues, it can be said that Buber offers valuable insights for a religiously based moral education. The value of these insights is enhanced by the realization that a congruence existed between Buber's life and the high ideals he recommended to others in his writings, e.g., the value of dialogue and the power of love. He was the epitome of the existentialist educator, a person of deep convictions and firm commitments. He was deeply involved in keeping up the spirit of his fellow Jews in Germany in the 1930s. He advocated Jewish-Arab coexistence in the new state of Israel. His less than orthodox propounding of Judaism lessened his influence among his people. Buber's deep commitment to the sanctity of the individual and to all of life was manifested in one of his last public gestures: begging the State of Israel not to execute the war criminal Adolph Eichmann.

It is interesting to note the interest in Buber's philosophy of moral education in the attempt to develop a feminine approach to ethics and moral education (Noddings 1984). In developing an ethics and a moral education of care Noddings relies on such Buberian concepts as encounter, inclusion, I-Thou relationships, receptivity, reciprocity, and the role of the teacher. Although Noddings explicitly rules religion out of her approach, the approach has much to recommend it, complementing as it does, the Western traditional ethics of justice and rights. In the next chapter the work of Carol Gilligan will be noted, who from another perspective argues for an ethic of care and responsibility.

MORAL EDUCATION AND ANALYTIC PHILOSOPHY: JOHN WILSON

For the past three decades the dominant philosophy of education in the English speaking world has been analytic. This form of philosophy attempts to avoid the systems building of other forms and to concentrate on logic, language, and arguments. Analytic philosophy is more interested in the tools of inquiry than in the objects of inquiry. The goals of this philosophy appear more modest than other philosophies in that it examines such issues as ambiguity and vagueness, definitions, claims, slogans, metaphors, and fallacies in reasoning.

The efforts of analytic philosophers of education have changed over the past three decades. Ryle's classic work the *Concept of Mind* (1949) made a careful analysis of such verbs as knowing and understanding. Hardie (1942) drew on the Cambridge analytic school of Moore and Wittgenstein in arguing for an approach to education that concentrated solely on language. O'Connor (1967) applied the principles of language philosophy to such concepts as values, value judgments, morals, and religion.

From its very beginning the analytic movement has devoted attention to issues related to moral education. Prominent scholars who have offered analyses in this area include John Wilson (1967), Israel Scheffler (1960), R. S. Peters (1966), and Clive Beck (1971). Two major research projects in moral education have been closely connected with the analytic movement: the Framingham Research Project at Oxford and the Values Education Project at the Ontario Institute for Studies in Education.

The major criticisms leveled against analytic philosophers have been the narrowness of their concerns and their refusal to take stands on important social and political issues. While some analysts contend that their type of philosophizing demands a value neutrality, in recent years analysts have begun to involve themselves in normative and practical problems such as social injustice, equality, personal and social freedom, nuclear war, and ethical problems relating to science (Rawls 1971; Nozick 1974). Since many analysts have thus moved to more normative concerns, there is now less distinctiveness in this form of philosophy. One remaining difference may be that the traditional philosophies still have greater concern for building an organized system of thought.

The work of analysts in the sphere of moral education has been valuable. Chazan (1976) has indicated the components of the moral sphere which have received attention:

> *Reason* (thinking, reason, deliberation, cognitive skills); *moral principles*; *autonomy* (choice, the individual, decision making); intentions (commitment, belief, concern); *action* (doing, behaviors, performance) (p. 28).

In this view the moral situation contains alternative choices between good or evil and right or wrong. The moral person makes reasoned choices after consideration of relevant moral principles, becomes committed to the choices, and acts accordingly.

John Wilson's Rational Utilitarianism

The choice of a representative analytic philosopher of education is not an easy one. Anthologies on this subject include many excellent analysts (Chazan and Soltis 1973; Cochrane, Hamm, and Kazepides 1979). My selection of the British philosopher, John Wilson, is based on his excellent writings on moral education for over two decades. John Wilson is Reader and Tutor in the Department of Educational Studies, and Fellow of Mansfield College, Oxford. Wilson is particularly pertinent for this book since he has also shown a particular interest in religious as well as moral education. Other analysts will be mentioned in this section where their principles complement or differ from Wilson's.

Wilson's thinking is based on the necessity of finding the rules or principles by which we can determine what morality is, what a morally educated person is, and what types of moral education are appropriate for developing this person. According to Wilson, the primary question in moral education is not about a specific authority such as a church or a political system or a set of values contained in classical writings. The basis for moral education:

Should consist in imparting those skills which are necessary to make good or reasonable moral decisions and to act on them. We are not primarily out to impart any specific content, but to give other people facility in a method (Wilson 1970, p. 470).

The Morally Educated Person   Wilson has made a sustained effort to describe the morally educated person. First of all, he accepts Aristotle's teaching that to act morally a person must act freely and with full consciousness, act for the right sort of reasons, and have right dispositions of mind. For Wilson, Aristotle's ideas translate into components or attributes which constitute the morally educated person:

an *attitude* of respect/concern for others
an *ability* to be aware of emotions
an *attainment*: mastery of relevant knowledge
an *attainment*: bringing to bear of the above components
a *decision* about what to do or feel
an *attainment*: translation of this decision into action
a combination of these produces right actions and emotions (Wilson 1970, pp. 470–471).

According to Wilson's careful analysis, the moral person makes choices on the basis of reasons which can be considered good. Good reasons are those which are autonomously or freely held, logically constructed, consistent, and impartial. Good reasons commit a person to a way of acting and take precedence over other opinions. The morally educated person accepts the reasons of a moral authority not because an authority has so stated but because the person recognizes that such acceptance is reasonable. The moral person considers authorities as useful in society but not as having the power to bind the consciences of individuals. It is only the intrinsic goodness of actions which binds a person.

Wilson makes the strong contention that these characteristics can be derived from an analysis of what we mean by morality. These characteristics also concern "all that one would want to include under moral education" (1970, p. 471). Such persons can also be described as autonomous, rational, reasonable, mentally healthy, having a strong ego, and reality oriented. Wilson recognizes that not everyone can be educated to this ideal but for him the very effort is worthwhile.

A careful reading of Wilson's writings indicates that his approach is not narrowly rational or intellectual as some of his critics have charged. He is also interested in emotions, the will, and feelings of obligation and commitment. While these are important attributes for a morally educated person, it is clear that for Wilson it is by rational or reasonable standards that these dimensions of human nature are ultimately to be judged. These non-intellectual elements do not help to define the moral person unless they are clearly and directly related to a competence that is rationally moral. While Wilson admits that all forms of affective thought and action require the alertness, the determination, and other rational components, he points out that:

> There have been plenty of alert and determined men whose morality was disastrous because their alertness and determination were not geared to the proper concepts and principles (Wilson 1979, p. 183).

Though Wilson's description of the morally educated person does not necessarily entail an explicit mention of a religious perspective, he believes that some forms of religious belief might find his criteria adequate. He recognizes that the precept "love thy neighbor" may be valuable for teaching the skills which interest him. What he is more concerned about is that people do not accept religious commands arbitrarily but rather because they fit human nature and the human condition (Wilson, Williams, and Sugarman 1967). Wilson contends that his criteria for moral education are met by those religious educators who make the authoritative transmission of received traditions and commands give way to the open and honest search for living truths.

Wilson's description of the morally educated person is paralleled by the analyses of his fellow countryman, Richard Peters. Rather than speak of components, Peters refers to essential moral principles that characterize the morally educated person. Peters describes four essential principles: 1) *impartiality*: one does not act arbitrarily but makes distinctions only where there are relevant differences; 2) *consideration of the interests* of others: one manifests a benevolent and kind attitude; 3) *respect for the freedom of others*: a person has good reasons for restraining people from pursuing what they take to be good; 4) *respect for persons*: one does not treat persons as functionaries, objects, or things (Peters 1979, pp. 131–133).

Peters goes beyond Wilson in his relating of moral education to social, political, and economic values: what he calls democratic values. Democracy is briefly described by Peters as:

> A way of life in which high value is placed on the development of reason and principles such as freedom, truth-telling, impartiality, and respect for persons, which the use of reason in social life presupposes (1979, pp. 468–469).

Peters admits that these principles are purely procedural and do not offer a blueprint for the ideal society. Yet he contends that these procedural values are at the heart of democratic social and political systems. For Peters:

> Democracy is more concerned with principles for proceeding than with a determinate destination and aims of education in a democracy should emphasize the qualities of mind essential for such a shared journey (1979, p. 482).

Peters has manifested an openness to religious values. He thinks that the religious perspective is a possible, though not an essential perspective within a democratic society. Religions provide helpful insights and sensitivities and give concrete embodiment to intimations about the human condition. The world religions offer wider perspectives and ways of life that "transcend and transform what is demanded by truth and morality" (Peters 1979, p. 473).

Wilson's Suggestions for Moral Education   John Wilson is keenly aware of the limitations of philosophy for directing the actual practice of moral education. He recognizes that empirical factors, common sense, and the sciences of psychology and sociology have important contributions to make. Yet he contends that philosophy is extremely valuable in determining important aspects of method in moral education.

For a proper moral education of children in a school setting a number of preconditions must first exist. Children must have emotional security both at home and at school. They should have certain habits, moral training, and a framework of rules and discipline. Lingusitic skills should also be developed. Children should be able to relate emotionally to other people and take part in rule-governed activities. Finally, they need the social structure of the school and a relationship with a teacher. Wilson makes large assumptions here since it is recognized that these conditions are lacking in many places. A relevant moral education for schools must also attend to what can be done where these conditions do not prevail.

Wilson addresses two major issues in making concrete suggestions for moral education in schools: the context and the content. The *context of communication* is for him more important than the content since moral education is more concerned with procedures or processes than with content. For Wilson context includes understanding the task of moral education, fostering communication, understanding the ground rules of the school, having a degree of self-government, dividing the school into small groupings, providing outlets for aggression, and having an authority figure within the school.

Though stressing context, Wilson also examines the *content* of moral education. Among the items of content Wilson lists understandings of concepts and meanings, knowledge of general facts of social sciences, knowledge of prevailing moralities in law, professions, government, a study of history, literature, music, arts, teaching about practical living, and opportunities to help others (Wilson et al. 1967, p. 411–412).

In a response to a critic who charged that he ignored content at the expense of method or form, Wilson replied that moral education demands both form and content. As to content he argued that educators should present "few, if any, items of content as definitely proven or known to be true" (1970, p. 181). These items should be presented as moral beliefs "more or less widely subscribed to, which merit inspection and verification in the light of proper methodology" (1970, p. 181). With regard to the content of moral education Wilson is very concerned that the moral beliefs which children hold be their own beliefs.

Wilson's approach to moral education is a broad one in that he makes suggestions beyond what can be gathered from purely philosophical analysis. One of the reasons for this is that one of his major works in this area was a collaborative one with a psychologist and a sociologist (Wilson, Williams, and Sugarman 1967). Wilson recommends that teachers and parents present their own moral codes in a clear and definite manner. If children reject these, they at least know what they are accepting and rejecting. Drills, rules, and formation of habits should also be utilized. Wilson contends that the hard facts about money, power, war, and economic efficiency should be included in moral education. The task of the moral educator, however, is neither to produce conformity to the values of society nor to impose the particular view of the teachers on them. The task is to produce neither conformists nor rebels but to instill respect for and a capability of applying moral principles (Wilson 1970).

Evaluation of Wilson's Theory of Moral Education

What the analytic philosopher has provided in the field of moral education is an elucidation of the structural dimension of the moral sphere, an analysis of the concept of the morally educated person, and the conclusion that the components of this sphere and person are multi-dimensional and complicated (Chazan 1976, p. 28). It is the contention of such analysts that other approaches to the moral sphere are simplistic in reducing the moral sphere to one particular dimension, (e.g., cognitive, emotional, or legal). Though there are differences among analysts, these general conclusions are well established.

One weakness in the analytic position presented by both Wilson and Peters is their attempt to justify their description of the moral person. While the starting point of their philosophy is ordinary language, it appears that they appeal to some sort of intuition in describing the qualities of the moral person. Their description of such a person is also culturally conditioned by the ideals of the democratic societies of which they are a part. There does not appear to be in this philosophy an adequate realization of differences among cultures in defining moral standards and norms.

Most analytic philosophers now recognize that their system emphasizes the rational at the expense of other dimensions of the person. In this regard Wilson's methods differ from others since he made suggestions from a broader scholarly base. Such collaborative efforts would appear to be essential for developing a comprehensive theory.

One final aspect of the analytic approach for evaluation is the appropriateness of this theory for a religiously based moral education. One insightful philosopher is of the opinion that:

> The complicated sense of the moral way which emerges from contemporary analytic philosophy closely parallels the liberal religious conception of moral man (Chazan 1976, p. 32).

According to this liberal religious tradition, religious persons must be moral persons: that is, they must be thinking, choosing, principled, and acting agents. The liberal religious view of morality emphasizes that morality must include deeds: commitment, passion, and the disposition to act morally. In this viewpoint great importance is attached to individual choice and decision making. Finally, the liberal religious viewpoint emphasizes the complexity of the moral life (Chazan 1976, p. 37–39).

Though Chazan's case is modestly made, one can still question its adequacy. Neither the analytic approach to morality nor the liberal religious view of the moral person does full justice to other elements of the human situation: irrationality, tragedy, unfreedom, culture, determinism, and sinfulness. Only if the analytic perspective shows a capacity to grapple seriously with these dimensions will it offer the hope which Chazan and others see in this valuable approach to moral education.

CONCLUSION: PHILOSOPHY AND MORAL EDUCATION

After this presentation of four different philosophical theories, it may be helpful to note some of the contributions and limitations of philosophy to developing an interdisciplinary approach to a secular and a religiously based moral education. One of the major values of philosophy is that it moves moral

education beyond mere moralizing—simply conveying opinions and judgments about what is moral or immoral in society. By attention to philosophies, moral education can base itself in careful analyses of such concepts as
morality, the moral person, the moral sphere or situation, the justification of
moral judgments and systems, and systematic treatments of diverse moral
problems. Philosophy also has the advantage of raising broader questions
about the nature of the good life and the moral person in terms that transcend
local or cultural boundaries. Finally, philosophy in a particular way has an
openness to religious values in that it is not circumscribed by the empirical
methods which dominate in such disciplines as psychology and sociology.

Moral philosophy is valuable in making educators aware that programs of
moral education must be founded on some theory of justification or criteria of
right or wrong. Unless such a theory is present in the system, what takes
place is not education but either a form of conditioning, training or indoctrination or a mindless relativism. It is important to recognize that how moral
judgments are justified determines to a large extent the objectives, content,
and methods of moral education. If, for example, moral norms found in
religious literature are viewed as the infallible will of God, a distinct form of
moral education is appropriate.

While philosophy is an important component for developing an interdisciplinary approach to moral education, its limitations must also be noted.
Philosophy cannot offer convincing proofs that something is right or wrong
nor does it offer a generally acceptable theory for justifying moral choices.
Philosophy is best at clarifying alternatives and presenting arguments for
different positions. Philosophy in itself has nothing to say about what kinds
of moral education will work in particular cultures or for persons at various
stages of life. It is impossible to draw specific principles from philosophy
itself for how moral education should take place. To develop specific principles and practices, it is necessary to examine the contribution of psychology
and social sciences, the realities of particular situations, relationships among
individuals, and the values of various organizations. While philosophy does
not present this type of practical information, it is, however, in a position to
make critical judgments about such information.

Four representative philosophies of moral education have been presented
in this chapter. All four can form the basis for a secular or a religious moral
education. An adequate religiously based moral education must be responsive to important elements in each of these approaches. Though religious
assumptions, norms, and principles do not have to be expressed in Maritain's
terms, a religious based moral education must attempt what Maritain attempted to do in finding a rational basis for moral theory and education. It is
important for moral theory and education to take account of pragmatic
consequences in making moral judgments. The educational approach of

pragmatism highlights the value of moral education through involvement in concrete situations. The existentialists' emphasis on freedom and the importance of personal relationships and encounters is a valuable component of a religiously based moral education. Finally, the clarification that analysts provide the field of education and their careful scrutiny of language and arguments will prevent moral education from descending into tedious moralizing.

CHAPTER 3

PSYCHOLOGICAL THEORIES
OF MORAL EDUCATION

As we have seen, many academic disciplines have converged in an interest in moral education. Its history and the philosophy are replete with attempts to answer the classic question posed to Socrates in the *Meno*:

> Can you tell me, Socrates, whether virtue is acquired by teaching or by practice; or if neither by teaching nor practice, then whether it comes to man by nature, or in what other way (Guthrie (Tr.) 1956, p. 115).

The challenge presented to Socrates has been particularly addressed in our times by the discipline of psychology. Though various disciplines have been involved, it can be safely said that in the past two decades the most extensive contributions to moral education have come from psychology and social psychology. The relationship between psychology and moral education is clear from the obvious consideration that programs in moral education must take into account empirical findings on the development of children, adolescents, and adults. The important research of Hartshorne and May was summarized in my earlier historical survey of moral education. Moral psychologists in recent years have built on or challenged this seminal psychological research (Wright 1971; Sapp 1986).

A research conference under the sponsorship of the Ontario Institute for Studies in Education, Toronto, on the role of psychology in moral education and development pointed to the kinds of questions with which psychologists are concerned:

> What are the skills and psychological dispositions that are required for moral action? What are some of the psychological constructs that may be related to morality (e.g., personality development, intelligence, character)? Can types of moral judgment be graded according to their degrees of "rationality" or "sophistication"? How does the capacity of children for moral development change with age? In what ways can the child's moral development be facilitated and enhanced? Are there some types of envi-

ronments or training conditions that are especially important for moral growth? (Beck et al. 1971, p. 14).

These questions adequately summarize the kinds of concerns which psychologists bring to the area of moral education. It is not my purpose in this chapter to discuss all the different responses that psychologists give to these questions. My limited purpose is to review how major psychological theories describe moral development and what implications they find.

In this chapter I will review five major psychological theories: behaviorism, psychoanalysis, cognitive-developmentalism, social learning theories, and humanistic theories. I neither espouse one theory over the others nor present a unified synthesis of these theories. The psychological pluralism which exists is best maintained for the time being because of the important insights which each theory brings to our understanding of moral development. An issue of the *Journal of Ethics* (1982) surveyed the field of moral psychology and limited its treatment to just two psychological theories: social learning theory and cognitive-developmentalism. Though these are two major theories, an exclusive dependence on them ignores important contributions from behaviorism, psychoanalysis, and humanistic psychology.

Though no synthesis of psychological theories on moral development and learning exists at present, I believe that efforts might be made in this direction. One way to approach such a synthesis is to begin with the most simple and most basic theory and then work into the more complex ideas. This attempt may bring to light helpful comparisons and contrasts among theories though no adequate or satisfying synthesis may result.

Since one of the purposes of this book is to examine moral education from secular and religious contexts, the theories presented will be examined for their potential to promote understanding in both contexts. What must be recognized at the outset is that tensions often exist between psychology and religion. This is especially true, for example, of Skinner's behaviorism and Freud's psychoanalysis, because of the negative attitude toward religion which both theories contain. The challenge and criticism of these theories, however, must be accepted by religionists along with the congruence that appears to exist between religion and humanistic or cognitive developmental theories. Perhaps it is only by dealing seriously with psychological opinions which view religion negatively in moral development that we can better see the proper role of religion and avoid some improper uses of it in this enterprise.

The basic strategy of this chapter is similar to that used in the previous chapter. Each psychological theory will be examined to determine how it describes the morally educated person. Then the theory's suggestions and implications will be analyzed and criticized. The new element in this analysis, not contained in most philosophical theories, is a description of how and under what conditions persons develop as moral persons.

BEHAVIORIST THEORY OF MORAL DEVELOPMENT

The moral person for Skinner is one whose behavior has been so shaped and controlled that he or she conforms in all actions to what is best for the survival of the culture. It is a basic philosophic contention of radical behaviorism that all behavior is determined and under the control of environmental factors. There is no such thing as an autonomous person since according to radical behaviorism people are totally controlled by the environment in which they live. Those things become good which contribute to the long term survival of the species. In this theory, since persons do not have control over their actions, they should be given neither praise nor blame for them. This is what Skinner means by going *beyond* freedom and dignity.

Moral Development   The behaviorist theory on the development of values can be considered the least complex psychological explanation of moral learning. It is Skinner's view that:

A person's behavior is determined by a genetic endowment traceable to the evolutionary history of the species and by the environmental circumstances to which an individual has been exposed (1971, p. 96).

Skinner believes those things are good which reinforce or reward the individual. Those things are bad which do not reinforce the individual. In the evolutionary history of the human race some things have become good and may be used to urge people to behave for the good of others. Thus it appears to be accidental that some things have become good or bad. The influence of the genetic endowment of the individual also plays a role in human behavior, though this endowment is secondary to environmental factors according to Skinner.

Moral Learning and Education   In this radical behaviorist view moral learning does not differ from other forms of learning. Learning is reduced to the shaping of an individual's behaviors. Desired behaviors can be shaped by suitable rewards and by structuring the environment so that the desired behaviors can be educed more easily. It is Skinner's contention that undesirable behaviors should never be reinforced, neither by attention nor by punishment. These behaviors have a surer chance of extinction if they are simply ignored.

Moral education for Skinner thus entails the use of the technology of behavioral modification through which social controls are placed upon the behavior of all persons. Unless these controls are enforced, it will be impossible to avoid the multiple catastrophes that afflict our culture: pollution, murder, wars, the breakdown of families, and general moral decay.

A Critique   Within a limited scope it is difficult to argue with Skinner's basic contention that behavior is shaped by reinforcements. Parents, teachers, and others often resort to methods of reinforcement to inculcate right behaviors. Skinner's criticisms of the use of punishment as an effective tool for shaping behavior also have some merit. At a strictly philosophical level, it is just about impossible to refute Skinner's major contentions about the nature, causes, and consequences of human behavior. This is so because of the difficulty of proving conclusively the existence of internal forces within persons which are not reduced to behaviors.

However, Skinner's radical behaviorism does not offer the complete psychological foundations for moral development and education. Experience with behavioral modification shows a significant and dramatic drop in behavioral change for many subjects once they have left controlled situations for rather short periods of time. Also, various interpretations are possible for explaining the effectiveness of behavioral modification. For example, individuals may modify their own behavior in given situations. It is also a fact that other forms of shaping behavior exist which are equally effective and based on principles diametrically opposed to behavioral principles. This convinces me that persons possess a high degree of flexibility with regard to the route they may take to better themselves. This flexibility also demonstrates that though persons may not always have the power to shape their environments, they can exercise some control over how they respond to factors within their environments.

Skinner's ideas on learning values are important for reminding us that there are certain limitations to human freedom. Freedom is not an absolute condition but appears to be a freedom to control environment and behavior in terms of individual psychological states. Our background controls our freedom. But it is *our* background and values that control us. We also recognize that no matter how strong our backgrounds, in some cases we have the power to make decisions contrary to our background and values.

Religious Implications   In a previous analysis of behaviorism (Elias 1983) I pointed out that of all contemporary psychologists, Skinner is the most ignored by religious educators. Many religious educators have taken into account the Freudian critique of religion and moral education. My speculation on this difference in treatment is that despite his determinism, Freud still speaks of an inner person and that this inner person affords some point of contact with religious views of the person. Grappling with the radical behaviorism of Skinner can, however, sensitize educators to the powerful influence of environment on moral learning. Skinner's work also exposes how some forms of religiously based moral education have utilized ill advised methods of control. The behavioral modification that Skinner proposes can have some place in a moral education situated in a religious context, as has been proposed rather extensively by Lee (1971; 1973; 1984). Lee does not espouse a radical behaviorism but rather a modified one in his comprehensive theory of education which takes into account both behaviorist and non-behaviorist theories.

PSYCHOANALYTIC THEORY OF MORAL DEVELOPMENT

While behaviorism focuses on the external actions of the person, psychoanalytic theory concentrates on the dynamics of thought and feelings within individuals. Sigmund Freud, the founder of psychoanalysis, assumed that a person's behavior could not be understood except through a knowledge of a person's motives, fears, feelings, and thought processes. Freud's basic insights on human development have been extended into the moral area by the influential ego psychologist, Erik Erikson. This section will treat the views of both of these psychologists on moral development and the development of conscience.

Freud and Moral Development

Development of the Moral Person Freud considered conscience a manifestation of neurosis rather than a sign of emotional maturity. Freud's theory of conscience can be described in terms of a number of functions. Conscience is more of an *accuser* and a *tormentor* than a guide. In Freud's view conscience acts as a *repressor* of conscious intentions and ideals which a person has but is afraid to manifest for fear of losing a significant relationship. Conscience is also a *censor* of forgotten memories that are sexual in nature and that often appear in dreams. Finally, conscience is a *reservoir of the taboos* which are necessary for restraining basically undesirable urges (Miller 1977).

Freud developed a theory of the origins of conscience which is essential for understanding his view of human development. This theory can be described in a series of interrelated actions performed by children and parents. Young children experience many frustrations, some due to parental control and others due to such factors as illness and physical discomfort. These frustrations are connected with oral, anal, and genital satisfactions. Such frustrations create hostility towards parents and others. Children repress this hostility in order not to lose the love of their parents. To repress this hostility they consequently model their behavior after that of their parents and take on the parental prohibitions as their own. However, when children go against these internalized prohibitions, they experience guilt since they know they are doing things of which their parents disapprove. Children also develop defense mechanisms to protect themselves against their own impulses when these go counter to the internalized wishes of their parents.

It is clear that in this theory conscience develops essentially in an unconscious manner. Unconscious conflicts determine the values and behaviors. Children develop an irrational superego (internalized parental values) from unconscious identification with parents and their prescriptions and prohibitions. In Freud's view the rational dimension of the person (ego) is pitted in a struggle with the desire for self pleasure (id) and with the superego. The later two forces are irrational and punitive.

As Freud further refined his theory of human development he paid more attention to conscious ego processes (Freud 1933). He brought the concept of self-esteem into his theory of conscience. He came to believe that persons also acted morally to achieve certain ideals for themselves. This positive aspect of ego ideals forms an important part of Erikson's theory of moral development.

The heart of Freud's theory of conscience is the superego. It is this dimension which integrates the various functions of conscience into one single and complex activity: repressor, dream censor, observer, tormentor, and ego ideal. The severity of the superego depends on the relationships of the person to significant others. The unconscious nature of the superego makes one helpless in the development of moral values.

Freud in the latter part of his life became very sensitive to the demands that a culture or civilization makes. He came to believe that the continued existence of society demanded repression and restraint on individuals in the areas of sexuality and violence. This part of his theory goes counter to his earlier emphasis on the importance of the development of the ego as rational, deliberative, reality oriented, and conscious.

A somewhat neglected aspect of Freud's theory of moral development is discussion of the defense mechanism of sublimation, which he considered a valuable form of repression. Through this mechanism persons can transform what might be immoral instincts of sexuality and violence into socially acceptable patterns of behavior. Sublimation, for Freud, is the essential factor in building important aspects of culture such as religion, art, and literature.

Moral Education Freud's concern was not directly with education but rather with therapy. He believed that one of the purposes of therapy is the integration of the superego with the ego. Therapy is to make one aware of the functioning of superego as repressor, accuser, censor, and tormentor and to bring a degree of consciousness to the functions of the person in morality. The person must recognize the values that should be integrated into the ego.

Though Freud did not direct much attention to formal moral education, his ideas were influential for A. S. Neil's experiment at Summerhill (Neil 1960). This school was based on the principle that education was intellectual and emotional because it involved both intellect and feeling. Education was to be directed to the psychic needs and capacities of the child. It was Neil's belief that all guilt feelings were an impediment to independence and true education. Freud's influence on Neil is apparent especially in the area of sexuality. Both Freud and Neil, however, overestimated the significance of sex. For Neil education appears to be a therapy to remove the guilt that parents and society have imposed on children.

Neil also took from Freud a negative attitude toward religion. There was to be no religious instruction at Summerhill because of its alleged propensity to increase guilt, inspire fear, and decrease happiness. Neil as well as Freud were interested in those forms of religion which stressed basic humanistic values.

The direct influence of Freudianism in education has not been great outside this well known experiment. Its indirect influence, however, has been considerable in promoting an understanding of instincts, interests, and tendencies. Freud's ideas have formed the basis for many interpretations of human behavior which have influenced educational theory and practice. Educationists who contend that the schools are repressive institutions often look to Freud for support.

Freud's theory is open to criticism in its treatment of the development of the moral sense in women. Because male development is presented as normative in Freudian theory, women are assumed to achieve a weaker sense of morality due to the development of a weaker superego. Freud based this contention on the dubious notion that value identification and value internalization is weaker in young girls because they do not experience the early frustrations with sexuality that occasion the development of a strong moral sense. Psychologists have also rejected Freud's portrayal of woman as the temptress and scorner of civilization who squanders men's psychic energies which might otherwise be used for greater cultural benefits (Gilligan 1982).

Erikson: The Development of Moral Virtues

In more recent times it is Erik Erikson who has presented the most influential psychoanalytic theory of moral development. The emphasis in his theory is on the power or "virtue" (Erikson's terminology) of the person to develop in a healthy manner. Although Erikson remains true to the basic biological orientation of Freud, he expands Freud's thoughts about ego and moral development. Because of the primary emphasis this theory places on the interaction of persons with social institutions, his theory is termed a psychosocial theory of development. In this section I will examine Erikson's theory of human development primarily as it affects moral development. In an earlier work I attempted to relate his theory to religious development and education (Elias 1983).

Theory of Moral Development Erikson has speculated about innate moral strengths or virtues which he contends must be nurtured at various stages of time in order for the person to develop morally. In each of the eight stages of life he presents there are conflicts, challenges, and crises to be resolved. If development is correct, then these are met by the emergence of inner strengths within the person. The emergence of these virtues takes place within three periods of ethical development. Erikson lists three distinct areas of development: 1) *moral learning* in childhood; 2) *ethical or ideological experimentation* in adolescence; and 3) *ethical consolidation in adulthood* (1975, p. 22).

The *roots of virtue* should develop in childhood. The first crisis that the child faces is that of *trust versus mistrust*. This crisis or turning point is brought on by a combination of physical, psychological, and social factors. To resolve this crisis the child must develop the pre-moral ego strength or virtue of *hope*, which Erikson defines as "the enduring belief in the attainability of fervent wishes, in spite of dark urges and rages which mark the beginning of existence" (1964, p. 118). Hope is the virtue that enables one to live in the world without the paralyzing fear that one will be overcome by negative forces. As in all of these crises the healthy person must achieve a balance of the positive and negative (trust and mistrust).

The next crisis that the child faces is that of *autonomy versus shame or doubt*. This crisis arises when parents attempt to place limits or controls on the child, including but not restricted to control over bowel functions. The virtue the child should develop at this turning point is *will*, "the unbroken determination to exercise free choice as well as self-constraint, in spite of the unavoidable experience of shame and doubt in infancy (Erikson 1964, p. 119). The development of will is essential for the acceptance of law and rules during one's entire life. Its achievement demonstrates that individuals can exercise freedom with a certain degree of restraint and control. The role of parents is extremely important in the development of this and other virtues of childhood. The creation of a sense of shame and doubt are positive achievements for conscience development so long as they do not prevent the positive emergence of will.

For Erikson the *onset of mortality* takes place during the years between three and seven when the child faces the crisis of *intiative versus guilt*. Freud had connected the onset of morality with the superego's internalization of parental values. Erikson accepts this notion but then places more emphasis on the new ego strength that emerges to handle the initiative versus guilt crisis. In doing this he also softens Freud's harsh view of the superego. The virtue required at the onset of morality is *purpose*, "the courage to envisage and pursue valued goals, unhibited by the defeat of infantile fantasies, by guilt, and by the fear of punishment" (1964, p. 112). While Freud saw the years between three and seven as dominated by the beginnings of sexual conflicts, Erikson places these conflicts within the broader attempt to grapple with play and reality. It is in this grappling that the virtue of purpose develops.

In the period of childhood spanning ages seven to twelve the major crisis a child faces is that of *industry versus inferiority*. For Freud this time was called a latency period because during it no major conflict dealing with the development of a biological organism occurred. Anna Freud gave more attention to this period and described it as a time when children develop a number of important powers and abilities. Erikson drew on her interpretation in focusing on the virtue of competence as the necessary power for resolving the conflict between industry and inferiority. Erikson described *competence* as "the free exercise of dexterity and intelligence in the completion of tasks, unimpaired by childhood inferiority" (1964, p. 129). This virtue includes the personal joy and satisfaction which emerge when one successfully develops a skill. It also lays the foundation for work skills in later life. Not being able to develop the skills associated with school and play may lead to a sense of inferiority.

One of Erikson's major contributions to the field of psychology is his theory of adolescence and the importance he ascribed to the stage of adolescence in moral development. While Freud considered morality a survival of infantile childhood mentalities, Erikson presented a theory of moral development throughout the life span. During adolescence moral development was connected with the crisis between *identity and role confusion or diffusion*. This conflict is to be resolved by dealing in moral terms with one's sexuality and one's belief system or ideology. The virtue that enables one to resolve this crisis is *fidelity*, described as "the ability to sustain loyalties freely pledged in spite of the inevitable contradictions of value systems" (Erikson 1964, p. 125).

Adolescents deal in moral terms with their developing sexuality. Sexual maturity involves the unifying of sexual organism and sexual needs, the integration of love and sexuality, and the coordination of sexual, procreative, and work productive patterns. Ego identity cannot be achieved unless it includes some dimension of sexual identity. Erikson places sexuality within the wider concern for friendship, relationship, and interaction with others.

Erikson, however, does not regard the resolving of sexuality as the most important moral element in the formation of identity. What has even greater moral import at this stage of life is the working out of personal ideologies or belief systems to which adolescents may commit themselves. The ethical problems adolescents face are centered around where they are to put their now developed hope, will, purpose, competence, and fidelity. Often adolescents pass through a moratorium when they refrain from making such commitments. Other adolescents gets bogged down in a state of role confusion or role diffusion. One thing is clear, however—during adolescence many young people gain the rational capacity to take a moral point of view and moral stands (Parks 1986).

For Erikson, it is only in adulthood that the *true ethical sense* develops when persons face the crisis of *intimacy versus isolation*. Freud had little to say about the peculiar crises of adult life except that the mature adult is one who can learn to love and work without either inhibiting the other (Hale 1981). For young adults the major task is the achievement of the virtue of genuine *love* which Erikson defines as "the mutuality of devotion forever subduing the antagonisms inherent in divided functions" (1964, p. 129–130). Although the capacity for love develops in adolescence, the achievement of the true intimacy of love is an adult task. For Erikson love has a true ethical sense when it:

Encompasses and goes beyond moral restraint and ideal vision, while insisting on concrete commitments to those intimate relationships and world associations by which man can hope to share a lifetime of productivity and competence (1964, p. 226).

The lack of proper resolution of this conflict leads to an isolated existence wherein persons are unable to make needed intimate contact or close friends.

A second ethical conflict in adulthood, one that is associated with middle adulthood, is the conflict between *generativity and stagnation*. With the achievement of personal and career goals many persons experience a sense of complacency with their lives. At this time one is challenged to remain generative, to show concern for what has been generated in one's personal or work life, to show interest and concern for the wider community. The virtue or ego strength that needs development at this time is *care*, "the widening concern for what has been generated by love, necessity, or accident; it overcomes the ambivalence of adhering to irreversible obligations" (1964, p. 131). The temptation to become absorbed in oneself in mid life inhibits the development of this care. One develops morally at this time only if one recognizes that a full life extends beyond the self and includes all those whom one is called upon to love.

The final ethical conflict between *integrity and despair or disgust* confronts persons in the latter stages of their lives. In the face of loss of physical strength, retirement from some forms of active engagement, and the death of loved ones, persons need to develop the virtue of *wisdom*, "the detached concern with life itself, in the face of death itself" (1964, p. 133). Wisdom holds together in a unified form an acceptance of the past, active living in the present, and a hopeful attitude towards the future. It also recognizes the circle of life: as we are born, so shall we die. It comes to realize that we are involved in a broader circle with others. The failure to achieve this wisdom results in succumbing to the manifestation of disgust which comes from a lack of hopeful attitudes towards all aspects of one's life.

Moral Development, Religion, and Education   Erikson, like Freud, considered human development from the perspective of the therapist. In educational terms he showed more interest in the influence of parents on the moral formation of children than he did on the role of teachers. Erikson is more interested in what should be going on in the developing person than he is in what others should do to foster this moral development. What Erikson presents is not a theory of moral development or an approach to moral education but rather a theory of the psychological virtues that are essential in any form of moral development. One can, however, gather from his theory some indications of an approach to moral education in both secular and religious contexts. In concluding this treatment of Erikson I will draw special attention to his appeal for religious educators.

What has recommended Erikson to religious educators is the seriousness with which he considers the role of religion in human development. The task of parents during the early stage of life is to provide the atmosphere and context in which basic trust can develop. Erikson contends that the virtue of hope is best engendered through religious faith. Religions foster this virtue by their stress on childlikeness in believers, their call for prayers for guidance, and their ritual celebrations. Erikson observes that "the clinician can only observe that many are proud to be without religion whose children cannot afford to be without it" (1962, p. 251). The virtue of hope begins in infancy and needs to be developed throughout the life cycle. One way of doing this is through participation in a religious faith.

Erikson recognized that religious faith can also be effective in inculcating the virtue of will and respect for law. He observes that:

There is a relationship between faith, will, religion and law. Organized religion cements the faith that will support future generations. Established law tries to formulate obligations and privileges, restraints and freedoms, in such a manner that man can submit to law and order with little doubt and shame. The relation of faith and law is an eternal question fraught with difficulty (1958, p. 257).

The parental role is crucial in teaching this virtue of will. Parents must be judicious as well as guided by the spirit of the law. They should gradually grant a measure of self-control to their children.

Children can be aided in their struggle for the virtue of purpose by parents who understand the need for play and ritual. It is a sobering fact for parents to recognize that the first values their children possess come from the internalization of parental influences. This is especially true of the first attitudes towards sexuality. For conscience to develop properly unity between parents in the family is required. Erikson warns of the danger of children internalizing contradictory values. Though he does not make the point explicitly, it is consonant with Erikson's thought that the unity of values found in religious traditions can aid parents in this important task. Psychological theory also makes it clear that the internalized images of both parents become the basis for images of God (Rizzutto 1979). These images are revised and refashioned as crises in life are negotiated.

Education for the virtue of competence takes place primarily in the context of the school. Children learn to use their intelligence and abilities to make and fashion things. These basic attitudes of workmanship and cooperation are necessary for school and for all of life. Moral education takes place through words and examples and also through involvement with producing things and developing skills. Teachers aid in the development of this virtue through their encouragement and assistance. A religious orientation can foster the development of this virtue by considering all human work as creative and cooperative activity with God in fashioning a world and contributing to the happiness of all. A religious faith which asserts the basic goodness of creation and of all human activity can assist persons in developing this virtue.

Erikson explicitly relates religion to the development of the virtue of fidelity in adolescence. Religious faith by pointing to the importance of true love and self-control can aid the young in dealing with the problem of sexuality. A commitment to a form of religious life may be a moratorium for the young as it was for Martin Luther in his youth (Erikson 1958). Erikson, however, issues a strong warning against imposing religious rituals on the young:

Young people in crises of faith chose to face nothingness rather than submit to a faith that to them had become a cant of pious words or a collective will, that cloaked only collective impotence; a conscience that expended itself in a stickling for empty forms, a reason that was a chatter of commonplace, and a kind of work that was meaningless busy work. . . . Many young people eager for an image of the future, find the confirmations and ceremonies offered by their parents' churches designed more for parents uplift than their own (1958, p. 99, p. 114).

The task of achieving love, though a lifelong one, is situated by Erikson primarily in young adulthood. All the great religions place human love at the heart of their teachings. This love includes sexual love as well as the love of friendship and comradeship. Both Erikson and religious traditions agree that one's capacity to love is the real test of ethical character. When religious persons witness this love in action, they are so overwhelmed by it that they consider it a manifestation and presence of God's love.

The midlife virtue of care has obvious religious dimensions. Care is related to the religious virtue of *caritas*, love for others. This virtue is manifested in adults' teaching their children about ideas and work. Religious traditions urge individuals to transcend their own concerns and those of their families to become involved in the broader community. The crisis of midlife is basically a spiritual one in which persons are challenged to make use of unused spiritual resources. Also, generativity has a special meaning for those who do not have children for religious reasons. About the generativity of religious celibates and monks Erikson notes:

> Where philosophical and spiritual tradition suggests the renunciation of the right to procreate, such early turn to ultimate concerns wherever instituted in monastic communities, strives to settle at the same time the matter of this relationship to the Care for the creature of the world and to the Charity which is felt to transcend it (1958, p. 267).

The integrity crisis, as described by Erikson, is replete with religious implications. The virtue of wisdom to be achieved at this time entails finding meaning in the face of fading life and ensuing death. This crisis, "last in the lives of ordinary men, is a lifelong and chronic crisis in *homo religiosus*. He asks questions about how to escape corruption in living and how in death to give meaning to life" (1968, p. 261). Persons of religious faith have no particular advantages over others in the face of this crisis but they do have the teachings of religious traditions and examples of religious persons which enable them to formulate satisfying immortality ideologies.

Conclusion   The ethical dimensions of psychoanalytic theory have been treated at some length for a number of reasons. This theory as described by Erikson and others is consonant with religious traditions of human development. Erikson has based his ethical theory on values which are emphasized in major religions of the world. This theory views moral development as an integral part of human development. It also places greater stress than other theories on the emotional and affective dimensions of human development.

Erikson's theory has not, however, been without its critics. The theory is stronger on the earlier period of life than on later periods. At times Erikson's analysis becomes little more than moralistic exhortation. Thirdly, there has not been sufficient empirical testing of the theory, since it is rather difficult to test the presence of the various virtues which Erikson proposes for each stage. Finally, feminist psychologists have criticized the theory for an alleged male bias which leads Erikson to place the resolution of the identity crisis before the intimacy crisis. They contend that the opposite situation holds true for many women (Gilligan 1982). Notwithstanding these difficulties, the theory has stood the test of time well. Secular and religious educators have found it a powerful heuristic tool for understanding both human and moral development.

COGNITIVE DEVELOPMENTAL THEORY
OF MORAL DEVELOPMENT

The major theory for explaining cognitive aspects of moral development is the Piaget-Kohlberg theory of development in moral reasoning. Piaget's *The Moral Judgment of the Child* (1965 ed.) was a milestone in research. This book was largely an attempt to counter Durkheim's theory that adult influence was dominant in the moral development of children. Piaget contended that Durkheim ignored the existence of spontaneously formed children's societies as well as the facts relating to mutual respect. Kohlberg's development and extension of this theory has dominated discussions on moral development during the past two decades. Many educators, including religious ones, have found this approach helpful for understanding in both secular and religious contexts. Recently, however, a number of serious criticisms have been made of this theory. These will be discussed later in this chapter.

Piaget's Theory of Moral Development

Exposition of the Theory   In his studies Piaget found evidence of development in moral reasoning. By examining the thinking of Swiss boys between the ages of four and twelve, Piaget attempted to arrive at an understanding of how children view such a simple thing as the rules of the game of marbles. He also examined their reaction to stories of moral events. What he found was that children between the ages of five and seven regarded rules as deriving from semi-mystical authority of older children, adults, and even God. When they became about ten, children recognized that rules were invented by children and thus they felt free to change them.

In a second experiment Piaget found that though young children could make a distinction between intentional and unintentional actions, they did not regard intention as important in determining the morality of an action.

Thus breaking ten cups unintentionally is worse than breaking one cup intentionally. Older children gave more importance to intention since they recognized that a falsehood which is meant to deceive is worse than one due to ignorance or mistake. This finding gave greater proof to the thesis of moral development.

Piaget also found growth in children's ideas about justice and punishment. The younger child saw the need for misdeeds to be balanced by punishment because of a view of justice as immanent or inherent in things: natural forces somehow are in league with people to ensure that the disobedient person will be punished. The older child considered punishment not so much as a balancing but as a deterence to future injustice.

It was these experiments which led Piaget to his basic theoretical position. The thinking of younger children is characterized by *moral realism* or a heteronomous morality. Young children tend to regard duty and the value attached to it as so important that it is binding no matter in what circumstance people find themselves. Young children based their moral judgments on respect for authority figures. This morality is one of constraint and absolutist thought patterns as well as immanent concepts of fairness and justice.

Older children, on the other hand, develop a *morality of cooperation or reciprocity* (autonomous morality) according to which they are aware of the opinions of others and recognize that rules grow out of human relationships. They become aware that morality is not only a matter of obeying authorities but also of evolving principles for achieving mutually agreed on and valued ends. At this stage social experience, especially peer interaction, becomes the instrument for movement to a more cooperative and reciprocal morality.

Piaget has offered some reasons for the movement or nonmovement from moral realism to a morality of reciprocity. Movement from one stage to the other takes place when children break out of egocentric thinking and begin to see the viewpoints of others. It is speculated that children make this movement because social interactions with peers force them to a degree of mutual respect. Thus the morality of cooperation or reciprocity may be thwarted by slow intellectual development or by a lack of social experiences in which mutual respect can develop.

Moral Education   Piaget did not see much value in the direct teaching of morality to children by issuing rules of behavior. In his view of intelligence there would always be a time lag between the performance of an action and reflection on the performance. Adult teaching only affects children's thinking about morality: it either retards this thinking or enables it to catch up with children's actual practice of morality. What enables children to develop in their moral reasoning is the interaction of their developing intelligence with the social environment. The danger of direct teaching of morality is that it might reinforce moral realism by calling for submissive obedience to adult authority and preclude young people from seeing the relativity and fallibility of viewpoints. It is the latter experience which enables children to develop a morality of reciprocity. Kohlberg, as we shall see, is more optimistic about the effectiveness of direct moral teaching.

Assessment and Critique of the Piaget's Theory In his review of research on the Piaget theory, Wright (1971) summarized the research on Piaget's theory with these conclusions. 1) The general view of age changes suggested by Piaget has been established by a number of studies in different cultures. 2) Evidence shows that the more intelligent the child, the more mature the moral judgment. The evidence, however, is not clear in the area of ideas about justice. 3) Studies have not substantiated the importance of social experiences for developing moral insight. 4) Little connection has been found between moral insight and other moral variables such as the ability to resist temptation and avoidance of guilt. 5) No significant differences have been found between moral insight in boys and girls. 6) Research on the ability of religious training is mixed. Some studies have found a high degree of moral realism in children attending church schools while other studies show that children are better able to apply the criterion of intention.

Piaget's theory has been the object of a number of criticisms. Scholars have questioned the emphasis on the positive aspects of peer interaction, especially Piaget's assertion that it often leads to excessive dependence on peer approval. Comparative studies of adult authority versus peer interaction have produced mixed results. Piaget's methodology has been criticized on several grounds: sample bias toward males and intelligent children; unwarranted inferences from stories and games such as marbles to more central moral issues and the equation of cognitive and moral ability. Many of these criticisms have also been made of Kohlberg's theory and will be discussed.

Kohlberg's Theory of Moral Development

It is a difficult task to present Lawrence Kohlberg's highly influential theory of moral development because in the past two decades he has made significant modifications. (It is reassuring to note that some developmental theories really develop themselves.) The source for this section will be the more recent revisions that Kohlberg (1984) has refined in response to critics.

Stages of Moral Development Kohlberg has agreed with Piaget on the basic process of moral learning. Like Piaget he accepts that moral learning takes place through the interaction of individuals with their environment. Furthermore, he agrees that people are active in their own learning processes and that this activity is of paramount importance. Kohlberg also agrees with Piaget in postulating various stages in moral development. For both researchers these stages describe the interaction of the person's structuring tendencies and the structural features of the environment.

The meaning that Kohlberg gives to moral stages is in the Piaget tradition. He contends that the stages of development occur in an *invariant sequence*. This means that under normal circumstances people either remain at the same level or move upward but do not move back to lower stages. Also there is never any skipping of stages. Secondly, the stages are arranged in a *hierarchical order* such that persons who reason at a higher stage easily comprehend the reasoning of persons at lower stages. Thirdly, the stages are a *structured whole*, (i.e., individuals are consistent in their stage of moral reasoning, regardless of the issues they face). Finally, the stages are concerned with the *structures* of moral judgment as opposed its content. The stages are concerned with the reasons persons give for their judgments and not the particular judgments themselves.

Kohlberg has presented what he considers are six culturally universal stages of moral development. The progression in these stages is from rigid moral reasoning about punishment and external effects of behavior to internal standards and motivations. In their development people move from fear of punishment to respect for laws and social enforcement to an internalized conscience which is based upon more complex reasoning and perceptions of the world and the need for justice. Not everyone reaches the highest levels.

Over the years Kohlberg has used different terminology to describe stages of moral development. The following terminology and descriptions are found in his latest work (Kohlberg 1984).

Preconventional Level

Stage 1: Heteronomous Morality   The main perspective in this stage is the naive moral realism described by the Piaget. The morality of actions is determined by their physical characteristics and consequences. Those actions are judged wrong for which one is punished by some authority.

At this stage "right" is determined by a literal obedience to rules and authority, by the avoidance of punishment, and by not doing physical harm. Persons at the stage of development are egocentric and incapable of recognizing points of view of others. At this level stealing is wrong simply because "you're not supposed to steal."

Stage 2: Individualistic, Instrumental Morality   At this stage persons regard right and wrong in terms of their own interests and in terms of fair exchanges, which, however, may necessitate a consideration of the interests and needs of others. Thus there is a recognition of perspectives other than one's own. Concern for fairness, agreements, equal exchange, and the like show an ability to be concerned with others in concrete terms. Fairness often means being just in giving others their due. Persons at this stage do not have an adequate means for deciding among conflicting claims or determining moral priorities.

Conventional Level

Stage 3: Interpersonally Normative Morality The rightness of human actions is determined by mutually trusting relations among people and a set of norms they are supposed to live by. At this stage people are concerned about others and about loyalty, trust, respect, and gratitude. Good behavior is that which pleases or helps others and is approved by them. Thus morality is primarily a matter of interpersonal trust and social approval. Persons at this stage have the ability to put themselves in the place of others. Behavior is frequently judged by intention and motivation.

Stage 4: Social System Morality Those actions are good which are approved by authorities or fixed rules and which maintain the social order. Individual interests are moral only if they are based on laws that apply equally to all in society. This stage was presented rather negatively in earlier formulations. In more recent writings Kohlberg has given it a positive description as the goal of civic education in schools. The goal of civic education is "a solid attainment of the fourth stage of commitment to being a good member of a community or a good citizen" (Kohlberg 1980, p. 459). Persons at this stage are concerned about contributing to society, the group, or the institution. Such persons move beyond interpersonal considerations to consider the needs of larger institutions. Kohlberg recognizes that within this orientation one finds some people whose primary allegiance is to a religious system. Commitment to religious systems such as natural or divine law are included within this form of moral development.

Postconventional Level

Stage 4½: Transitional Stage Kohlberg has often recognized that in the transition from stage 4 to 5 some persons are at a level which is postconventional but which is also not completely principled. At this stage the right is both personal and subjective. Emotions play an important role and conscience is arbitrary and relative. Individuals see themselves as standing outside of society and capable of making decisions without reference to it. A lack of clear principles in making choices characterizes this stage (Kohlberg 1981, p. 411).

Stage 5: Human Rights and Social Welfare Morality   Right actions at this stage are whose which safeguard individual rights and standards agreed to by a particular society, even when these are in conflict with the concrete rules and laws of the group. The social system presents a contract freely entered into by each individual to preserve basic rights in society and to promote general welfare. Some fundamental rights such as life and liberty are recognized as necessary for society, regardless of majority opinion. In this morality a concern for the rights of minorities is clearly recognized. Moral reasoning at this level shows awareness of the relativity of personal values and the need for procedures to arrive at consensus in a democratic and constitutional manner. It also recognizes the possibility of changing unjust laws. Kohlberg's recognition that these goals are rather lofty for civic education in schools led him to his more positive formulation of stage 4 morality.

Stage 6: Morality of Universalizable, Reversible, and Prescriptive General Moral Principle(s)   Persons at this stage decide what is right according to self-chosen ethical principles by appealing to logical comprehensiveness, universality, and consistency. People are motivated by the universal principles of justice, equality, and respect for human dignity. Respect for human dignity may at times even entail breaking rules or violating societally recognized rights (e.g., giving a lethal drug to a dying person at his or her request). Kohlberg now recognizes that this stage remains more a theoretical hypothesis based on Platonic idealism rather than an empirically confirmed one (Kohlberg 1982, p. 523). The most recent manual designed for testing individual stages of moral development does not include this stage.

Kohlberg on Moral Education   Educators have been attracted to Kohlberg's theory of moral development, especially because he has drawn educational conclusions from the theory and has set up educational experiments to test it. Moral education in this system is vastly different from shaping behavior through reinforcement or focusing on the dynamics of parent-child relationships. In his earlier writings Kohlberg (1971) presented an approach which he termed Socratic and developmental. In this view moral education came down to the stimulation of the natural development of moral judgment. Kohlberg contended that it was only this indirect method that respected the autonomy and dignity of the individual. For him persons should be free to develop along the lines that nature directs.

The first step is the Socratic step of creating dissatisfaction in students about their present reasoning. This is done by describing to them conflicts where the students' present principles offer no ready solution, (e.g., is it right to steal if a person is hungry? is it right to take the life of a person who is in extreme pain?) When students recognize that they have no answer to these problems, they are exposed to agreement, disagreement, and argument about the situation with their peers. By exposure to such reasoning at a stage above their own ability, persons are challenged to move to a higher stage of moral reasoning.

In a later essay Kohlberg (1980) developed an approach for the schools which is not only Socratic and developmental but also indoctrinative, to use his own terminology. The method is called indoctrinative because it advocates that teachers present rules of behavior. Yet Kohlberg wants the students to participate in rule-making and in a process of upholding values. In this manner moral education becomes civic education, having as its goal the formation of the good citizen and member of society. His concept entails the governance of a small high school community by participatory or direct democracy. Rules are to be made and enforced through a community meeting, one-person-one-vote, whether faculty or student. Kohlberg advocated this change to counter the narcissism and privatism of the culture of the late 1970s. He drew on Dewey's conception of democratic and participatory education. In his theory the school becomes the crucial institution by which the values of society are transmitted. Kohlberg realistically understands that there might not be a carry-over from the school community to the out-of-school situations and institutions.

Though his use of the term "indoctrinative" is unfortunate, Kohlberg's recognition of the social role and potential of the school for moral education is a valuable one. This reformulation of his theory comes rather close to the views of Durkheim from which Kohlberg once distanced himself (Kohlberg 1971). A fuller consideration of the role of the school in moral education is discussed in the next chapter. Also, in chapter six I will present a fuller explanation of an educational approach which uses Kohlberg's theory.

While Kohlberg's research efforts and educational suggestions have primarily concerned adolescents, he has made some suggestions pertaining to adults. He reports on research with college age students which shows that some of these students make the transition from stage four to five at this time. He suggests that the lives of such leaders as Gandhi and Tolstoy show some moral transformations which take place in the forties and fifties of peoples' lives may have represented changes in moral judgments. Kohlberg has also observed that educators should direct more attention to adults because it is adults who make the decisions which will make our society what it is (Kohlberg 1977, p. 199).

Critique of Cognitive Developmentalism　The Piaget-Kohlberg approach to moral development and education has dominated discussions in moral psychology for the past two decades. Recently, however, a number of serious criticisms have been leveled against the theory. Kohlberg has been criticized for centering too exclusively on the virtue of justice and ignoring other important moral virtues (Peters 1981). Peters suggest that because children cannot grasp a principled morality, they learn good habits, especially virtues of self-control and moral courage. Kohlberg's definition of morality is considered by many to be culturally biased towards North American liberal culture (Sullivan 1977). Gilligan (1982) has pointed out that Kohlberg has drawn on an exclusively male sample thus causing him to define stages in a masculine manner which stresses rights and justice and thus to minimize an ethic of care, responsibility, and love. Gilligan also accuses the theory of male bias because she has found in her research that the majority of women are situated at level three while men tend to reason at level four. To her the ordering of these two stages manifests a male bias. Kohlberg has also been accused of exaggerating the role of reason at the expense of affect, personality, habit, and expectations of consequences (Aronfreed 1971). Finally, the Kohlberg methodology has been criticised for lack of sufficient validity and reliability as well as lack of evidence for the higher stages (Kurines and Grief 1979; Gibbs, 1977).

Kohlberg's work has also been reviewed by theologians and religious educators. Hauerwas (1980) makes several criticisms from the perspective of Christian theology: the emphasis of the theory on living autonomously is contrary to the idea that we are to live our lives as a gift of God; the religious life should involve learning to imitate rather than, although not excluding, acting on principles; the Christian moral life is ultimately not one of development but of conversion. These criticisms form the basis of Dykstra's (1981) Christian alternative to Kohlberg, which will be examined in chapter five.

Though these criticisms of the Piaget-Kohlberg theory all have some merit, I do not believe that they have sounded the death knell for moral stage theory or for the value of such a theory for a religiously based moral education. The basic insight that there is a general movement from heteronomy to autonomy is a valuable principle for moral education. Though the importance of moral reasoning may be exaggerated in the theory, one cannot deny its centrality. Though justice may not be the only virtue, it is certainly the most important one in public life and morality.

Religious educators have found much of value in this theory. The educational enterprise has a strong rational component. Although reason is not the only factor in moral development, there are certain dangers in any theory that does not appeal to reason as central to moral education. Failure to attend to reason risks making education manipulative and indoctrinative. The Kohlberg approach also affirms values which are important in religious traditions: freedom, responsibility, rights, relationships, law, and equality. Religious educators add distinctive religious virtues and motivations (Elias 1983).

My opinion of the Piaget-Kohlberg theory is that it provides a typology of ways in which persons engage in moral reasoning. The evidence for rigidly defined stages does not appear conclusive. Persons may go through stages in their early development. But once persons attain a certain degree of maturity and experience, they appear to base their moral reasoning on various justifications which appear to correspond to Piaget-Kohlberg stages. What determines the form of reasoning might include factors of personality, affect, habit, and expectation of consequences. It is these factors which form the basis for social learning approaches to moral development and education.

SOCIAL LEARNING THEORIES AND MORAL EDUCATION

The treatment of social learning theorists is logically placed after the behaviorist, psychoanalytic, and cognitive developmental approaches to moral development. This logic is based on the fact that social learning theory is a family of theories which attempt to combine a modified behaviorism with either psychoanalytic theory or cognitive developmentalism in an effort to explain all learning, including moral learning, through various processes of socialization. Social learning theorists are eclectic in drawing on concepts, hypotheses, and methodologies from various psychological theories. Some theorists use the psychoanalytic constructs of identification, frustration, aggression, and dependency while others develop their own constructs, such as modeling and imitation. Social learning theorists also utilize the findings of cultural anthropologists.

Major social learning theorists who espouse a psychoanalytic orientation include Miller and Dollard (1941), Sears, Maccoby, and Levin (1957), and Aronfreed (1968; 1976). Social learning theorists who take a more cognitive orientation are Bandura (1977) and Rushton (1980). Both of these approaches agree that the focus of investigation of all social learning theory is the whole spectrum of the socialization process by which people learn directly or indirectly to conform to cultural expectations. Despite their differences, all social learning theorists concentrate on observable behavior. They also stress the laws which govern the acquisition, maintenance, and modification of behavior. Finally, these theorists have a preference for understanding behavior through experimentation and the scientific method (Rushton, 1982).

Social learning theorists assume that behavior is determined not through stage development but within social situations and contexts. These theorists do not look within individuals for structures or virtues but rather examine the environmental factors and consequences in their lives. They emphasize the influence of social conditions and cultural expectations in moral development. If changes come about in a person's life, these are explained not so much through internal maturation or development but rather through sudden changes in social situations, family structures, peer group expectations, or other environmental factors.

Social Learning Theory of Moral Development

Though the starting point of social learning is a form of modified behaviorism, the theory has developed considerably through dialogue with other learning theories. The following are some of the basic principles common to social learning theories: 1) all behavior, including moral behavior, is learned as a result of many independent processes; 2) there is no age-related sequence of stages, since persons are infinitely malleable and changeable in learning; 3) moral development is the growth of behavioral and affective conformity to moral rules; 4) the motivation of morality is rooted in biological needs as these receive either rewards or punishments; 5) in the last analysis morality is culturally relative; 6) basic moral norms are the internalization of external rules; 7) the environment supplies the experiences and the rewards which are necessary to teach children and adults how to behave in society.

Social learning theorists have outlined social processes which they believe contribute to the learning of moral behavior. They recognize, first of all, the power of classical conditioning in the learning of emotional responses. In this process emotional states such as fear and anxiety are responses to stimuli in the environment. Classical conditioning is used to explain the acquisition, elimination, and modification of a variety of emotional responses. It is reported that the emotion of empathy was induced in young girls when adults joyously said "There's the light" and hugged the child. These children were more likely to accept hugging and pleasure than the candy which was offered them (Aronfreed 1971).

Social learning theorists contend that observational learning through modeling accounts for the learning of many pro-social or moral behaviors. Research has shown that people can learn behavior patterns merely by watching others perform them. Actions can be reinforced or inhibited by observing reinforcements and punishments given to others. Persons can also acquire conditioned emotional responses to stimuli which accompany a painful stimulus to another. A number of studies have shown that children readily internalize behaviors of generosity or selfishness to which they have been exposed (Rushton 1976). Another study has demonstrated that children who saw someone give in to temptation were later unable to resist, whereas those who saw a person exhibit self-control were later able to resist temptation (Grusec et al. 1979). The power of observational learning among adults is reported in a study which showed how the example of models helped induce persons to donate blood (Rushton and Campbell 1977).

The influence of reinforcement and punishment has been studied extensively by social learning theorists. The power of reinforcement has been presented in Skinner's research reported in the first section of this chapter.

Although some social learning theorists have hypothesized that the mere exposure to a model is sufficient for learning the responses displayed, most theorists do not think that stable behavioral patterns can be developed without reinforcements (Rushton and Teachman 1978). On the matter of punishment there is some disagreement. While Skinner and others do not consider it a valuable process for shaping positive behavior, Eysenck (1977) has argued that punishment delivered for antisocial behavior decreases the frequency of cheating, stealing, and selfishness. Rushton (1982) presents a balanced view on this matter in his judgment that:

> From punishment people undoubtedly do construct appropriate rules of behavior, and these serve to guide their behavior in the future. Mild punishment can be effective in aiding children to generate their own self-regulatory controls. Both social norms and their internalization require judgment of what is wrong as well as what is right (p. 437).

The effectiveness of verbal procedures such as instructions, preachings, and reasonings is also a matter of dispute among social learning theorists. Hoffman (1971) contends that the method of induction by which parents give explanations and reasons to persuade children to change their behavior is more effective than discipline through power assertion or love withdrawal. Rushton (1982), however, theorizes that methods of induction are effective only if they are paired with previous positive or negative reinforcements or with the example of a model. All recognize the need for more research in this area before generalizations can be made.

Social learning theorists with a psychoanalytic orientation appeal to the process of identification to explain some aspects of moral development. Parent identification refers to the process by which children so identify with their parents that they praise or blame themselves according to whether or not their behavior corresponds with that of their parents. Some research indicates that children selectively identify with their parents and more easily identify with external behaviors than with internal values. Parents need to be more than passive identification models in order for children to accept prohibitions against stealing and lying (Hoffman 1971).

The psychoanalytic concept of internalization of values is also utilized by some social learning theorists. Persons internalize the values of others if they act independently of external sanctions rather than out of fear of detection and punishment. The explanatory power of internalization has come under considerable criticism ever since Milgram (1974) demonstrated that people often behave in ways that contradict their professed and presumably internalized values. They even at times obey outrageous requests made by respectable authority figures. Such criticisms do not, I believe, demand the total rejection of the process of internalization but indicate that the process, like all other processes, is a weak one. There are examples of people who have so internalized values that they can resist external pressure and support.

Cognitively oriented social learning theorists have offered a social theory of moral judgment. Experiments have shown that children's moral judgments shift in the direction which they had seen modeled. Children change from an initial rule to the modeled rule (Rosenthal and Zimmerman 1977). Social learning theorists also point to experiments of this nature to deny the sequential stage development theory of Kohlberg.

Social learning theorists have introduced the concept of self-reinforcement to explain the apparent absence of external reinforcements to explain some actions. This process is a specific and more intricate form of modeling by which persons imitate another's way of distributing praise and blame. What results from this process is a form of self-regulation and control. This type of behavior is found more often in adolescents and adults than in children.

Bandura's Theory of Moral Development

Bandura (1977) has presented the most consistent social learning approach to moral development. He is rather critical of the stage theory of Piaget and Kohlberg and he explains moral development through changes in social situations. At first children are exposed to necessary controls on their behavior, even of a physical nature. As children mature, social sanctions are increasingly used instead of physical ones. Bandura contends that:

Successful socialization requires gradual substitution of symbolic and internal controls for external sanctions and demands. After moral standards of conduct are established by tuition and schooling, self-evaluative consequences emerge as deterrents to transgressive behavior (1977, p. 43).

In Bandura's theory, as children grow older parents begin to use forms of moral reasoning with them. They also appeal to legal codes and penalties with adolescents. Children also learn how to get around moral consequences. Older children and adolescents have other sources of moral judgment and conduct besides their parents. Other adults, peers, and various types of symbolic models also have influential roles to play. Furthermore, televised modeling is influential in learning values in contemporary society. In Bandura's opinion, conditions of social learning are so varied in most cultures that it is impossible to speak of stages and types of moral development.

Moral judgments in this theory are social decisions made on the basis of many factors. Standards of moral evaluation come from precept, example, and the direct or vicarious experience of the consequences of transgressive actions. Exposure to different models alters moral judgments in several ways. Models transmit ideas and preferences, emphasize the importance of certain issues over others, and provide justification for some actions and avoidance of others.

Assessment and Critique of Social Learning Theory

Any discussion of moral psychology must give serious attention to the experiments and ideas presented by social learning theorists. These theorists represent a common sense approach. It is undeniable that we are shaped as moral persons through our interaction with others and through the social situations in which we make moral decisions. Though the attempt by social learning theorists to explain as much as possible on these grounds is a valuable one, the theory has a number of weaknesses which must be recognized.

Social learning theorists are limited by their commitment to an exclusively empiricist understanding of the scientific method. By focusing almost totally on observable behavior and not sufficiently attending to reports and analyses of internal states, these theorists ignore a great deal of important data for understanding moral development. The importance of emotion, intention, motivation, and moral reasoning are not easily accounted for in these theories. They offer a better explanation of the learning of moral behavior in the earlier years of life than they do for later development. The theories do not appear to deal adequately with the more complex learning that takes place in adolescence and adulthood. The critical question about such theories is whether or not they advance much farther than the determinism and mechanism of behaviorists theories.

Notwithstanding these critical questions, social learning theories need to be taken with greater seriousness by moral educators, even those wanting to include a religious perspective. These theories emphasize the importance of parents, teachers, and peers in the learning of moral values. The moral and religious commitments of those who deal with the young may have more effect than direct educational methods. The value of social learning theory has been recognized by a number of influential religious educators (Nelson 1987; Westerhoff 1976; Marthaler 1978).

HUMANISTIC PSYCHOLOGY AND MORAL EDUCATION

The final group to be considered are psychologists commonly known as humanistic psychologists. Also called existential psychologists or Third

Force Psychologists (behaviorism and psychoanalysis being the first two Forces), they take an optimistic view of human potential for personal and interpersonal growth. The major humanistic psychologists are Gordon Allport, Victor Frankl, Abraham Maslow, Rollo May, and Carl Rogers. This group has been most influential in combatting some of the deterministic tendencies in behaviorism and psychoanalysis. Although the theory is primarily one that focuses on therapy and counseling, some the some humanistic psychologists are also concerned with education.

Although humanistic psychologists accept learning through conditioning as well as learning in response to drives within individuals, they assert that we cannot fully understand persons from these perspectives alone. In fact, they contend that exclusive concentration on external conditioning and innate drives leads to a rather abstract way of talking about persons and their development. Humanistic psychology examines the whole spectrum of human behavior: self, motives, intentions, identity, relationships, values, and freedom. These concepts are used to fashion personality theories which place considerable emphasis on human freedom and personal interdependence.

One of the distinctive features of humanistic psychologists is that they give much more attention to adults than they do to children and adolescents. All of the other theories of moral education focus primarily on pre-adults. Humanistic psychologists and educators are more concerned with adult issues and problems. Thus in the area of moral development they have a number of distinctive contributions to make.

Humanistic Theories of Value Development

Humanistic psychologists usually use the more general term values and do not often speak specifically of moral values but moral values are included in their discussions. These psychologists are also only indirectly concerned with questions of learning moral values through an educational process, since their main context is therapy and not education. Maslow and Rogers, however, have made noteworthy attempts to apply their theories to the realm of education.

The Morally Educated Person Rogers' concept of the morally educated person has to be inferred from his conception of the fully functioning person. The fully functioning person is open to experience, lives in an existential manner, has trust in self, and exercises creativity. To become a morally educated person in his viewpoint is to assume total responsibility for one's choices and the consequences of these choices. At the heart of his theory of the fully-functioning person is a description of the process of valuing by which persons become fully functioning.

When Rogers speaks of the process of valuing, he restricts himself to the concept of values as preferences of individuals. He does not speak to the question of what he calls objective values, (i.e., values which are objectively preferable) (Rogers 1969, p. 241). He draws a contrast between infants who have the locus of valuing within themselves and adults who often have introjected value patterns. Infants value hunger and pain negatively; they value food, security, and new experiences in a positive manner. While infants value things in an instinctive manner, adults often introject the values of others: sexual desires are wrong, obedience is bad, communism is bad. Rogers thus believes that the valuing process in many adults is faulty since the majority of adult values are introjected from other individuals. Because the source of adult values is often outside adults, they feel insecure and easily threatened in their values.

Rogers believes that adults must recapture some aspects of the infant's valuing process. They must establish the focus of valuation within themselves and allow themselves to be open to what they are immediately experiencing. They must be willing to express negative feelings, trust their own organic inclinations, and be willing to correct any mistakes they make. Adults should be willing to get feedback from others. The moral task of adults is to move from facades and oughts to meeting the expectations of others. They should value being real, self-directing, expressive, and open to deep relationships (1969, p. 253). To achieve these values is to become the fully-functioning person that Rogers sets as the highest human ideal.

Rogers believes that the valuing process appears to be similar to the existential position that individuals in the exercise of their freedom decide what is morally right. Human freedom gives to human endeavor a moral dimension. What Rogers provides is a psychological description for this philosophical position. He asserts that modern persons no longer trust religion, science, philosophy, or other systems of beliefs. He also asserts the possibility of universal human value directions emerging from the experience of the human organism. It is his contention that if all persons get into contact with their organismic valuing base, theirs can be "an organized, adaptive, and social approach to the perplexing value issues which face all of us (Rogers 1969, p. 255).

Maslow's Theory of Value Development   Maslow's approach to value development is implicit in his theory of personality development. According to Maslow, the goal is to become self-actualized, (i.e., to bring into existence all potentialities). Maslow's self-actualized person has some similarities to fully functioning person of Rogers. Such persons have clear and efficient perceptions of reality; they are open to experiences, have wholeness, spontaneity, objectivity, creativity, a democratic character, a fusion of concreteness, and an ability to love (Maslow 1968).

One interesting feature of Maslow's theory of personality is his attention to religion. He contends that persons need "a framework of values, a philosophy of life, a religion or a religion surrogate to live by and understand by. . . ." (1968, p. 206) Maslow is critical of many practices of institutionalized religion, especially rituals, for their tendency to become forms of idolatry. For religion to be humanly beneficial, it must be intellectually credible, morally worthy of respect, and emotionally satisfying (1964, p. 43). Maslow's humanistic approach to religion may not satisfy all, but it does show a deep respect for a religious dimension of life.

In comparing the personality theories of Rogers and Maslow one major difference can be noted. Though both take a rather romantic and optimistic view of human potential, Maslow deals more extensively with the problem of human evil. He recognizes that falling away from one's nature and the commission of crimes against one's nature register in the unconscious and cause a despising of the self (1968, p. 5). Evil is a product of limited selfish visions and understandings, Maslow believes that people have within themselves the power to deal with evil and do not have to resort to extra-human forces to deal with it.

Humanistic Education for Moral Values

Maslow has argued against the desirability and even the possibility of a value-free education. Healthy education is education toward the development of all human potentialities. Such an education must be universal, ubiquitous, and lifelong. It is Maslow's view that education must be concerned with higher and spiritual values, and to ensure this it should deal with these age-old questions:

> What is the good life? What is the good man? The good woman? What is the good society and what is my relationship to it? What are my obligations to society: What is best for my children? What is justice, truth, virtue? What is my relation to nature, death, to aging, pain, to illness? How can I live a zestful, enjoyable, meaningful life? What is my responsibility to my brothers? Who *are* my brothers? What shall I be loyal to? What must I be ready to die for? (1964, p. 52).

Though Maslow eloquently raised the ethical questions, he gave little direction on how this value oriented education should proceed. Maslow's context remained that of therapy. By extrapolating from therapy to education, I would construct an educational situation for Maslow along the lines of a continuum of safety, person, and growth. The task of the teacher would be to make growth more attractive, minimize the dangers of growth, make safety less attractive, and minimize the fears of defensiveness, pathology, and regression. Once the proper environment has been set up, then persons can work out their hostilities and other personal problems. The movement to higher values can come after this. Though persons cannot be forced, they can be coaxed (Maslow 1968, pp. 53–54).

Rogers deals a bit more directly with the educational problem since he has attempted to apply his basic theory to education for personal growth and freedom. Also, there are some connections between the values clarification movement and theories of humanistic education.

Rogers concentrates on the teacher's role as a facilitator who attempts to be real and genuine in relationships with students. Facilitators are to be accepting, prizing, and trusting persons who possess empathetic understanding. The facilitator sets the initial mood or climate of freedom and gives students the freedom to arrive at their own moral values. Facilitators should accept the feelings and reaction of the group. The moral educator is the non-directive person who allows students to arrive at their own values. (In chapter six I will present a fuller discussion of the theory of values clarification and related approaches.)

Critique of Humanistic Moral Education

There can be no doubt about the merit of this form of education. It is refreshing to move away from the world of determined environments, stages, and innate propensities to a respect for human freedom. No one can quarrel with the goals and the aims which this education offers to the educator. One can, however, question some of the assumptions and point out what may be deficiencies.

The view of human beings presented is individualist and romantic. Ideals of what they may become at their best must also be accompanied by a treatment of those factors, both internal and external, which inhibit, retard, or prevent this development. Humanistic psychology makes a powerful act of faith in a particular view of the human person—a romantic and idealistic view—and does not grapple with biological, social, and political forces which should enter into this vision.

Many religious educators are attracted to this theory, and with good reason. There is a certain religious quality about the writing of humanistic psychologists. Liberal religious faiths can find much here to applaud. Yet there are deficiencies in the theory when it comes to determining the good and offering justification for what is morally good and what is morally evil. It appears that something is of value if it leads to greater mental health and growth. At its heart this assertion may contain an absolute relativism which is in reality inimical to many religious faiths. In truth, the same can be said about the other psychological theories presented in this chapter.

Conclusion

In this chapter I have presented five significant psychological approaches to understanding moral development and behavior. Each of the theories has implications for moral education. It is not necessary to choose among them. Each explains some important factors about moral development and behavior. Though all theorists present their views as an adequate and comprehensive understanding of moral development, it appears that each theory has only a part of the truth because it focuses mainly on one aspect of development. Behaviorists attempt to explain moral *behavior* by appeal to reinforcements. Psychoanalysts focus on inner *drives, emotions,* and *conflicts* and see these as critical in moral development. Cognitive developmentalists give greatest attention to *rational processes* or moral reasoning. Social learning theorists look both to *environmental factors* and to additional processes by which behavior is modified, especially modeling and imitation. Finally, humanistic psychologists attempt to focus on *the whole person* as a developing organism.

No approach to moral education, either secular or religious, can be sound unless it takes account of these psychological theories. Psychologists in this century have offered many possible ways of understanding human development and thus enhance our understanding of how persons develop morally. They have focused on the individual. What we now need to do is to look at the other side, the social. What influence do social forces play in the development of moral values. As we shall see in the next chapter, this is an even more complex question to pose and to answer.

CHAPTER 4

THE SOCIAL SCIENCES
AND MORAL EDUCATION

Thus far in this book I have treated moral education from three different but related perspectives. First, a brief history of moral education has focused on attempts to base a moral education on either secular or religious grounds. Secondly, four different philosophical positions were described with their implications for a secular or religious moral education. Thirdly, five psychological theories which describe moral development were described, together with general implications of these theories for the practice of moral education. Criticisms have been offered of these various theories, with the result that no one theory is considered as having all the answers in this complicated enterprise of moral education. The purpose of this chapter is to examine theory and research in the social sciences on moral socialization and education. The social science disciplines which focus on moral education are primarily sociology and, to a lesser degree, anthropology.

The approach taken to moral development by the social sciences can best be described as attempts to explain moral socialization, or socialization into moral values. To be sure, there are some similarities between sociological theories and psychological theories in this area of study. A distinction, however, can be made. While psychology looks primarily to the individual or private lives of individuals, the social sciences study collective life—groups, communities, institutions, structures, as well as entire societies and cultures. The particular emphasis of the social sciences is the effect of social events, the distinctiveness of subcultures, and significant differences among groups. Thus the importance of the social science contribution to our understanding of moral development and education is an illumination of the social contexts in which persons are morally educated. The social sciences take it as axiomatic that persons are to a large degree shaped by social contexts.

In the social sciences the language of morality and education is usually, but not always, replaced by the language of values and socialization. The understanding of the term values, however, is a matter of dispute. Most social scientists explain values functionally by analyzing them in terms of their contribution to the establishment of a social, political, or economic system.

Other social scientists take a reductionist view of values and discuss them in terms of the ideology of the ruling class (Marxist interpretation), constraints placed on the superego by society (Freudian interpretation), or genetically determined social responses relating to behavior (behaviorist interpretation). Although these reductionist views tell us something about values, they tend to explain away precisely what they set out to account for. For the purposes of this chapter it is therefore stipulated that values are personal choices or preferences made under the influence of various social contexts.

The organization of this chapter differs from that of the previous two chapters. The focus here is not so much on grand theories but rather on the various social contexts or institutions in which persons are socialized. Some general theories are presented in the first part of the chapter. In the latter part of the chapter I will concentrate on social contexts in which moral socialization and education takes place. Specific attention will also be given to the little research that exists on adult socialization in values.

THEORIES OF MORAL SOCIALIZATION

The primary thrust of social theory is to explain how societies are maintained and how changes are brought about. Social theories attempt to understand our experiences in society and our ideas about the world in which we live (Craib 1984). Though social theorists recognize that there are conflicts between individuals and society, they contend that persons cannot develop properly as social beings without the socialization which society provides. My interest in social theory in this section relates primarily to an understanding of how society influences the moral values which persons choose. This problem has been addressed by a number of influential social theorists.

The classical theory of moral socialization and education is Durkheim's *Moral Education* (1961). (I will make only some general comments about this theory now since a fuller treatment will appear in the section on the school's role in moral socialization.) This work and the general theory of morality offered by Durkheim is still at the center of debate among sociologists of morality and education. Durkheim contended that morality is a social phenomenon created by societies to provide for their maintenance. Societies socialize their members into a core of values which are necessary for the maintenance and development of society.

Durkheim is considered the founder of the *functionalist theory* in sociology. This theory analyzes institutions in society and society itself in terms of the overt and latent functions they perform for individuals and groups. Function is a broad way of speaking of the usefulness of institutions in society. From a functionalist perspective, morality in society is to preserve order. Moral values serve to provide stability and to integrate individuals into society.

Durkheim's functionalist theory finds expression in a value consensus according to which societies are maintained by the transmission of a nucleus of values from one generation to another. According to this theory every group in society has a core of relatively stable values and norms on which members concur. The task of socialization is to transmit these group values, which make up the collective conscience, and to elicit personal commitments to them. All the institutions of society contribute to this socialization process by transmitting generalized conceptions of what is desirable (values) and standard ways of acting (norms).

A fuller explanation of moral socialization, which builds on functionalism, is found in the *phenomenological approach* of Berger and Luckmann (1966). This work attempts to explain how individuals internalize the social reality of the society in which they are socialized. Socialization in this theory is defined as the "comprehensive and consistent induction of an individual into the objective world of a society or a sector of it" (1966, p. 130). Primary socialization takes place in childhood while secondary socialization occurs throughout adult life as persons move into other sectors of society. Primary socialization is in many ways an unconscious activity, especially in the earliest years of life. The chief process of socialization is a subjective internalization of the values and norms. In other words, by taking on the roles, values, and norms of others one takes on their social world. Socialization includes both cognitive learning and affective or emotional learning. Socialization, especially that of a secondary nature, is not a mechanical process since there always exists a dialectic between one's own self definition and one's identification by others.

In recent years a group of social theorists called *critical sociologists* have radically challenged the concepts of moral socialization of the functionalists and to a lesser degree of the phenomenologists. The functionalist approach is criticized for failing to point out the importance of such elements as ideology, power, and class in the process of socialization and education (Apple 1979; Giroux 1981; Giroux and Purpel 1983). A number of themes relating to moral socialization can be identified among this group of critical sociologists of education. They emphasize the power of individuals to shape their own social reality and moral values. They reject the view that social and moral consciousness is merely a reflection of social reality. They raise issues of how class, power, and ideologies influence what is accepted as morally correct. Critical sociologists draw extensively on Marxist and neo-Marxist analyses of society and offer a powerful critique of conventional ways of analyzing values in education.

Most of the research I will deal with in the treatment of societal institutions comes from the functionalist orientation because this theory has dominated sociological studies of education. In certain areas, especially with regard to schools, I will discuss some of the critical analyses that have been offered by sociologists. The work of these sociologists has not led to many empirical studies in the area of moral socialization. Instead their work is more in the form of a radical critique of the theories and research of the dominant functionalist paradigm in the sociology of education.

Culture and Behavior: Anthropological Perspective

Though it is not always easy to distinguish between sociology and anthropology, the latter discipline includes a more explicit cross-cultural perspective which is important for understanding social processes in moral development. Culture is viewed as the wide variety of customs and forms of social life which characterizes human activity. Anthropologists also raise the important issue of cultural and ethical relativity for moral educators.

The application of anthropological concepts and methods to the study of educational processes has been a rather recent one. The major thrust in this effort has been to determine the effects of culture on individuals and to determine how learners adapt to different environments. Anthropologists view education as synonymous with the process by which a person learns his or her own culture. From the perspective of a society, education is the process through which cultures perpetuate and attempt to change themselves; education is concerned with the transmission, conservation, extension, and reconstruction of culture (LaBelle 1972, p. 528).

In their concern with inculturation in values, anthropologists describe persons as evaluating individuals who talk and argue about values and who show by their behavior that values are important factors in deciding what persons do or not do. It is also their contention that every society promotes a set of values that give meaning and purpose to group life, that can be symbolically expressed, that are in continuity with past values, and that appeal to both reason and emotion (Kluckhohn 1962, p. 298).

When one considers how persons are socialized in different cultures, one must face some of the most perplexing problems in philosophy and the social sciences, e.g., the issues of cultural and ethical relativity. This is an extremely important issue in moral education since traditional moral education has assumed that there are certain moral universals which are recognized by all cultures. The existence of universals has generally been challenged by anthropologists, who have taken two basic positions on this issue: absolute relativism and moderate relativism.

Absolute relativism is associated with the well known statement of Ruth Benedict (1956) on ". . . the existing and equally valid patterns of life which mankind has carved for itself from the raw materials of existence" (p. 278). This position, stated in sweeping fashion, is not considered tenable today because it is recognized that its logical implications include the acceptance of any cultural pattern, (e.g., slavery, Nazism or cannibalism). This view also precludes any moral evaluation and criticism of cultural patterns.

Most anthropologists espouse an ethical relativism which has room for some universals or near-universals across all cultures. A prominent anthropologist's statement on this issue is accepted by most anthropologists:

> Every culture has a concept of murder, distinguishing this from execution, killing in war, and other "justifiable homicides." The notions of incest and other regulations upon sexual behavior, of prohibitions upon untruth under defined circumstances, of restitution and reciprocity, of mutual obligations between parents and children. . . (Kluckhohn 1962, p. 276).

In Kluckhohn's view such universals arise from similarities in human needs and human responses or responsibilities. Such similarities arise from the nature of the human organism and the human situation and come close to producing "conditional" or "moving absolutes." For the anthropologist the universality of values does not mean their absoluteness but merely means that these values are ascribed to at most times in all cultures.

The position of moderate relativism recognizes that a pluralism of values is found in the cultural world. Such pluralism results from a number of factors: ignorance, mischance, different situations, and different perceptions. Ethical conceptions are related to what people believe to be the facts of the situation. Scientific knowledge yields some facts but it must be recognized that the activity of empirical science also carries its own value commitments.

Kohlberg is a vigorous opponent of both forms of ethical relativity. He contends that he has established universal moral concepts, values, or principles. He ascribes differences between individuals and cultures to differences in stage or developmental status. Kohlberg points to cross cultural studies on his theory as evidence that cultural universals do actually exist. He further contends that different moral stances arise from various stages of moral development, some of which are less advanced than others (Kohlberg 1971; 1984).

The debate over moral relativism is a valuable one because it raises questions about the fundamental basis of mortality. Chapter two touched on this debate in the discussion of the various philosophical positions. Kohlberg's contention that he has conclusive empirical evidence invalidating the concept of moral relativism is not on strong grounds, given the growing criticisms against this theoretical position. It is clear that the broader the definition of moral universals, the greater the intuitive acceptance there is of them by people in general. Yet morality is basically about lower level principles of action, and this is where there are significant differences among cultures. It is difficult to offer a moral basis by which one is to judge among competing moral positions at this level. Thus some form of moral relativism would appear to be indicated.

Moral relativity tells us something about the complexity and plasticity of human nature. Morality is thus to be seen as a social creation of cultures to deal with evolving needs and situations. Some may be depressed by this realization, but it is possible to find in moral relativity reason for optimism and hope (Wong 1984). Moral relativity is a recognition that our moral values are only in part determined by specific historical and cultural environments. If morality evolves from culture to culture, we gain a new perspective on the possibility of moral reform and even revolution. Moral relativism is an incentive to moral tolerance and to the development of an approach to education which truly respects the truth in all positions.

Given a relativist perspective, it is clear that there is a great difference between moral education in traditional (folk) societies and modern (mass) societies. In folk societies there are close family ties, traditions are important, and religious sanctions reinforce them, especially through communal ritual celebrations. The young are given a strict moral education into the values of the society. A clear-cut set of norms exists along with a considerable amount of authority and constraint. A premium is placed on conformity. Yet a study of such societies also reveals the existence of many deviants from the norms.

Moral education in mass or pluralistic societies is a more complicated task. In these societies norms are vaguely defined: different groups of people have different sets of norms; they have many different roles to play. The potential for greater mobility is common and thus there is exposure to various value systems. Tradition is of less importance in such societies, where the possibility of developing an autonomous moral character exists. The other side of the coin is that such societies may suffer harmful consequences from the lack of clearly defined social norms (e.g., crime, suicide, drug addiction, and mental illness).

In presenting these two types of society I do not want to judge the one as good and the other as harmful for moral development. While it is true that there is more freedom in most modern societies, it is also a fact that others are totalitarian wherein chances for free moral development are less. At the heart of issue between folk and mass societies is the definition of the ultimate goal of all socialization and inculturation: Is the ultimate goal the production of persons who conform to the norms of society? Or is the development of free and autonomous choice the chief goal? Are the aims of moral education to be primarily individual or social? It is clear that in most of the literature on moral education from a sociological perspective, social aims rather than individual aims have received the greatest attention. It is on this point that the critical social scientists raise questions about the nature of society and the socialization processes which maintain existing societies.

Moral Socialization and Religion

The implications of social and cultural theories on moral development have been indicated by several religious educators. Nelson (1967) described the transmission of religious values and beliefs in terms of cultural transmission. His thesis in this now classic work was that:

Faith is communicated by a community of believers and that the meaning of faith is developed by its members out of their history, by their interaction with each other, and their relation to the events that take place in their lives (p. 10).

Social science theory has also been the basis for the development of a cultural approach to religious education (Westerhoff and Neville 1974). An attempt has also been made to show a correspondence between the religious concept of catechesis and socialization (Marthaler 1979). In all of these theories attention is not on the school but rather on the rites, rituals, myths, symbols, beliefs, and values of the religious community. Extensive consideration is also given to the family's role in this religious inculturation.

Most forms of religious education have approached morality by assuming the absoluteness of moral norms. Religious ethics usually appeal to universal principles of morality, known through an examination of biblical or church traditions. Ethical relativity has been viewed as a strong threat to religiously oriented ethical systems. The situation has changed in recent years with the debate by religious ethicians over situation or contextual ethics. The question of the role of moral absolutes in religious traditions will be further discussed in the next chapter.

Another implication of the social sciences for religious education is that this education can no longer presume that a religious ethic is reinforced by other institutions in society. Religious bodies in a modern pluralistic society have some of their ethical teachings reinforced and others rejected. A religious education for moral maturity must take into consideration its own attempt to inculcate a countercultural ethical system.

MORAL SOCIALIZATION AND THE FAMILY

For all people the process of socialization begins within a family. Social scientists are agreed on the crucial role that the family plays in the socialization of children. The family's role is stronger in folk societies than it is in modern ones because in the latter there are more agencies of socialization, often with diverse sets of values.

The family's importance in moral education comes from the fact that children so identify with the family as a group that its ways become part of their ways. The family is the first reference group whose values, norms, and practices the child refers to in evaluating the behavior of self and others. The pattern of interaction among the family becomes the model for the child (Parsons and Bales 1955, ch. 2).

Attempts have been made to classify families according to value and personality formation. Researchers have identified three types of families: adult-centered, child-centered, and adult-directed. The adult-centered family is run by adults for adults, and children take on the role of miniature adults. Within this type of family it has been found that children learn the morality imbedded in rules but do not seem to internalize much of it. The child-centered family is more attentive to children than to adults in that parents satisfy the needs of children before their own needs. The adult-directed family places greater emphasis on self development and individual growth. The latter type of family has greater potential for fostering personal and moral development than the former types (Gans 1962, pp. 54–60).

Another study of family types presents three different patterns (Baumrind 1971). In the authoritarian family pattern the parent is dominant. In the permissive family the child is dominant. In the authoritative family there is a reciprocal, interactive relationship in which forces exerted by the parent and child are in a state of tension. This latter pattern is associated with higher levels of competency and responsibility, based on observation and teacher reports.

In examining socialization within the family, one must attend to various forms that exist. One study has focused on the various types of socialization within families. First, children are educated by parents through teaching information, values, attitudes, skills, and sensibilities. Secondly, children educate parents by interpreting a culture to them, making parents look into themselves and their own development. Although there has not been much research in this area, it is clear that children educate their parents about developments in the child's world. Thirdly, parents educate parents about such issues as their own needs and perceptions, children, love, discipline, and power (Leichter 1974).

Of the many processes of learning that take place in the family those that are most closely connected to socialization are labeling and evaluating. Within families evaluations are constantly made and norms of behavior are recommended and even reinforced. Evaluations are made directly or by indirection, innuendo, or nonverbal communication. Evaluations that take place within the family have a way of leading to the development of self-concepts.

One extremely important role of the family in moral education is that of educational mediation. Educational mediation is the process by which family members translate and interpret educational experiences for one another (Leichter 1974, p. 214). This mediation can be in the form of direct teaching, coaching, or in indirect forms. The family, especially in the early years of formation, mediates the values of other agencies of education. Parents constantly evaluate peer group values, television, and the school. In time children mediate or convey to their parents perceptions and information from other educational agencies.

Leichter (1974) also reviews the research which has attempted to relate family socialization with social class differences. Higher and lower classes have been differentiated in various ways: knowledge and comprehension of the surrounding world, verbal and conceptual sophistication, assumptions about patterning and controllability of the environment, and values of activism versus fatalism, as well as future versus present orientation. This research has shown the effect of patterns of family life upon outlooks on life, views of societies, degrees of success motivation, parental consistency, and authoritarianism.

The research in this area is inconclusive and the assumptions built into the research have not always been clearly identified. It appears that most of the research takes as its starting point how well families socialize children for life in schools. Since there certainly are class differences in the preparation of children for school, family socialization patterns must account for at least some of these differences.

Limitations of the Family in Moral Socialization

It is recognized by historians of the family that in the past two centuries the family's role in socializing the young has gradually decreased. Other agencies now socialize and control the young (Shorter 1975, pp. 5–19). Histories of the family show that modern families differ from traditional families in a number of significant ways. New agencies and institutions have arisen that compete with the family in influencing and controlling the moral behavior of children. The boundary between the family and the surrounding community has become less rigid. The family exercises less control over the choices and values of adolescents. In modern family life a greater emphasis is placed on freedom, self-expression, self-realization, creativity, and spontaneity.

The waning influence of the family on the values of the young has some support in research done within the social sciences. Research on political values shows that family influences diminishes if individuals join groups which are personally significant to them, such as friendship cliques and families of spouses with values that conflict with those of parents (Hyman 1959, pp. 52–55). Research has also shown that values learned in family settings are often not adequately internalized and thus do not become operative in other situations. Research on the power of other agencies, such as peer groups and media, show that family influences can be challenged by other sets of values (Coleman 1974). Studies on adult development and socialization also indicate that persons change values from one social situation to another (Sloan and Hogan 1986).

On the other hand, some research does exist which shows that there is more convergence between values of children and those of parents. At times there is considerable overlap between the values of parents, children, and children's friends. This is especially true in similar socio-economic backgrounds (Alpert and Richardson 1980). It is also reported that parental influence is likely to be stronger in moral and social values, whereas peer influence is stronger in peripheral matters such as taste in music, entertainment, and patterns of interaction with persons of the same or opposite sex (Conger 1977).

From a societal perspective the family is seriously limited in the values it forms in the young. Durkheim (1961) contended that the family is not an effective place for the moral education of children for life in society since it is primarily a place of emotion, affection, and forgiveness. He did not see in the family the potential for discipline needed for the moral education suitable for life in society. There appears to be some truth in this contention, even though empirical studies are lacking to substantiate it.

MORAL SOCIALIZATION IN THE SCHOOL

Children spend many years in schools where they are expected to be introduced into the knowledge and ways of society. The schools serve many purposes, both individual and social. A certain tension exists among individual and social purposes. The making of the good and autonomous person may at times be at odds with developing the good citizen of a society. In this section we will examine the role of the school in the moral socialization of children and adolescents.

Durkheim's Sociology of Moral Education

The strongest case for the role of the school as an agency of moral education was made by Durkheim in his classic work, *Moral Education* (1961). In this work the French sociologist attempted to develop a new secular morality based on his understanding that individualism was the core value of modern society. What was essential for a moral society was respect for authority. As mentioned earlier, Durkheim developed this theory in a society which was becoming less dependent on the force of religion as an instrument of social control. In developing his theory he proposed three elements of moral education: discipline, attachment to social groups, and autonomy or self-determination.

Durkheim argued that the school has the potential for imposing *discipline* and good order as well as for fostering group purposes in which individuals are subordinated to the group. By discipline Durkheim meant the ability to restrain one's egoistic impulses and to do one's moral duty. The school in its structure can make up for the deficiencies of the family in moral education. It can utilize effective punishment and promote *attachment to social groups*. This attachment is described by Durkheim as warm, voluntary, and positive, done not out of external obligation but out of willing attraction. The third essential element in a school's moral education is autonomy or self-determination. Durkheim described the *autonomy* which schools can foster as the freedom to know and keep the rules of the school and of wider society. Durkheim also argued that it was important for the schools to administer punishment to rule breakers in order to inculcate a respect for authority. The methods of his proposed moral education are those of authority, even though he attempted to introduce tempering features to respect individuals' freedom of conscience.

It was Durkheim's contention that the sense of moral obligation, moral consciousness, respect, and obedience that develops in the child arises from life in society and contact with the rules of various groups, especially the school. Social rules are transmitted to children through external pressures exercised on them. As children move into larger and more diverse social groups, their conformity to rules lessens. A basic assumption of Durkheim was some sort of homogeneity among individuals. This assumption led him to give less attention to individual and developmental factors, for which he has been criticized by Piaget and others.

Though there are many features of Durkheim are incontestable, the theory has serious weaknesses. The major criticisms have come from Piaget (1965). Critics doubt whether Durkheim sufficiently attended to the freedom or autonomy of conscience. His theory may result in a compromise of personal morality through identifying it too closely with the norms of the state or society, with the accepted opinions in society, or with a conservative collectivity. Durkheim thus seems to place greater emphasis on constraint in morality at the expense of freedom and cooperation. In dealing with the normal education of children, Durkheim seemed to consider children as belonging only to an adult society, which has the right to make them conform to its rules. The individuality of children and the importance of their own groups was given little attention. Durkheim gives authority only to society and to those who represent it.

Durkheim's theory opposes the general direction of contemporary education. Contemporary theory, at least in the Western world, focuses chiefly on the need for autonomy in persons and only secondarily on the needs of society. This is so because psychological theory has dominated methods of child raising and the pedagogy of the schools. Grappling with Durkheim's theory forces educators to challenge what may be the excessive individualism found in many contemporary educational practices.

The value of Durkheim's ideas as a corrective, however, is shown by a change in Kohlberg's attitude towards Durkheim's theory. In an article published in 1971 Kohlberg argued strongly against the theory and pointed to Russian education as the proper fulfillment of Durkheim's theory. In a 1980 article, however, he accepted the critical role of the school in fostering a civic education which is not merely Socratic and developmental but also indoctrinative (i.e., direct teaching of rules). In this article, which was discussed in the previous chapter, he accepted the views of such functionalist sociologists as Durkheim and Parsons to the point that the schools should foster a system-maintaining perspective in which children learn to be concerned about collective goals. What separates Kohlberg from Durkheim in this latter viewpoint is his proposal that such an education should utilize the participatory democratic education fostered by Dewey (Kohlberg 1980).

Kohlberg is right in seeing the influence of Durkheim educational views in Russian education. The great Russian educator A. S. Makarenko was influential in developing an educational system that was based on a rehabilitative strategy of dealing with large numbers of uncared for and unattached children who caused social upheaval and civil strife in Russia between 1919 and 1929. The practical thrust of his educational philosophy was the attempt to establish in the young a psychological commitment to the social structure of the human community and a dependence upon it first through children's collectives and then through membership in larger communities and organizations and finally through total integration into the overall social structure.

Durkheim's ideas also suffer from an excessive rationalism. His moral theory attempted to eliminate the symbolic and the religious. He argued that:

We must discover those moral forces that men, down to the present time, have conceived of only under the form of religious allegories. We must disengage them from their symbols, present them in their rational nakedness (1961, p. 11).

What is left when the symbols of religion are eliminated is society, which he describes as a set of ideas and sentiments. In eliminating the symbolic, Durkheim does not provide a means by which moral sentiments and commitments can develop. Also, in contending that art, literature, and music are not sufficiently grounded in reality to play a role in moral education he makes moral education overly rational and does not explain the intensity of feeling needed for moral life. For him the two important curricular areas are science and history because they lead to an understanding of and confrontation with reality.

Talcott Parsons: Schools as Instruments of Moral Socialization

The functionalist theory of Durkheim has found a powerful proponent in the influential work of the American sociologist, Talcott Parsons (1959). He believes the moral purpose of the school is to produce responsible citizens in the school community. Schools are so managed that students are to exhibit respect for teachers, consideration and cooperativeness in relation to fellow students, and good work habits. In elementary schools teachers should attempt to foster unity between cognitive and moral goals. The good student combines both qualities. According to Parsons the task of schools is to develop in students commitments to capacities which are needed in school as well as in future endeavors. A major achievement of schooling is the fostering of independence, (i.e., the capacity to take responsibility and make decisions in coping with new and varying situations). Parsons contended that progressive education has emphasized the moral purposes of schools over the cognitive purposes. He proposed a better balance between the two.

Parsons contends that the elementary school should perform a number of key functions in society: the emancipation of the child from the primary emotional attachment to the family; the fostering of an internalization of societal values and norms at a step higher than can be learned in the family; the provision for the evaluation of student achievement; the selection and allocation of resources in keeping with the adult role system. The high school continues to evaluate student achievement and has an important role in the selection and preparation of persons for specific roles in society. During the high school years the peer group and youth culture take on added importance.

Functionalist sociologists have emphasized that schools are instruments of moral socialization both through the explicit and the hidden curriculum. The hidden curriculum refers to the unconscious shaping of children's behavior in adapting them to the needs of society (Dreeben 1968; Jackson 1968). Schools teach the general qualities that are necessary for adult performance in society: obedience, punctuality, respect, orderly work habits, and ability to follow instructions. According to Jackson the central characteristics of school life are: the crowds, the praise, and the power. Learning to live in a school classroom is learning to live with one's own age group and to be under an impersonal power. Dreeben emphasizes that in school children learn to live under an authority.

In the past two decades a reaction has developed in educational circles against functional analysis. Critics argue that this analysis has a conservative bias and prevents utilizing the potential of schools for bringing about changes in society. Marxist analysis has been used by some to show how schools function in many societies to impose repressive values of a capitalist society (Bowles and Gintis 1976). Schools are criticized for fostering the values which are needed to keep a repressive capitalism in existence. They sort people into various roles in society and promote the virtues needed by capitalist elites. Thus the radical contention is that moral socialization in schools is under the explicit and more often implicit control of elites (Giroux and Purpel 1983).

This debate between functional and critical sociologists on the role of schools in society has polarized analyses of schooling and moral socialization. It appears that both views exaggerate the influence of schools in shaping the values of students. Evidence does not exist to substantiate the strong assertion that the schools, in isolation from other agencies of socialization, have the power to perform the ascribed functions. The connection between the schools and wider society would appear to be looser than both viewpoints allow. Many of the qualities fostered in school represent what is needed in a good school organization as well as in the wider society. The limitations of schooling in moral socialization need to be recognized (Hurn 1978).

Empirical Research on Moral Socialization in Schools

The previous analyses of schooling have been for the most part at the theoretical level. Other studies examine schools through empirical methods. The research of political scientists shows that the schools play a powerful role in fostering existing social and political values, especially in the area of democratic values (Hess and Torney 1967). It has also been shown that children learn to respect and admire political authorities and idealize these figures. The reason for this is that children have security needs which are met in this way. Children also identify God with country (Easton and Hess 1962). Other research on schools indicates that in cognitive learning the schools can only reinforce family values (Greeley 1976). Studies on school athletics and extracurricular activities indicates that schools promote values in these areas.

The research base for the application of critical theory to an analysis of schooling is growing. An ethnographical study by Anyon (1980) concluded that attitudes toward work differ in working class schools and middle class schools. In the former children are presented the values of workers in a capitalist society while in the latter children are presented with the value of managers and bureaucrats. The study concludes that such educational methods tend to reproduce the relations which presently exist in capitalist societies.

College Students and Values   Empirical research has also indicated changes in values that result from college attendance. It has been found that college has a liberalizing effect on students' religious and political views, though colleges vary in their impact (Feldman and Newcomb, 1969). A major research project with college students studied changes in religion and values over five decades (Hoge 1974). In this study Hoge documented a single linear trend that had three visible components. 1) There was *increased individual and personal autonomy among college students*. College students in recent years are more like adults than students in past years. 2) There have been *changes in moral orientations*, mostly from commitment to detailed moral codes to more generalized and flexible moral orientations relating to dominant values. These new codes include a greater degree of tolerance regarding details of moral codes. 3) There has been the emergence of *a self-conscious youth culture*. This development began in the 1920s and became stronger after the Second World War.

Besides this linear pattern Hoge also found a back-and-forth pattern in the students' religious and moral values which he contended responds to short-term events and pressures. Commitment to religious values were strong in the 1920s, dropped to a low point in the middle or late 1930s, increased in the early 1940s until a high point was reached in the early 1950s. From that time through the 1960s and early 1970s there was a decline, with some indications of a rise in the middle 1970s. A possible interpretation of this data is that traditional religious and moral commitments have been strongest when other traditional commitments—to family, nation, and existing social order have been strongest. The study also found that college students were more susceptible to influence of social and economic situations than the general adult population.

Hoge's findings are confirmed by other surveys of college students (Yankelovich 1972; 1974). These studies stressed changes in values from the late 1960s to the early 1970s. The studies contend that there are a number of permanent and major values trends: 1) changes in sexual morality in the direction of more liberal sexual mores; 2) a lessening of automatic obedience to and respect for authorities of all kinds; 3) less inclination to follow church and organized religion as a source of guidance for moral behavior; 4) less patriotism and allegiance to national ideals. These studies revealed a greater concern for personal self-fulfillment and preoccupation with self over family, employer and community. This broad cultural analysis concluded that trends in individualism, desire for autonomy, and emphasis on personal fulfillment would continue for a number of years. The studies also concluded that obedience to authority, personal sacrifice, and traditional sexual morality would progressively weaken.

It cannot be inferred from these studies and from others that the college experience alone is responsible for all of these trends. Family background or other variables might explain some changes in the past few decades. The few studies done on non-college young adults have found that the cultural gap between college and non-college youths appears to be closing. Studies have shown that while non-college youth tend to be more conservative in the area of moral values than college youth, the differences between them narrowed considerably in the 1970s and 1980s. While at one time it was clear that attendance at college did correlate with more liberal moral values, non-college youth are now becoming more liberal in moral values, perhaps because of the development of a pervasive youth culture.

Summary: Moral Socialization in the Schools

Though I have attempted in this section to isolate the influence of the school as separate from other agencies of moral education, it is obvious that in reality this is impossible to do. Notwithstanding this problem, conclusions can be drawn about the role of the school for moral education.

The schools foster moral education by giving students basic cognitive skills. Skills in conceptualizing and problem solving can aid in understanding moral ideas and can foster an approach to moral problems that is thoughtful and not impulsive. Secondly, schools provide an area where students will have to handle personal and social relationships and the power of rules in their lives. There is no doubt that handling these adequately leads to greater moral awareness and development. Thirdly, the school may have a negative effect on moral development by promoting a sense of failure and a negative self-concept. With these negative attitudes students can only with difficulty develop the insight into themselves and the empathy into the lives of others necessary for moral development.

MORAL SOCIALIZATION AND PEER GROUPS

It is now generally accepted that peer groups constitute a distinct social group that influence human development. Children and especially adolescents interact in peer groups. These groups range from a small play group to a large organization such as Girl or Boy Scouts. These groups vary but the chief characteristics are their voluntary nature and collective influence. Peer group relationships are usually transitory although deep and lasting relationships can develop. Peer group influence is usually related to school because it is connected with school activities where many of these groups form.

Peer groups are treated in this chapter with regard to their socializing effects. They assume greater influence as children move into adolescence. Generally speaking, peer groups reflect and reinforce many of the values of the adult society: competition, honesty, cooperation, and responsibility. These groups often present what behavior is expected of a boy or a girl. Peer groups supply their members with social norms as well as affective support. Children learn a great deal about sexual matters from their peers thus building on the sex roles which they have learned within the family. Peers also teach adolescents how to become independent of adults by giving them opportunities to try on new social roles and identities.

A major study of the transition of adolescents into adulthood pointed out a number of harmful developments in the growing influence of peer groups over other socializing agencies (Coleman 1974). This study contended that peer groups were unsuitable for fostering movement toward adult goals and weakened the lines of communication across generations. The report took a negative view of organized youth groups because they segregated adolescents from the real world of adults and thus kept them immature. This work describes a distinct youth culture in which young people are segregated from adults in a culture which emphasizes inward-lookingness, psychic attachment, drive toward autonomy, concern for the underdog, and interest in change. The report decried the fact that many young people are so assimilated to this culture that they decide to remain in it rather than to enter the adult world.

A balanced view of peer groups and youth culture is that they possess both healthy and harmful dimensions. An evaluation of the effects of these groups may depend on how one judges the values of contemporary society which the youth either wish to assimilate or reject. Social science research in this area, as in all other areas, is not value free. Many social scientists have been more sensitive to the proper socialization of youth into the dominant society. Other social scientists have seen in the youth cultures forces that might bring about radical changes in the values of society (Friedenberg 1959; Keniston, 1970).

Empirical Research on Peer Groups and Moral Socialization

Researchers have attempted to determine the influence of peer groups on personal and moral development. Because no major study has been done in this area, I will depend on a number of small studies done on different types of samples. One study showed that adolescents typically conform more to norms of friends than to norms of parents as family members, students, or members of a peer group (Goodman 1969). Adolescents have been found to be more peer-compliant in choices perceived as having high relative importance in the eyes of peers, and parent-compliant in choices perceived to be more important in the eyes of parents. When the issue was seen to be relatively unimportant to both parents and peers, peer conformity dominated, but where the choice appeared to be important to both peers and parents, parent conformity ranked higher (Brittain 1967–68). Another study by the same researcher (Brittain 1971) found that adolescents make choices between parental and peer values. Peer values are followed in matters of status and identity, while parental values are followed on larger societal issues. It was also found that parent values were chosen in the dilemmas which adolescents rated as most difficult. The quality of interaction with parents is considered important since it has been found that the lower the quality of adolescents' interaction with adults, the higher will be the peer group involvement (Iacovetta 1975).

Several studies have attempted to make comparisons between parental and peer group influence. One study found that adolescents receiving a high degree of support and control by parents tend to conform most to parental expectations (Weigert and Thomas 1972). In a comparative study Lasseigne (1975) found that the influence of parents was significantly greater in 1974 than in 1964 and that there appeared to be a lessening of dependence upon the peer group among adolescent girls over that period. In matters related to moral courage, responsibility, loyalty, honesty, and friendliness adolescents were influenced by the opinions of their peers to a significantly greater degree than they were by their parents. In a study which asked "With whom would you consult in a complicated life situation?" both boys and girls listed their mother first (Kon and Losenkov 1978). From a study utilizing a sample of over nine thousand adolescents Curtis (1975) concluded that:

While parental opinions are clearly preferred to those of friends, it is also true that parental opinions become devalued during the adolescent life cycle. . . . A gradual independence from parental perspectives is achieved while the influence of friends remains relatively consistent but rarely more important than that of parents.

Curtis's conclusions are confirmed by other research. Siman (1977) found that parents actually play a more significant role in influencing adolescent behavior than one would think. This study contends that the peer group acts as a filter for parental norms as shown by a comparison of parental standards of individual group members against an average for parents of group members. The peer group serves to reinforce parental behavior and standards for the adolescent, resulting in greater parental influence over individual behavior. While peer group influence operates in a direct manner by setting standards for dress and social behavior, it also functions in an indirect way by affecting individual reactions to the behavior and standards of other significant persons in the adolescent's environment.

Researchers have also attempted to study the direct effects of peer groups on moral judgments. In an experimental study Lefurgy and Wolshin (1969) showed that adolescents of both sexes and of either realistic or relativist moral orientation will respond to immediate, face-to-face peer pressures with dramatic shifts away from their initial orientations. Their research showed that adolescents were more consistently susceptible to progressive development rather than to retrogressive change. Thus when disequilibrium induced by peer pressure in a developmentally advanced direction is resolved through the subject's accommodation in the direction of that influence, it tends to be of longer duration than if the influence is in a regressive direction. Another study done with male and female students of high school age showed that participation in a peer group discussion of moral judgment brings about increases in individual levels of moral judgments (Maitland and Goldman 1974). The study also found that greater social conflict and pressure to agree with group consensus in discussions of moral judgments induces greater change in the level of moral judgment of individuals than less conflicting and less consensus-oriented open-ended discussions of moral issues.

It is not easy to offer a simple summary of research on this subject. Some obvious conflicts exist in the research. It appears that parental influence remains strong under favorable conditions and in areas that do not directly impinge on adolescent and youth culture. There is a domain within the life of adolescents, directly related to social group norms and expectations, where peer pressures are particularly influential. The research on the value of peer groups discussion for promoting advancement in moral judgment offers a helpful suggestion on a way in which effective moral education might be done in the adolescent years.

This discussion on peer group influences has focused on children and adolescents. The matter of peer group influences on adults is a more complex one, and one that has not been well researched. Some research on adult socialization will be presented in another section of this chapter.

MASS MEDIA AS MORAL EDUCATORS

It is recognized that in the twentieth century the mass media have emerged as a major factor in socialization. Mass media include newsprint, comics, radio, records, tapes, films, photographs, and especially television. The influence of the mass media is more anonymous than socialization through family and school. The media are guided primarily by utilitarian motives for they are supported by advertising. It is recognized that media values often are in conflict with those promoted by other agencies of socialization in society. My treatment of the media in this section will be confined to television since it is recognized by many as the most powerful mass media.

An Analysis of the Television Curriculum

The information environment in which we live is greatly controlled by television. In many ways this medium shapes the modes and patterns of communication of the society in which we live. Most people get a large amount of their information about what is happening in the world and about what is valuable from this medium. In light of this it is important for moral educators to analyze the different forms of communication, interpret their social and psychological effects, and develop other educational environments and experiences which would balance, reinforce or counter the effects of this medium.

Postman (1979) has presented an insightful analysis of the educational curriculum of television. The TV curriculum according to his analysis, has the following characteristics: attention centered, non-punitive, affect centered, present centered, image centered, narration centered, moralistic, non-analytic, non-hierarchical, authoritarian, contemptuous of authority, continuous in time, isolating in space, and immediately and intrinsically satisfying. His basic contention is that the schools should rethink their educational task in the light of the powerful TV curriculum which is actually the first learning experience of children.

In his analysis Postman points out a number of harmful effects of the TV curriculum. It produces persons who are strong on intuition and feeling but weak on reflection and analysis. TV is inimical to conceptual, segmented, linear modes of expression such as speech and writing. The powerful imagery of TV often does not provide ground for debate or ambiguity. The message of TV commercials directs the search for time-compressed experience, short-term relationships, present oriented accomplishments as well as simple and immediate solutions. TV is biased, Postman believes, against scientific and logical thinking, the engendering of a sense of history, and the advancement of critical thinking. What he proposes as an alternative school curriculum is one which is subject centered, word centered, reason centered, future oriented, hierarchical, secular, socializing, segmented, and coherent.

Postman with insight notes how TV uses religious and moral parables, (i.e., narratives with moral implications). TV has something of the power of religious communication since it deals with values through emotion-packed situations. Commercials are likened to parables in their attempt to teach the means of resolving human problems. It is Postman's contention that the "masters of the media have quite simply preempted the functions of religious leaders in articulating the moral values by which we ought to live" (1979, p. 98).

As a socializing agency the media expose children and youth to adult culture. An analysis of values presented by TV shows that it emphasizes the middle class urban industrial culture. The mass media socialize persons into the consumer society but they also teach persons how to play and be family members (Greenberg 1980).

If we make a comparison between the media and the schools it is clear that the schools and media socialize the young into different cultures. The school promotes the nineteenth century Protestant middle class tradition: conservative, asexual, lower-middle brow music and literature, and lower middle class social but non-political community service (do-gooders), small town culture in which home, school, and church are the pillars of society. The media, on the other hand, promote the twentieth century non-Puritan culture of show business and the latest in dress, music, cars, and even politics. Schools usually present the media as uncultured, uncouth, and unwholesome because of the portrayal of a large amount of sex and violence. In the media schools are usually presented as dull, stodgy, and unfashionable. While schools preach production and participation, the media promote consumption and spectatorship.

In this analysis schools are at their best in teaching modes of formal communication, basic schooling, and social as well as occupational skills. Media allow children to learn what is going on in the present world of culture and politics. From the media one learns ideals, basic values, and the mood or ethos of the dominant culture.

The analyses of TV offered by Postman and others do not deal explicitly with moral education, though much of their analysis does relate to the learning of values in general, including moral values. A rather negative appraisal of TV from the perspective of moral education is offered by Sullivan (1980). He contends that TV in North America entraps children into the commodity culture of capitalism by exploiting their lack of power to react critically to TV, especially to the commercials. He considers TV a miseducational environment since it directs children to the ulterior objective of selling products. Television advertisements encourage children to serve their own needs and to be preoccupied with them. Friendly figures like Ronald McDonald and Burger King act as figures who can be trusted. Sullivan calls on moral educators to create in children a post-critical perspective which makes them aware of values already assimilated unconsciously. It is his contention that a crisis of values now exists in consumer capitalist countries which should call forth from parents and educator strenuous efforts to develop critical consciousness in all persons, especially children. His call is for a media literacy which would enable persons to uncover the hidden curriculum of the mass media.

Empirical Studies on Mass Media as Moral Educator

The above analyses of TV come both from a content analysis of what appears on TV and the analyses offered by social scientists and educators. A more difficult task is the ascertaining of the precise effects TV has on the moral behavior of individuals. Some of this research will be reviewed in order to present a more complete picture of TV's role in moral education.

As might be expected the social science research on the effects of TV on moral development are inconclusive. Most of the attention of the research has focused on the relationship between TV and aggressive or violent behavior (Comstock et al. 1978). The work reports that laboratory and field studies show a correlation between TV watching of violent activity and subsequent aggressive behavior. This finding is corroborated by research based on self or second-hand reports. Many have argued for positive programming to promote pro-social values. There are some studies which show that specially designed TV programming can stimulate the acquiring of pro-social behaviors such as sharing and self control, the reduction of fearfulness in phobic children, and the learning of simple intellectual skills.

Two issues can be raised with regard to these findings and recommendations. The validity of the research can be questioned on the basis that there is no guarantee that the results of field studies, laboratory studies, and self-reporting studies tell us about actual aggressive or behavior. One can also question whether or not the effects of such viewing are long lasting. Spokespersons for the TV industry have also pointedly indicated the weaknesses of the studies. Finally, it is always difficult to design studies in the social sciences which have validity and also maintain the canons of professional ethics of researchers.

The question of media promoting pro-social values in a pluralist society is also a difficult matter. What are the pro-social values to be promoted? Have the media the right and the responsibility to promote these values through programming? The media certainly do promote values because no educational endeavor is value free. The basic conflict is whether or not TV can be as profitable as it is in some countries, if it restricts itself to pro-social values and eliminates its direction towards violence, immediate impulse gratification, and persuasive techniques.

The debate over violence on TV in the 1970s raised a number of important questions that remain unresolved. How are the rights of the public and the rights of TV networks balanced? Television should have some accountability to the public interest. If it is shown that it is not in the interest of children to be exposed to a certain type of programming, what actions can citizens take? Consumer advocacy groups have attempted to deal with this problem at the political level. Notwithstanding the political issues, those involved in moral education should also address this matter.

An attempt to deal with the TV experience from the perspective of moral and religious values has been developed by Media Action Research Center. In a 1980 publication it set a number of goals. The goals of this five level program (from child to adult) are: 1) to help participants look at cultural values in contrast to biblical values; 2) to assist persons to use TV as a values clarification resource; 3) to be intentional about content, values, and the presence of TV; 4) to develop critical viewing skills; and 5) to help people to move to new decisions for their lives. The criticisms made of TV are the standard ones: confusion of fact and fantasy, stress on consumerism, exploitative view of human sexuality, poor images of persons. Unfortunately the program does not pay enough attention to the potential of TV for dramatizing positive values.

An Assessment of Media as Moral Educator

There is no doubt that moral educators must take cognizance of the power of the mass media, especially TV. There will never be conclusive social science evidence on the power of this medium in moral education, either viewed in isolation or in connection with other forces. But in the meantime persons must act on their own insights, the opinions of experts, and the research which is presently available. The power of this medium calls for formal programs to utilize the potential for good and to minimize harmful aspects. People need to become aware that TV teaches while it entertains. What must be examined are its intellectual, emotional, sensory, and content biases. Questions to be raised about TV and other media include: what attitudes are fostered? what types of behavior are approved and disapproved? who determines what we see? where does the money come from? what political interests are controlled by the media? what methods of persuasion are used in advertising?

The only way for educators to use the mass media effectively is by fostering a commitment to critical thought by emphasizing the powers of reason and imagination, by providing a study of the best minds of the past and present through their writings, by promoting a tradition of constant criticism and review, and by placing all things within a critical and comprehensive vision.

It is my belief that formal religious education can be a powerful instrument for such a critical approach to the mass media (Elias 1986, ch. 4). Because religious education in the informal settings of family, church, and media is conducted chiefly through parables, myths, stories, and rituals—with their strong emotional appeal—a formal religious education is required to emphasize critical rationality and thought. What is needed is a balance between the proclamation of the Christian message and the practical rationality of the Jewish tradition. Schools should rediscover the method of mutual criticism that emphasized the importance of publicly articulated reasons for moral and religious actions. In this tradition "what counts is reason, ubiquitous, predominant, penetrating." It was not the authority of the rabbis that counted but "the timeless, impersonal reasons for ruling as they did" (Neusner 1973, p. 234).

MORAL SOCIALIZATION IN RELIGIOUS BODIES

Until rather recently it was taken for granted that religious bodies such as churches and synagogues had considerable influence in shaping the moral attitudes and behaviors. All religious institutions promote a moral code to which members should adhere. Religious institutions provide moral education in direct ways, through teaching and preaching, and in indirect ways, through worship and the ethos of the community. Some religious bodies have their own schools in which moral education is explicitly related to religious education. The role of religion in moral education has been so strong that some claim that unless morality is founded on religious principles, it will collapse. Durkheim's attempt to develop a secular morality for the schools was in response to this particular fear.

The processes by which religions foster moral education have been studied by social scientists. Geertz (1973) has described how religious bodies transmit both faith and values to their members. In his symbolic-functionalist approach to understanding culture he explains how the powerful symbols of myths, stories, and rituals shape values, attitudes, and behaviors. For him religion is defined as:

> (1) A system of symbols which acts to (2) establish powerful, pervasive, and long-lasting moods and motivations in men (3) by formulating conceptions of a general order of existence and (4) clothing these conceptions with such an aura of facticity that (5) moods seem uniquely realistic (p. 90).

In this theory of religion values come out of direct experience with a symbolic system which includes a view of what is good. Individuals in early years assimilate in a somewhat unconscious manner this symbol system with its inherent value implications. As persons continue to participate in their religious faith they are summoned to internalize and live out the implications of their religious faiths in a more conscious manner.

It is true that not all members of religious bodies always abide by the prescribed moral norms. Often within the same institution there are serious differences of opinion on certain issues, (e.g., divorce, birth control, smoking, abortion, and war). In recent years studies have shown that many people consider themselves good members of their religious institutions even though they depart from some of the ethical teachings of their religions. For example, Catholic youths between the ages of 15 and 30 were questioned on their acceptance of church teaching on birth control, remarriage after divorce, legal abortion, euthanasia, premarital sex, and homosexuality. The study concluded that only on abortion on demand (51%) and homosexuality (77%) did a majority agree with the official teaching of the church (Fee, Greeley, McCready, and Sullivan 1981, p. 13). This does not necessarily mean that these young persons have not been influenced in many other areas by the ethical teachings of their church. But it does make us realize the increasing limitations on the moral authority of religious bodies.

It is clear that for many people moral socialization does not include direct influence of a religious institution. In modern societies there are people of religious beliefs and people of no religious beliefs. Also, it would be difficult to establish one particular set of beliefs on which moral education might be based in society in general. Notwithstanding this, it is important to recognize that many people base their moral life on particular religious beliefs. Thus religious bodies form the environment for socialization and education in moral values for many persons. The moral environment of religious groups varies greatly, extending from authoritative transmission of a received tradition of rules and regulations to an open and free search for truth. Many religious educators favor an approach to moral education which would help persons make up their own minds about moral beliefs, while utilizing the traditions and norms of religious bodies as helpful guidelines. This does not mean that there are not other approaches to moral education which are more directive and authoritative. In the next chapter I will discuss various approaches to religious education developed within Protestant, Catholic, and Jewish faiths.

Research on Religion and Moral Education

One issue relating to religious bodies that has received attention from social scientists is the relationship between religion and moral behavior. One might hypothesize that religion would foster more acceptable moral behavior or lead to higher standards of moral judgment or reasoning. Little research has been conducted on this subject. Though the following conclusion was reached on the research done on this topic before 1970, the judgment probably still stands today, as will be made clear in the discussion which follows.

> The evidence does not encourage the view that in its general influence religion strengthens the conscience. This is no way to deny that individuals have been morally transformed by their Christian convictions. It is merely to say that as far as most believers are concerned the existing evidence shows that Christian belief and practice influence behavior in the direction of social conformity rather than in the direction of personal moral growth (Wright 1971, pp. 232–233).

One example of such negative research findings on religion and moral education is reported by Kohlberg (1971). He found that respondents, regardless of denomination, make remarkably little use of religion in coping with moral dilemmas. He found, however, that in less religiously pluralistic societies like Turkey, more religious concepts were used in responses. Kohlberg recognized that some studies have shown that persons rely on religion for their moral beliefs. Yet he contends that his research project has not found this on any significant scale. Kohlberg concludes that religious education in the churches and synagogues has no specifically important or unique roles to play in moral development as opposed to the role of the family or school.

The difficulty with interpreting these research findings is that no clear distinction is made between types of religious environments and their influence on moral education. For example, the research on the relationship between religion and prejudice showed that some types of religion fostered religious prejudice while other types did not (Allport 1966). Also, it must be recalled that Kohlberg's research is school oriented and concerned with moral reasoning. The context and the form of research may influence students against religious responses.

Some comparative research has been done on the differing moral attitudes among members of religious institutions. A rather extensive study was conducted by the National Opinion Research Center (NORC) in the middle 1960s on moral issues (Greeley 1976). The study presented persons with dilemmas about dress, marital affairs, bribery, stealing, grades, damage to property, tax evasion, cheating, lying, and embezzling. An analysis of the data showed that in general there were no significant differences among Catholics, Protestants, and Jews in their responses to these dilemmas. Whenever there were significant differences on an item, Protestants took the strictest moral position and Jews the most lenient position, with Catholics generally in the center (p. 241). The research is not conclusive and scholars have called for more controlled studies to determine the relationship between religion and morality (Spilka, Hood, and Gorsuch 1985).

In an extensive review of studies on the relationship among religion, prejudice, and personality, Dittes (1971) reported some significant findings. A number of studies have established a correlation between pro-religious attitudes and conservative social attitudes towards capital punishment, sex, and divorce as well as racial and domestic social politics. A few studies, however, have found that religious persons have more liberal attitudes than non-religious persons. Dittes was not impressed with the scientific rigor of the studies he reported on and cautioned that such studies need to be interpreted carefully. It is his view that studies need to differentiate between a *consensual* religious faith (extrinsic religion) in which one merely belongs to a religious group and a *committed* religious faith (intrinsic religion) in which one is truly committed to the beliefs of the religious body). He believes that it is only the latter that correlates with lack of ethnocentrism and prejudice as well as with a mature personality. A subsequent study using this distinction has verified that a committed religious faith does enhance the level of moral judgment (Ernsberger and Manaster 1981). Sapp (1986), on the other hand, has found that the distinction does not appear that clear and that results are inconclusive about the effects of intrinsic and extrinsic faith.

Research on the influences of religious bodies on moral development has not yielded any definitive findings. The great difficulty with this research lies in the effort to isolate particular variables in the study and to arrive at agreed-upon operational definitions of important variables. Many interacting factors are involved in the development of moral values. Studies more sophisticated than those designed at present are needed to arrive at firm conclusions.

ADULT SOCIALIZATION IN MORAL VALUES

The term socialization usually refers to the introduction of children into the values of a particular culture. In more recent years social scientists have used the concept to explain changes in adult life. In general terms they have attempted to determine how adults develop throughout the life span. Socialization takes place because of the demands of others, role or status change (marriage, parenthood, widowhood, retirement), occupational entry or shift, developmental changes in family (early years, parenthood, empty nest, divorce, death of a spouse, geographic or downward mobility (due to sickness, retirement or widowhood). It is also clear that in adult life many persons alter the moral values in which they were socialized as children or youth.

An early study of adult socialization reported these general changes in adulthood (Brim 1966): a shift from emphasis on values and motives to an emphasis on overt behavior; a movement from an idealistic orientation to a realistic one; an attempt to synthesize old material rather than gather new material; learning how to handle conflicting situations; and socialization for increasingly specific tasks.

Attention to moral development among adults has recently come from Kohlberg's theory which contends that moral development among adults seems to result more from transactional effects of experience on development and less on maturational factors as in the case of children and youth (Kohlberg and Kramer 1969). The important transactions in adulthood take the form of experience with conflicting ideas, the questioning of identity, and the recognition of the need for making and then living with irreversible moral commitments and the acceptance of sustained responsibility for the welfare of others. It is Kohlberg's belief that the higher stages of moral reasoning are reached only with the accumulation of experiences that occurs when adults confront conflicting loyalties and live in a broad and pluralistic social situation.

It must be recognized that Kohlberg's treatment of moral development remains within the parameters of his psychological theory and thus pays more attention to internal dynamics of the developing person than to the effect of specific environments or situations on adult value changes. Research on the effects of these environments is not extensive. In an earlier section of this chapter I reviewed research relating to young adults, especially college students. Additional research on family influences were also treated.

Some scholars argue that the Kohlberg theory is not broad enough to extend to the complexity of adult life. Sloan and Hogan (1986) have offered the rudimentary theory based on changing self understandings throughout adulthood as adults face moral decisions in ordinary life. Though the theory has not been empirically tested, it does offer some fruitful hypotheses.

According to this theory every activity in life is a source of moral conflict. Thus moral problems come from individual's concrete life. Moral deliberation takes place within a community and is not a solitary process. Our present dilemmas relate to past experiences which we now find as inadequate. Our moral development and decision making is related to all aspects of our lives. Individuals under stress are more likely to regress to less advanced moral stances, thus the term development may not be the best language to use to explain moral life in adulthood. A major study of changing adult values documented significant changes during the life span (Lowenthal, Thurber, et al. 1975). This cross sectional study of lower middle class adults showed the following: 1) young adults emphasized values that reflected expansiveness and high expectations in contrast to older adults who emphasized self-limitation and reduction in frustration; 2) young adults emphasized personal achievement and happiness while those in middle age and old age were more concerned with coping, personal caring, leading a religious life, and making a contribution to society; 3) younger adults put more emphasis on achievement or instrumental values while middle-aged and older adults emphasized expressive values and interpersonal relations.

Socialization in Values in Work and Employment

In order to develop the thesis that adults change values during their life span, it might be helpful to look at a powerful environment: the world of work. Individuals are socialized into work organizations. Various means of control exist in all organizations to enforce standards of performance. Organizations set norms not just for persons when they are at their place of employment but also for their off-work lives. In fact organizations have a way of setting norms for spouses and children of their workers (Whyte 1961; Kanter 1977).

Although work and the learning of moral values have not been the subject of research, some research exists on the effect of work on personality where parallels can be drawn for socialization into values. Reports indicate a correlation between the complexity of one's job and one's off-job psychological functioning, ranging from valuation of self-direction to self-esteem to authoritarian conservatism to intellectual flexibility. Job complexity in these studies is determined by the degree of complexity of one's work with things, with data, and with people. Kohn and his associates confirm research which establishes that environmental factors affect cognitive learning not only in childhood and adolescence but also in adulthood (Baltes and Schaie 1976).

Though no research is reported on the relationship between job complexity and values, self-concept or social orientation, Kohn confidently predicts that research would establish this relationship. In his view intellectual flexibility is intimately related to values, self-concept or social orientation (Kohn 1980, p. 203). Thus it appears that it is a reasonable hypothesis that where work is central to people's lives, it affects their self-concept, values, and social orientation.

When one moves from this general thesis about the effect of work on psychological constructs to the specific area of moral values, the research is even more tentative. It is clear that in the world of the modern organization and in other forms of work men and women face many challenges to moral values and attitudes for which they have not been adequately prepared (Velasquez 1982). It can be assumed that under the pressures of these situations persons may significantly alter their moral perceptions and values. The world of work presents many opportunities for decision making and is thus a powerful socializing agency for adults.

In reviewing the literature on adult socialization in moral values and attitudes, I have become convinced that this is largely an unresearched area. Many questions need to be raised about adult life. The Kohlberg theory of development through interaction with persons and events provides a formal framework. Yet this framework is developmental and it is not clear that we can call changes in moral values, attitudes, and behavior in adults "developmental" in the sense in which he has defined the term. Stage theory would appear to have limited application to adults.

The one type of research that does exist on adults about morality is found in studies of sexual practices (Kinsey et al. 1948; 1963) and blue collar crime (Velasquez 1982). These surveys indicate some moral values and attitudes. The general direction of such studies is towards liberal and flexible views in morality.

A related issue concerns the ethical standards of various professions. In recent years greater attention has been given to these concerns although research is not extensive (Lebacqz 1985).

The conclusion to this section is that though we have a common sense impression that in adulthood significant changes do take place in moral attitudes, practices, and values, we do not have an adequate way of conceptualizing these changes or understanding them. The theory and research in moral development has not taken adequate account of the moral sphere. Perhaps there are no patterns to be found beyond the general one of flexibility and liberalism. Yet this pattern is not universal since such movements as the Moral Majority foster the development of more conservative moral attitudes among adults.

SUMMARY

It is extremely difficult to summarize or to make conclusions about the social sciences. I have tried to describe the general theories that are operative in moral socialization. The structural-functionist view is still the predominate theoretical perspective. Recently, however, it has been challenged by a group of critical sociologists who look beyond functions and structures to examine the broader social influences and effects. All general theories agree on the influence of environmental and institutional factors on moral socialization. More research is needed to establish the extent of this influence.

I have also presented research on important social agencies of moralization: family, church, peer group, work, and the media. The difficulty with research is the impossibility of isolating the separate effects of these agencies. There is general agreement that all of these agencies influence moral socialization but it will take more sophisticated research methods to determine the exact influence of each agency. The research on family influence appears the most convincing since it is rather extensive. The research in other areas is less definitive and not easily separable from family influences.

The conclusion from this chapter for moral educators is that they need to be aware of the power of all social forms of moral education and to recognize the limitations of formal schooling as a separate agency of moral education. Schools do have an influence but they are only one among many factors. Moral educators often need to see themselves in various roles with regard to other agencies. At times they will want to challenge values learned from other sources; at other times they will merely reinforce values.

Religious educators face the same tensions about morality as other educators. These educators have the added problem of dealing with the moral teachings of religious bodies and the socialization that has taken place in these bodies. In the next chapter I will examine more carefully the theological and religious issues that religious educators face in the area of moral education.

Fernhout, Harry
" Moral Education as
grounded in Faith " J. of Moral Ed
Vol. 18, 3. pp' 190-202, Oct. 1989

CHAPTER 5

RELIGION AND MORAL EDUCATION

Given the close connection that most people make between religion and morality, one would expect that moral education would be a major focus for theologians and religious scholars. This, however, is not the case. No recent scholar comparable to Dewey, Maritain, Kohlberg, Erikson, or Durkheim has written a major work on moral education from a theological perspective. For the past few years I have been puzzled by the relative silence of theologians on this particular topic. One theologian has pointed out how remarkably shy theologians have been about entering into debates about theories of moral development, noting that no theologian took serious note of Piaget's work until 1978 (McDonagh 1980, p. 320). Another theologian, decrying the fact that moral development has been left to psychologists and educators, has attempted to make a specific contribution to moral development and education (Hauerwas 1980).

Several reasons for the surprising lack of works on moral education from a theological perspective exist. There appears to be a division of labor between theologians and religious educators according to which the latter handle practical matters such as methods while theologians concentrate on theoretical and speculative matters. Recently, however, a field of practical theology has been delineated which gives specific attention to education (Browning 1983). Also, theologians who are interested in moral issues and who are of a practical bent have traditionally directed their attention to other activities of religious bodies. Thus Protestant theologians usually deal with the contexts of preaching and counseling. Catholic theologians have traditionally related their writings to the work of priest-confessors. Jewish theologians have concentrated more on education because of the strongly ethical nature of Judaism. Extremely few theologians, however, have developed their moral theories with a view to contexts of education, either within specific or outside schools.

Lawrence Kohlberg (1971, pp. 23–24) provides another possible explanation for the relative silence of theologians and religionists. He contends that only two academic disciplines—developmental social psychology and philosophy—can make scholarly generalizations on moral education. The generalizations of scholars in other disciplines, including theology, have merit only in so far as they can be reduced to social psychological or philosophical generalizations. Kohlberg makes this statement on the value of theological contribution to moral education:

> A Catholic theologian and educator may have a great deal of interest in, and working knowledge of, the aims and processes of Catholic moral education. This knowledge will be of use to non-Catholic educators, however, only insofar as the Catholic educator has formulated a conception of morality that is defensible by reference to moral philosophy, rather than Catholic theology, and insofar as he has studied the development of such morality in terms of the general methods and concepts of developmental social psychology (1971, p. 23).

Kohlberg sums up his argument with the assertion that "anything worthwhile any of us can say about moral education requires us being simultaneously a social psychologist and a philosopher" (1971, p. 24).

A suspicion about this idea arises when one realizes that Kohlberg classifies himself as a social psychologist and a philosopher. It is my view that scholars in other disciplines can say something worthwhile about moral education, even in the form of scholarly generalizations. Historians, social scientists, scholars in the humanities, including religion and theology, can also engage in studies which add to our knowledge of moral education concepts and theories which cannot be reduced to philosophical theories or psychological generalizations.

A number of observations can be made on Kohlberg's position vis-a-vis theology. First, the usefulness of a particular theology is to be judged not merely by what it says to those outside the system, even though such a criterion is a helpful one in the overall analysis of a moral system. Secondly, Kohlberg is right to press for a justification of a moral system on rational grounds. Thirdly, theology's contribution to moral development and education should not be restricted to the issue of the justification of a moral system. There are many significant contributions that theology can make, as will become clear.

In this chapter it is my intention to review some recent works of theologians and philosophers of religion. Specifically, I will examine what four groups have written on the relationship between religion and moral education: philosophers of religion, Protestant theologians, Catholic theologians, and Jewish theologians. In the previous chapter I have reviewed social science research on the relationship between religion and morality. This discussion will continue in this chapter. There will obviously be some repetition of ideas in this treatment, but I believe that the differences uncovered will justify this repetition.

PHILOSOPHERS OF RELIGION AND MORAL EDUCATION

In this section I will present and critique the theories of writers interested in the relationship between religion and education. These writers might best be classified as philosophers of religion since they do not write out of the perspective of any explicit religious tradition or theology. Many of these philosophers are situated within the analytic tradition in philosophy which places an emphasis on the language of religion and morality.

Viewed philosophically, there are several possible relationships between religion and morality (Wallwork 1980). Firstly, the connection between religion and morality can be metaphysical in that all things are by nature dependent on God, religion, and religious faith. Secondly, the relationship can be logical in that the one is deduced, inferred, or derived from the other. Thirdly, the relationship can be psychological in that religion is needed for the buttressing of morality or because the moral sense develops chronologically in children from the religious sense. The first two questions are purely theoretical in that they entail an analysis of concepts while the latter question is partly empirical since it requires observed data for its verification.

Another attempt to understand the relationship between religion and morality has posited four possibilities: 1) the moral and the religious are independent of each other; 2) religion and morality are the same; 3) religion is necessary for morality because it provides moral standards and an incentive to be moral; 4) religion and morality are complementary, (i.e., though they are two different domains, from the very beginning of life there is an intertwining of the two) (Nelson 1973).

From Wallwork's and Nelson's classifications it is clear that the relationship between religion and morality can be viewed as either a theoretical issue involving logic or an interpretation of language and reality, or a psychological and empirical issue involving the testing of such constructs as development and motivation. Although philosophers attempt to focus on the conceptual issues involved, they often appeal to psychological factors. Given these considerations a number of approaches can be examined.

Total Independence of Religion and Morality   Some philosophers argue that morality cannot be based on religion because the two are logically distinct forms of discourse (Hamm 1979). From this position it follows that moral education cannot be based on religion and that religious instruction should not substitute for or supplement moral instruction. Interestingly enough, Hamm also concludes that moral instruction can legitimately be taught in all schools, including public schools, because of its total independence from religion.

Hamm presents a theoretical argument for this position. Morality enjoys an autonomy with regard to religion. He argues that religion includes dogma, priesthood, ceremonies, images, books, and public assemblies. Although he admits that a symbolic interpretation of religion such as Paul Tillich and other liberal theologians offer might include a moral element, Hamm contends that our ordinary experience tells us that there can be a knowledge of the good without a knowledge of religion. He also appeals to common experience for proof that religion is not even needed as the motivating force for ethical conduct. Finally, he asserts that religion may even obscure the central notions of morality by providing false motivation or by reducing freedom to heteronomy—dependence on others for one's moral judgments. The empirical data on this issue is inconclusive, though none is cited by Hamm who merely appeals to what he terms ordinary experience. In the previous two chapters I indicated some of the problems with establishing firm conclusions when it comes to establishing an empirical connection between religion and morality.

What Hamm and others who argue for the independence of morality from religion have established is merely that morality can have justifications other than the religious, a point which was argued by Durkheim, Dewey, and other scholars. What they have not proven is that religion cannot form a basis for morality and thus for a particular form of moral education. These critics are right in pointing out that some forms of religion lead to harmful moral development and behavior. Yet it cannot be contended that all forms of religion are harmful. Though there may not be a logical connection between religion and morality, the two may be related in other ways as alternate approaches argue. Given the state of empirical research in this area and the complexity of human motivation, it is still possible that morality can be related to religion and that moral education can have a religious basis.

This relationship between religion and morality has given rise to a number of approaches to moral education. Some of them were treated in previous chapters: Dewey, Wilson, Skinner, Kohlberg and others. In the next chapter additional approaches which apply this assumption will be treated.

Metaphysical Relationship Between Religion and Morality   According to this viewpoint a necessary metaphysical relationship exists between religion and morality. Morality has no other justification except with a religious faith. Like everything else, morality depends on God or a "ground of being", in Tillich's expression. God's existence is as necessary for morality as it is for the rest of the universe. This viewpoint takes two forms. In one, a knowledge of God is explicitly required for the content of moral standards. In the other, such an explicit knowledge is not required, because the relationship between the two is in the very nature of things (Wallwork 1980, p. 274).

The argument for a metaphysical connection between religion and morality is basically made on religious grounds. The rules and principles of conduct which mark the moral life are considered indissolubly, and even logically, tied into a wider system of religious beliefs. They are justified through an authoritative revelation in sacred writings, in the person of Jesus or another moral teacher, by divine grace given by God through the church, or by grace given by God to the individual mind through the operation of conscience. The appeal is made to one or more of these theories in order to establish a metaphysical connection between religion and morality. Ultimate justification, however, is in God, an omnipotent and omniscient creator.

Questions raised about this theory of grounding morality exclusively on religious faith include: Does such a being as God exist? Is such a being good? Why should we obey the commands of such a being? Is the revelation to be taken as God's word? These questions indicates that we are forced to present rational arguments for the justification of morality besides purely religious arguments. It cannot be simply asserted that what God reveals defines what is good, for from a description of the origins of moral laws one cannot infer whether they are good or right. Merely because people believe that God is the source of moral laws is no justification for them since the truth of these laws must be judged individually. In a real sense knowledge of morality is logically prior to knowledge of God (Hirst 1974).

The position that knowledge of the moral depends on an implicit belief in God because divine grace is needed to live the moral life does not offer any more hope for establishing a metaphysical connection. It is clear that many persons perform morally good actions without any religious motivation or consideration. To assert that there is a divine aid which they are unaware of merely resolves the problem by broadening the definition of grace and extending God's activity even to those who are unaware of it or who do not believe in it. If all persons have the grace through conscience to do what is right, then it appears that by positing a religious interpretation, nothing substantial is added to a rational or secular justification of morality.

This theory of the metaphysical connection between religion and morality underlies orthodox religious approaches to moral education which are found among Protestants, Catholics, and Jews. A description of these theories follows.

Religion and Morality Are the Same   A third position about the relationship to religion and morality consists in reducing the religious to the moral. This theory, common to many liberal theologians and progressive educators, proposes that religion is a major orientation to life, a concern for the wholeness of reality and for the highest values. Matthew Arnold expressed this viewpoint in his definition of religion as "morality tinged with emotion" (Arnold in Kaufmann 1961, p. 103). In this form of religious humanism the deity becomes a symbol for our highest human ideals, and religious assertions announces an allegiance to a particular set of moral principles.

This almost naturalist resolution of the problem is found in the writings of educators who contend that the goals of morality and religion, and therefore of religious and moral education are basically the same. This belief was expressed among some liberal Protestant religious educators in the early part of this century and it also found place in religious education circles during the heyday of secular theology and the Death-of-God God theology in the 1960s.

In criticism of this viewpoint, it should be noted that an analysis of the concept of religion shows it to be far more extensive than mere moral principles. This is not to deny that a moral stance is at the heart of the religious vision of many world religions. Yet a phenomenological and functional analysis of religion shows that all forms of religion contain meaning and belief systems, organizational patterns, and modes of life, all of which cannot be simply reduced to the moral without unduly extending the meaning of the moral or narrowing the definition of the religious.

The import of this discussion thus far is to recognize that one does not do justice either to religion or to the moral by reducing the former to the latter. While moral education may be one part of religious education, it certainly is not all of it, and not even the most essential element of religious education. *Religion and Morality as Complementary* The soundest philosophical position is presented by Wallwork (1980) who contends that religion is neither necessary nor sufficient for the justification of morality but that the two are mutually related. Morality must ultimately be justified on rational grounds. Religion can play an important role in the justification of moral principles since religious convictions profoundly affect how persons justify moral judgments. In his view religion provides believers with the following: 1) additional arguments on behalf of moral principles which are ethically justifiable (e.g., actions are declared to be against the will of God); 2) alternative perspectives on, and assessments, of morally relevant facts, such as an interpretation of human nature which sees a relationship to God as basic; 3) religious influences on moral judgments which add distinctive obligations and virtues such as the Jewish requirement of charity and the demands of Jesus in the Sermon on the Mount.

Wallwork insists that the obligations of religion include both religious and moral elements. The evangelical counsels of the Catholic tradition (poverty, chastity, and obedience) are closer to the religious side. In such concepts as sin, repentance, and reconciliation, moral and religious meanings are fused. Religions often require a greater degree of self sacrifice. The symbols, myths, and stories of the religious tradition qualify the dispositions, affections, and intentions of a religious person's moral character. Wallwork concludes that religion affects moral judgment in ways missed by the sharp delineation of the two realms.

Although Wallwork does not draw educational implications from his discussion of the relationship between religion and morality, he does present some useful guidelines. Moral education must include an appeal both to rational principles and to religious teachings. A religiously based moral education includes a relationship to God. Within religious traditions it must make use of the powerful laws, examples, rites, symbols, and stories of the tradition. All of these ideas will be found in more theologically based theories to be treated in the following sections.

PROTESTANT THEOLOGIANS AND MORAL EDUCATION

The salient characteristics of Protestant moral theology have been analyzed by Gustafson (1978). Drawing on his analysis some generalizations can be made about the approach of Protestants to moral theology and thus to moral education. Protestant ethics is essentially a biblical ethic. Protestant moral theologians depend to a great deal on Scripture for their ethics. They deal with such issues as the authority of Scripture and the relevance or application of Scripture to practical moral matters. The strength of this ethic is that it emphasizes God's action, gives clear guidelines on many issues, calls persons to faith and repentance, and presents a strong motivating and inspiring force. This ethic is both challenging and reassuring.

Yet the very biblical nature of Protestant ethics raises problems. What is the authority of Scripture in the moral realm? How are the moral teachings of the Scriptures relevant to many contemporary issues? A biblically based ethic may be suitable for members of the Christian community but it is not suitable for addressing persons outside the tradition on moral issues that touch on public morality and policy.

In dealing with the Bible two general tendencies have developed within Protestantism. An orthodox or fundamentalist mentality looks for ultimate moral guidance from specific teachings of the Bible. A more liberal tendency focuses on the general teachings about faith, love, repentance, grace, and sin without expecting to find precise guidelines within the Scriptures. The danger in the fundamentalist orientation is a rigid orthodoxy unresponsive to the complexity of moral situations; the danger in the liberal orientation is a relativist ethic without clear guidelines. The liberal tradition has led to forms of situation ethics in which little place is given to moral norms.

Protestant ethics tends to be historical in that it takes as its starting point not an immutable human nature but the facts of religious history where God is described as commanding or forbidding certain actions. This has led some to the orthodox or sectarian view that the Christian community must follow Jesus and should feel no need to show how Christian ethics is a value for all persons. This differs from the Catholic emphasis on natural law which is viewed as binding on all persons. In its more liberal version Protestant ethics is historical in that it consists of an interpretation of how God is acting in current events in history. The strength of this approach is that it has an openness to change because it sees God's present action as relevant to ethical decision making. The disadvantage of the approach is the relativization of ethics that may result and the difficulty of making universal moral claims.

Contemporary Protestant ethics tends to be existential. Many Protestant ethicians emphasize the fact of human freedom and the need to confirm personally one's moral choices. The ethic is also existential in that it stresses the uniqueness of each moment of real choice rather than focus on an enduring pattern of life or norms. Some classical Protestant theologians who stressed this dimension were K. Barth, P. Tillich, R. Bultmann, Reinhold Niebuhr, and H. Richard Niebuhr. One of the criticisms made of this existential ethic is its lack of philosophical grounding in comparison to a Catholic moral law ethic. A general criticism is its failure to provide substantive guidance for moral choices and clear reasons for these choices.

Some recent attempts have been made among Protestant ethicians to find a stronger philosophical basis for ethics. James Gustafson, Stanley Hauerwas, and Craig Dykstra are prime examples. It is also these theologians whose work has the most implication for moral education, as will be seen below.

The issue of moral authority is a complicated one in Protestantism. In most Protestant churches there is no clear institutional authority as in Roman Catholicism. The Scriptures have authority, but there are debates over its application to particular moral issues. Statements are made from time to time by particular churches but acceptance by general membership is rather rare. Ultimately moral teaching rests on biblical authority and with the authority of the Spirit of God working in individual consciences. The final authority is clearly the individual's informed conscience.

I have chosen to discuss three contemporary Protestant theologians who have explicitly related theology to moral education. These theologians are presented as representatives of a more liberal approach to religious ethics in their attempts to remain faithful both to a religious tradition and to contemporary knowledge and understandings.

Education for Creative Responsibility

James Gustafson (1970) attempted in an brief essay to deal with the relationship between religion and morality. His description of the moral person is that of one who takes responsive and creative action for human well-being, and gives of self to others in the world. Moral persons are both responders and inititators of actions. Gustafson sees the task of moral education as the development of persons who are capable of responsible moral action. Moral education should relate itself to all dimensions of the person: beliefs or convictions, character traits, affective and emotive aspects, motives and intention, and the capacity to make moral judgments.

Gustafson argues that religion can make some modest differences in a person's moral behavior. Although he admits that there is no logical or psychological connection between religion and morality, he contends that religion does provide for many persons a justification for morality in general as well as for particular moral actions. Gustafson makes the case that believing certain things about God does and should affect moral behavior. He also contends that the religious teaching that God is love and loves us can be a strong motivating factor for persons to love God and their fellow men and women.

Gustafson summarizes his probing essay with these conclusions about the relationship between religion and moral education. First, moral training without religious training is a clearly a reality. Secondly, religious training does not guarantee that a person will become a moral person. Thirdly, the primary purpose of religious training—trust and belief—is clearly distinct from moral training. Fourthly, a religious training directed at fostering trust and belief can foster certain things which are clearly relevant to moral life: attitudes, dispositions, sensibilities, motives, and intentions. Finally, Gustafson affirms that a religious moral training is not confined to authoritative rules of conduct or to sanctions of punishment and reward in eternity but rather has as its purpose the development of autonomous and morally responsible persons.

Gustafson's treatment is certainly a balanced one, making as he does only modest claims for the role of religion in moral education. If anything, he seems to have understated the case for religion to counter the exaggerated claims of many religionists for the role of religion in moral education. Perhaps since this essay was originally a lecture given at a general symposium of scholars, he may have understated some elements of a religious moral education. Also, I find his use of the word training a bit jarring, indicating perhaps a failure to deal with moral or religious education fully. The use of this word seems to foster the view that such education is the authoritative passing on of rules, a position which he decries. Furthermore, he pays little attention to the various ways in which religion produces the attitudes and dispositions that he recommends. He should address the educational role of religious worship and cult, the life and witness of a religious community, and the mediating forces of religious family and community in moral development. Gustafson covers these element in other writings, but explicit application to moral education does not greatly occupy even there.

Education for Christian Character

A sustained theological effort to deal with moral development and to a lesser degree to deal with moral education has come from the Lutheran theologian, Stanley Hauerwas (1980). He presents a Christian ethic of character and narrative as an alternative to Kohlberg's theory of moral development. Hauerwas attempts to combine a biblical theology with a philosophy of the life of virtue as narrative. He depends on Alistair MacIntyre's (1977) reformulation of the Aristotelian theory of virtues in the moral life.

Hauerwas admits that theologians have too long left the analysis of moral development to educators and psychologists. He believes that a theory of moral development is contained in any theory of morality. He suggests that the Christian language of spiritual growth, growth in holiness, the pilgrimage of the self, faithfulness to the way, and perfection all speak in relevant ways about the development of the moral self.

Hauerwas posits three differences between moral development theory as described by Kohlberg and the Christian moral life. First of all, the goal of the Christian moral life is not to achieve moral autonomy but rather to view life as a gift of God and to accept this gift in a spirit of dependence and obedience. Christians should not seek autonomy but "rather to be faithful to the way that manifests our conviction that we belong to another" (1980, p. 444). Secondly, Christian life involves imitating another rather than, although not excluding, acting on principles. Christians learn about the moral life by imitating others and by direction from a master. Thirdly, the Christian life is not really one of development but rather one of conversion in which growth takes the form of a narrative. In their moral life Christians recognize that they are sinful and thus must convert and undergo radical conversion.

Drawing on MacIntyre's reformulation of the Aristotelian tradition Hauerwas develops an ethic of virtue and character to describe Christian moral growth. Character is formed by training the self to live according to the Christian story. The moral life is the attempt to conform human lives to God's way. The ethic of character and virtue does not believe in a single moral principle governing the moral life such as justice or utility. Rather it recognizes that there are many values and virtues for which we must provide a coherence in our lives. Moral integrity is achieved by attempting to live a narrative or story line which guides us through many, often incompatible, duties and virtues. In this theory moral responsibility is determined by how true a person is to the personal narrative of individuals. This viewpoint acknowledges the possibility of regression, degeneracy, and sin.

The concept of the moral life as narrative, which Hauerwas takes from MacIntyre, is central to this theory. By this concept he attempts to show that moral decisions are not isolated from personal and social history. Character develops only if people acquire a narrative story which provides the skill to fit actions into a coherent account sufficient to claim one's life as one's own. Lives are narratives that chart the way to live coherently amid the diversity of human experience and conflicts within individuals and with others.

Hauerwas finds several educational implications in his ethic of character, virtue, and narrative, most of which are presented in opposition to the cognitional approach of Kohlberg and others. Hauerwas contends that Christians have always prescribed a form of moral development or training in their communities. For Christians moral growth often entails encouraging a stand for God's justice against the state's justice, as in the matter of warfare. Christians need to tell very often an alternative story which can be learned only from the Christian tradition.

In keeping with the narrative dimension of his ethical theory, Hauerwas suggests that rather than have students focus on moral dilemmas (as Kohlberg proposes) they should be helped to understand the stories or images through which people should live their lives. He suggests that the best moral education might be through reading novels, which are often moral narratives. Students can also be encouraged to write descriptions of persons whom they admire. They might also study the lives of the saints. If moral dilemmas are used, the major focus should be on the kind of individuals the actors are or should be. He recommends that dilemmas be presented in the context of our own historical circumstances. Finally, Hauerwas suggests that we should connect moral training with aesthetic and liturgical training, for these areas help us to see and understand the power of human life as narrative.

Hauerwas deals well with the formation of the person who makes moral decisions within the moral self. However, he tends to overlook rational processes. He does not express enough critical awareness of the religious traditions and the biases and ideologies which they may possess. Even with the guidance of religious traditions, it is still difficult to determine what the response to God should be in a particular case. It is not clear that a person who is aware of the Christian story will *necessarily* act differently from others. Hauerwas describes the biblical ethic but does not adequately integrate it with the philosophical Aristotelianism. Finally, I would question whether this rather sectarian approach to Christian moral education best prepares persons for moral life in pluralist society. While Hauerwas prefers the primary stance of a witness against the values of secular society, I prefer an ethic and a moral education which is in dialogue with the best elements of the secular tradition, looks for points of agreement with general public morality, and reserves the right of dissent on issues where there are both religious and rational reasons to oppose particular societal policies, structures, and systems.

Visional Ethics and Moral Education

Craig Dykstra (1981) has offered the most sustained approach to moral education working out of a Protestant theological perspective. He presents his approach as a Christian alternative to Kohlberg and relies heavily on the work of Iris Murdoch, Stanley Hauerwas, and H. Richard Niebuhr in developing a visional ethics. Dykstra's work is particularly valuable in developing the components of a Christian education based on a visional ethics. This work is rich in theological, philosophical, and educational insights and deserves a wide reading among all educators, especially religious educators.

Dykstra offers criticisms of what he terms Kohlberg's juridical ethics. First, Kohlberg is wrong in reducing all virtues to justice. His concept of justice is weak when compared to the biblical concept of justice, which includes relationships with God and intersubjective responsibilities. Secondly, Kohlberg has exaggerated the cognitive dimension of morality at the expense of such affective dimensions as the capacity for empathy, respect for others, and imaginative interpretations of nature and meaning. Thirdly, Kohlberg exaggerates the importance of the use of dilemmas for moral development. A moral education that emphasizes basic attitudes towards life and moral vision is considered preferable. Finally, Dykstra rejects Kohlberg's claim that faith is grounded on moral reason, arguing that the opposite is the case: moral reasoning requires faith.

As a Christian alternative Dykstra proposes a visional ethics which has both religious and philosophical justification. This ethics is mystery-encountering rather than problem solving. The world of nature and humanity is seen as a mystery which is open to the transcendent reality of God. Visional ethics considers moral goods as values which cannot be reduced to empirical facts. Through these goods we are directed to the Good. Visional ethics deals with sin and evil, from which we are released by our faith in God. This ethics is concerned with the development of character, the moral quality or pattern of our lives. Character is best described as the story which one tells about oneself and which reveal a person's fundamental convictions. Each story includes the incidents, persons, settings, images, metaphors, and beliefs which have shaped the individual. Characters and stories are formed within particular faith communities where people are shaped by the community's story, history, rituals, and language. Finally, visional ethics should include responsible action which entails reactions to what is going on in the world, an interpretation of events in the world, an accountability to the past and future, and solidarity with members of the community.

Dykstra's visional ethics emphasizes the role of imagination. Like Hauerwas he prefers to speak not of development but of pilgrimage, formation, and sanctification. Moral life includes experience of and response to the revelation of the mystery of God. Such an experience leads to a change of character, i.e., a fundamental way of seeing and living. Making sense of the world is an imaginative experience using individual symbols and those of religious tradition. An imaginative experience causes a transformation from a groping and intuitive discovery, to a verification through analysis and interpretation, and finally to the emergence of a new insight.

The moral education that Dykstra prescribes as consonant with this visional ethics is accomplished in two general ways: through the disciplines of the church and through intentional educational experiences. The moral disciplines are repentance, prayer, and service. Repentance or conversion is preferred to self improvement. It is a gift of God through which the self is transformed because one must depend on God and be receptive to others. Repentance is an activity of God which is ever available because it is needed throughout life. Prayer shapes people morally as it opens them to the activity of God. Through service they are morally transformed since service demands a presence and commitment to others which exposes persons' vulnerability to others, accepts an equality with them, and shows compassion for them. For Dykstra these disciplines are lived out in the worship of the church throughout a person's life. Thus church life is a place for moral growth.

Dykstra gives explicit attention to moral education in the church. For him Christian education (which is almost synonymous with moral education) is the introduction and incorporation of persons into the realm of church experience. Education specifically involves investigating, sharing, and taking responsibility for Christian experience. The mode of Christian living within the church is the chief force for moral education.

Dykstra sees the role of teachers as particularly significant. Not only should they be good models of Christian living but they must also be receptive, attentive, and present to learners. In representing the community, teachers have specified tasks: 1) to discover who and what are conflicts for the learners: loved ones, neighbors, enemies, and strangers; 2) to provide resources for exploring the various dimensions of their struggles; 3) to stimulate actual encounters between persons in conflict, provide situations for encounters, raise questions about such encounters, and encourage persons to full exploration of such encounters; 4) to provide time and space for students to struggle on their own; 5) to provide opportunities for story telling and interpretations of encounter experiences; 6) and to provide opportunities for action.

I have covered Dykstra's theology extensively because it is the most thorough effort to ground moral education on theological and philosophical principles. I think that moral educators within church settings and to some degree within secular settings can find helpful suggestions in his work. Nevertheless, there are some criticism and correction that I would like to offer.

Dykstra has made too sharp a contrast between juridic ethics and visional ethics. If moral education is to deal with people's problems at an interpersonal and societal level, considerations of justice, law, rights, and duties are important. The danger of visional ethics as presented by Dykstra is that it fails to take into account the full range of moral problems in society. At many junctures the ethic is similar to the caring ethic of Carol Gilligan (1982) and Noddings (1984). This form of ethic is most appropriate at the level of personal and interpersonal relationships but in dealing with societal, economic, and political issues it is essential to bring in the language and concerns of justice, rights, obligations, and laws.

Dykstra's dependence on Hauerwas creates another problem. He appears to assume that life in the church is morally educative by itself. What is missing here is an awareness of the prejudices, weaknesses, distortions in the Christian story and in the way in which it is preached and lived. The ethical system proposed and the education related to it appears to lack principles which are truly self-critical and self-correcting. While imaginative thinking is a helpful component in moral growth, there still remains the important rational and cognitive task of examining, investigating, and evaluating.

While I share Dykstra's vision that moral education takes place in churches through the disciplines of repentance, prayer, and service, there is enough of an empiricist in me to want some kind of evidence that this really happens. The structure of these activities appear suited to promote moral growth. Yet other structures within religious bodies seem to me to prevent moral growth: prejudices, authoritarianism, dependency, guilt-inducing activities, denial of the right to dissent, legalism, and pietism. Do the disciplines of the church overcome the effects of these structures? An adequate theory of moral growth within the churches must also look to dysfunctions and latent functions of church life.

Dykstra suggestions for intentional moral education in Christian churches are sound and flow naturally from his theological and philosophical vision. Yet I feel that he has attempted to distance himself too far from Kohlberg and other secular educators who offer a variety of methods, which I feel are relevant to church situations. Dykstra is right in insisting on a particular form suitable for church situations. As will be seen in the next chapter, his approach is also advocated in another form by secular educators.

CATHOLIC THEOLOGIANS AND MORAL EDUCATION

Gustafson (1978) has delineated some of the characteristics of Catholic moral theology in his attempt to distinguish it from the approach found in Protestant authors. Since Catholic moral theology developed as a separate discipline in an effort to guide priests in their role as confessor and judge, it has traditionally had a juridic flavor. Catholic moral theology also developed with a special connection with canon law. A separate Christian ethics is a more recent development in Protestantism. In recent years an effort has been made to develop a more biblically centered moral theology which has more connections with systematic theology (Curran 1977; Haring 1961–1966). Notwithstanding this trend, there is some truth in the over-simplification that Catholic ethics is a natural law ethic while Protestant ethics is a biblical ethic. This is true more of official Catholic church ethical teachings than it is of the work of a growing number of Catholic moralists.

There is a strong rational and natural law thrust in Catholic moral theology. Important questions include what is the moral law? How is it known? What is the role of human reason? What are the purposes of the moral law? Even those moralists who attempt to develop a more biblically based ethic still give a strong place to a revised or modified rational or natural law ethic. One of the advantages of the natural law ethic is that it addresses all persons since it does not appeal only to revealed truth for its basic premises. The Catholic Bishops' pastorals on Peace and War and on the American economy are based both on biblical teachings and on natural law reasoning.

There have been critics of the natural law ethic from both outside and inside the tradition. Its proponents are charged with advocating a static view of the moral order, making unwarranted claims for absolute certitude, and having a bias for the physical nature of actions over the personal meaning of actions. The debate over natural law has been argued chiefly in the area of sexual ethics and bio-ethics. A strong argument against natural law ethics is that very often its conclusions have not been arrived at by persons outside the tradition of natural law, thus weakening the tradition's reliance on human reason alone as a determiner of right and wrong.

Many efforts have been made to modify natural law ethics by joining to it a more biblical and social science approach. Studies have shown evidence of changes in moral teachings on such issues as usury, abortion, and contraception. Some theologians have argued for a more dynamic concept of natural law; others have attempted to show its biblical basis. Catholic moralists recognize that they should listen to the entire community of Christians to formulate moral teachings. A renewed theology of divine grace among contemporary theologians has softened the somewhat legalistic nature of Catholic moral theology. These attempts at revision have brought about a convergence with Protestant moralists in that both groups try to deal with relativity and change while remaining faithful to the authority of the churches and Scriptures.

Catholic moral teaching is authoritative. The church offers its teachings by appealing to its members and to the community for obedience and compliance. If polls in recent years are to be believed, however, a large number of Catholics do not obey a select number of rules. The role of theologians is a delicate one in that their work is examined by Vatican authorities to test the fidelity with which they promote church teachings. While the area for dissent is theoretically wide (i.e., all non-infallible teachings), the recent effort of the Vatican to declare Charles Curran, a moral theologian at Catholic University of America, unsuitable to teach Catholic moral theology appears to narrow considerably the area of dissent.

The quest in recent Catholic moral theology is for responsible openness. This quest is difficult to reconcile with the tradition's emphasis on the certitude of moral principles and the authority of the church. Some Catholic moralists have argued for a responsible openness by making the consequences of actions as important as, or more important than, the principles. In doing this they have looked to the human sciences for data about certain moral actions (Milhaven 1970). This has happened in the area of sexual ethics where a personalism has attempted to modify absolute judgments on such issues as masturbation, homosexuality, birth control, and even abortion. Thus the same type of relativism found in Protestants now exists among some Catholics. Offical church teachings and the opinions of other theologians oppose this personalist and relativist tendency.

As an example of Catholic moralists, I have chosen three who have shown a particular interest in moral education. These three scholars are representative of many Catholic moral theologians. I will present an assessment of them after their major ideas are expounded.

Moral Education and Community

Enda McDonagh has recognized that theologians have been tardy in dealing with issues raised by social science theory and research in moral education (1980). In his view of the moral person he emphasizes that moral behavior is relational and communal as well as personal. Critical of theories which set the goal of morality as the development of self, self-actualization, self-perfection or personal holiness, he insists that morality be viewed in terms of summons and responses which take place in relations and communities. Thus moral analysis and education must focus on both poles of person and community.

McDonagh recognizes that there has always been a close interaction between religion and morality. Religious faith entails a pattern of moral living. He goes so far as to assert that the moral lives of religious persons reveal the character of the God whom they worship, with the result that deficiencies in moral behavior reveal deficiencies in religious faith. He describes the relationship between the moral and the religious as a dialectical or creative interaction in which one challenges, confirms, condemns, and eventually transforms the other. He sees value in maintaining the two traditions of religion and morality because they can purify each other.

McDonagh is critical of some forms of moral education, including Kohlberg's, which concentrate on methods of promoting cognitional growth. Like many others he questions Kohlberg's exclusive focus on justice, rights, and claims, and suggests that attention be given to other issues and attitudes, as well as to virtues and values. In his viewpoint moral education must deal with the great moral issues of the world and face up to the darkness that is found in persons and societies. Moral education at the most profound level is about conversion to enable persons to do things in community with others. For religious persons the ultimate aim of moral activity is prayer, "the turning to the Ultimate Other [Who] empowers the recognition of and response to its incarnate presence in the neighbor (hood)" (1980, p. 341).

Moral Education for Critical Balance

John O'Donohoe (1980) has presented some reflections on the teaching of ethics and moral education in his analysis of moral development theory in the light of recent developments in Catholic moral theology. He describes theological ethics as "an attempt to discover the human by a diligent examination of the meaning and content of the Christian faith commitment" (p. 378). He describes a change in Roman Catholic moral theology from a deductive, abstract, and universal approach to one that is dynamic, concrete, particular, and adjustable. The former approach gives certainty and security at the risk of anti-intellectualism, authoritarianism, and dogmatism. The second approach emphasizes personal growth and personal responsibility but runs the risk of relativism, subjectivism, and antinominianism. O'Donohoe recognizes good and bad points in both and calls for attempts to achieve a critical balance.

O'Donohoe espouses an approach to theological ethics which he finds in the theologians Karl Rahner and Bernard Lonergan. From the former he derives a threefold task for moral development and formation: 1) to help persons deepen their personal and ecclesiastial commitments; 2) to convince persons that their moral responsibility goes beyond assimilating detailed instructions about right and wrong; 3) to teach persons to make moral decisions which do justice to moral principles seen and comprehended in existential situations. From Lonergan he draws the goal of moral formation: giving people attitudes which should be operative in evaluating rules involved in responses in faith to the initiatives of God.

In the light of a shift to a more subjective ethics, O'Donohoe contends that many Catholic moral theologians have been interested in Kohlberg. He offers some criticisms of Kohlberg's theory: lack of consideration of specific content, overemphasis on the role of reason, failure to deal with virtues other than justice, and the juridic notion of morality. O'Donohoe notes that

Catholic moral theology emphasizes charity and conversion, both of which are lacking in Kohlberg's approach.

O'Donohoe draws a number of implications for religious and moral education from this analysis. Firstly, educators should be concerned with both content and personal development. Secondly, Christian moral life is part of the process of personal spiritual conversion. Thirdly, educators should teach rules and information about the values which the rules intend to articulate in such a way that persons can handle norms and the values behind them in the particular situations. Finally, educators should foster a connection between moral development and faith development.

Moral Education and Imaginative Ethics

The most detailed effort by a Catholic theologian to deal with issues of moral development and education is found in Philip Keane's *Christian Ethics and the Imagination* (1984). Keane has specifically applied his theory of imagination to the realm of moral education. His work is more a review of developments in theological disciplines in the past two decades than a wholly original contribution. His major contribution, for the purposes of this book, is his contention that the teaching of morality might be enriched by a moral theology of the imagination. In this area his treatment is in dialogue with Kohlberg and his theological critics.

Keane's effort is to balance what he considers the over reliance of moral theologians on discursive, logical, and positivistic reasoning. The "more of moral theology" is found in the work of the imagination. He feels that imagination has advantages over other themes which contemporary moralists use to get at the "more of moral theology," such as story, virtue, character, and vision. Imagination entails attention to the aesthetics and shows how music, art, literature, and beauty can attribute to moral perception and judgment (pp. 16–17).

Situating himself in the Aristotelian tradition, Keane views imagination as "the basic process by which we draw together the concrete and the universal elements of our human experience" (p. 81). Imagination enables us to play with or hold together insights from our previous knowledge and tradition, and also remain open to new insights and images. Imagination allows a playful suspending of judgment which opens us to new experiences and truths. In the moral sphere imagination allows both tradition and our new experiences to coexist and, as it were, to play together in our consciousness.

Moral imagination is related to intuitive ways of knowing, (i.e., emotional reactions of attraction and/or repulsion), and human learning experiences but is not reducible to any of these. Keane depends on Dewey for the insight that imagination comes from human learning experiences. Works of art influence our capacity to imagine in such a way that learning through artistic works cannot be explained by logical processes.

Keane's theory does not dispense with the necessity of moral principles but sees them in a new light. Understanding and coming to accept moral principles entails the imaginative process of discerning principles, playing with ideas, and making appropriate connections. Imagination also enables people to arrive at the deeper meaning of these principles and to apply them to specific cases or issues. While moral imagination may deal with past stories, traditions, and myths, its main thrust should be directed to envisioning alternative futures.

In Keane's view it is the added dimension of moral imagination that will produce a spiritual, religious, and Christian ethics. Christian ethics is chiefly about presenting people with a vision that will motivate them in their lives. Imaginative ethics depends on biblical insights, symbols, and myths to inspire people to live the religious vision. Decision making is greatly aided by the creativity and vitality that comes from moral imagination.

Keane believes liberal arts are at the center of an imaginative moral education. Language skills, especially the learning of a foreign language, and the study of the classics foster the life of the imagination. Even the study of science can be done in an imaginative manner.

While recognizing many of the criticisms of Kohlberg, Keane would not go as far as Hauerwas or Dykstra in saying that in moral education the Christian story, symbols, and traditions should be central and not moral reasoning. Here he shows that he remains in the centrist Catholic tradition of focusing more on reasoning and natural law ethic than on a biblical ethic. He also recognizes with many Catholic scholars that the content of Christian ethics need not come from Christian sources alone. Keane sees value in Kohlberg's work for Christians if it is enhanced by direct reference to Christian sources which will soften its apparent rationalism and lack of attention to affectivity.

Keane suggests that moral reasoning be supplemented by education through the arts and reflection on relationships. Education in sexuality should utilize concrete and positive images of healthy sexuality. An imaginative approach to social justice would make use of social justice experience, games, audio-visual material, and personal asceticism. The presentation of fresh new images may be more valuable than debating moral dilemmas or even discussing personal moral crises.

While Keane makes a strong case for moral imagination in fostering moral education, he recognizes that this is only a partial answer. Moral imagination must be engaged in dialogue with moral principles. At times the poor and fanciful images of the imagination need correction by reasoning about moral principles.

Assessment of Roman Catholic Approaches

The traditional Roman Catholic approach to ethics and consequently to moral education is to focus on moral reasoning, natural law reasoning, the teaching authority of the church, the learning of moral principles, and moral decision making. Moral education has been viewed as a rational enterprise for the formation of conscience. Freedom of conscience is recognized but it is stressed that this conscience should be properly formed by the teaching of the church.

The three theories I have presented in this section attempt to supplement these traditional approaches with a more biblical ethic of vision and character, and also look at the way in which the church as a whole forms its members morally. This is especially true of McDonagh's emphasis on morality as gift and response. These ideas thus have some connection with the work of the Protestant moralists Hauerwas and Dykstra. I believe that this coming together of Roman Catholic and Protestant ethicians is helpful for both groups. Yet I believe that the attempt of Roman Catholic ethicians to develop a more visionary ethic based on Scriptural sources has introduced some helpful tensions into ethical writing which has repercussion on moral education and formation. The two traditions—ethics of vision and character and ethics of natural law reasoning—are in tension.

I do not want to deal with particular positions of the three Catholics ethicians I have treated. Rather I would like to point out some of the problems with making too great a contrast between an ethic of character and vision and an ethic of moral reasoning. Story, image, liturgy, and tradition will not suffice to provide moral education. Biblical and liturgical structures often include elements which incorporate prejudices and biases that contradict Christian principles of justice and love. Even when the images and stories present valuable ideals, there is much thought and reasoning needed to move from these ideals to the concrete problems of human life. Exclusive attention on these elements may develop an ethical community which is narrowly sectarian and unable to deal with social pluralism in contemporary society.

No one can deny the power of symbols, metaphors, imagination, stories, and images in influencing character. Yet the same scriptures contain laws and obligations which move us into the realm of moral reasoning, deliberation, and justification. It is not a question of one approach over the other but a combination of approaches, and a recognition of the limitations of both. In proposing approaches to moral education we need to be a bit more modest both about our claims for reason and about our claims for imagination (Elias 1986, ch. 4).

What Roman Catholic ethics and moral education stand for should not be lost in the attempt to incorporate a biblical ethics of vision and character.

Firstly, natural law ethics takes its stand on a basis that is common to Christian and non-Christian. It thus attempts to avoid a sectarian approach to ethics. Secondly, this ethic puts a great emphasis on decision-making processes and thus attempts to give concrete guidance to individuals in their personal and social lives. Thirdly, this ethic has been interested in determining the rightness or wrongness of individual actions and thus in fostering responsible action. Fourthly, the Catholic approach is not just interested in proclaiming the story; it also wants to reason and argue about the meaning of the story and its applications. Of course, there are Protestant ethicians who make these same points against the overemphasis on a Christian ethic of vision and character. Yet it has been the strong mark of Roman Catholic ethics to stress moral reasoning in which all persons can participate.

JEWISH THEOLOGIANS AND MORAL EDUCATION

In Jewish ethics some of the same tensions exist as are found in Protestant and Catholic ethics. Judaism has a strong tradition in ethics which is based on the Hebrew Scriptures and the Talmud and which includes specific laws, rabbinic discussions, and homiletic literature. Along side of this there are efforts to develop an ethic of reasoning which can deal more effectively with contemporary issues. The situation with Jewish ethics becomes even more complicated because ethical issues are related to the concern of Jewish identity, especially in countries outside Israel.

In the classical Jewish view of the moral sphere the distinction between religion and morality is nonexistent and almost inconceivable for "the living reality of Judaism has always been that religion is unthinkable without ethics, and ethics are intrinsically intertwined with religion" (Yaron 1975, p. 232). God is the source and object of both spheres. Within classical Judaism even ritual was assimilated to the moral. Ritual deals with moral obligations to God while ethics treats our relationship with one another (Hofmann 1982, p. 57). Because of this identity between religion and morality in classical Judaism, the study of the written texts became the chief form of moral education for all.

Did the classical Jewish ethics recognize something like natural moral law or knowledge of what is moral? Some consider the question irrelevant since they see the larger purpose of Judaism in terms of postulating "an entirely new language system which denied the religion/morality dichotomy" (Chazan 1980, p. 301). Another opinion (Hofmann 1982) appeals to the view of Rabbi Yanatron which suggests the possibility of ethics without the Torah. Yanatron contended that in the absence of a revealed Torah "we would have learned modesty from the cat, aversion to robbery from the ant, marital fidelity from the dove, and conjugal deportment from the rooster" (In Hofmann 1982, p. 57). What the Torah adds to natural moral knowledge is the details of commandments, a universally agreed upon ethics, a definiteness and constancy in ethical practice for the community, the possibility of a sanctified life by following the ways of God, a religious motivation for ethical behavior, and a rational ground for ethics, namely, a person should do good to fulfill the purposes of God's creation.

In moral life individuals have intentionality and free choice. Humans are to imitate the actions of God which are conscious, intentional, and willful. Free will is based on the religious teaching on the nature of God. "Thus the role of man's intentions and choice in the moral-religious sphere was at least an issue and probably an assumption in the classical perspective" (Chazan 1980, p. 302).

The classical Jewish ethic is collective and nonindividualistic. The ethical and godly life is rooted in a definite tradition and context. This is another reason for the study of texts. The Jewish ethic is based on the collective nature of the Jewish people. God is affected by the actions and prayer of a people.

Finally, the classical Jewish ethic is of a practical nature rather than contemplative. The laws, practices, parables, and stories are aimed at influencing daily routine and behavior. Concern with intentions and motivations, are subordinated to stress on specific actions and behaviors which embody moral principles and a moral life style. The emphasis in the tradition is on study because it is only proper study that will lead to moral actions.

Jewish ethicians and educators, like Christian educators, have entered into a dialogue with Kohlberg's theory of moral development and education. A number of analyses have been offered. Rosenzweig (In Chazan 1980) contends that Jewish education and Kohlberg are complementary since both are essentially concerned with justice. Another analysis (Chazan 1980) contends that the two approaches are more dissimilar than similar. Chazan suggests these major differences. While Jewish ethics focuses on a normative, substantive life style and behavior style, Kohlberg is concerned fundamentally with moral reasoning. Jewish ethics does not recognize the autonomy of the moral sphere since it sees it as intrinsically connected with religion. Jewish ethics has more concern for tradition and community development. Jewish ethics is based on legitimate principles of behavior and not on dealing with moral dilemmas. Finally, Jewish ethics does not recognize the hierarchical notion of moral development.

For Felder (1984) the crux of the problem between Jewish ethics and Kohlberg lies in the issue of autonomy. Kohlberg appears to consign a religious ethic, which places ultimate moral justification in laws, to a stage four morality. The moral autonomy which Kohlberg describes as the ideal for the post conventional stage of development would not appear to be open to religious persons who live their lives by laws and rules. Felder solves this problem at a theoretical level by describing a seventh stage of moral development in which persons allow their autonomous, principled judgment to be challenged by an ethical system such as a religious covenant. Felder seems unaware of Kohlberg's hypothetical stage seven, a stage of faith. I also do not believe that Felder has resolved the problem. A resolution lies not within the Kohlberg system but within an understanding of the place of autonomy in Jewish ethics.

For my treatment of Jewish ethicians who are concerned with moral education I will draw on the excellent article by Dorff (1980). This study presents three ways in which Jewish ethical thinkers have dealt with the study of texts for the purpose of leading to action. One of these scholars is Martin Buber; but because I have already covered his ideas in chapter 2, I will restrict my discussion to Samson Hirsch and Abraham Kaplan.

An Orthodox Approach to Jewish Moral Education

Samson Raphael Hirsch was the nineteenth century founder of the neo-Orthodox movement which combined supernaturalist theology and strict observance with a study of secular subjects. His system is similar to the classical Jewish education described by Chazan (1980).

The content of moral education is clearly the learning of the Jewish law which is the law for all humankind. The Jewish law is studied within a framework to enable students to deal with new situations not covered by existing laws and also to enable them to see ultimate goals of morality in such a way that they would subordinate to them immediate immoral gains. As to the methods in teaching, Hirsch advocated making primary texts available to students for these are at the center of the educational enterprise. The Torah is the immutable word of God. Hirsch rejected the critical, historical approach to the tradition.

Moral education has as its purpose the development of individual's power of judgment, including the ability to weigh values and to reconcile moral conflicts. Hirsch recommends the study of the Talmud for this purpose. Dorff considers it noteworthy that the text of the Talmud is preferred over the codes. Prescriptive codes offer less opportunity for rational discussion while the Talmud, because it records not only differing opinions but also the reasons each side gives for its decisions, would foster logical thinking and critical judgment.

The study of texts can be a strong motivating factor for moral action, according to Hirsch. He believes that the texts will foster the desire to be moral and to avoid what is vile. Texts are motivational by providing both positive and negative examples for students. The texts are also motivational for Hirsch because in them students encounter teachers for whom the Bible, codes, and Talmud are the eternal and indisputable word of God.

For Hirsch there are moral values attached to the study of texts. Study is an end in itself; striving for intellectual perfection is an act of pure duty. Although he recognized that right doing is the test for right knowing, Hirsch argues that intellectual perfection is an end in itself, including religious and secular learning. Learning for Hirsch is not just a moral value in itself but it also inculcates other moral values. He includes such values as "obedience, the readiness to comply with a superior will, the consequent exercise of self-control, the punctual and most perfect possible performance of duties imposed, the pleasure of work and pure joy in work done, self-disciplined serenity, modesty, sociability, friendliness, and team spirit in addition to care, caution, exactitude, and circumspection" (Hirsch in Dorff 1980, pp. 183–4).

Hirsch was aware of some limitations in moral education conducted through textual study. If the teacher is a poor model, then the study will not produce its desired effects. Hirsch also recognized that secular studies would foster some values counter to those in the Jewish tradition: vocational goals, self-fulfillment, competition, and ambition to win praise. Yet he does recognize a number of moral values in secular schooling: training for a livelihood, education in present-day civilization, general knowledge which might be helpful for understanding Jewish ideology and law, logical skills, and the knowledge of science and history which would make knowledge of Jewish law and history all the more impressive. Any contradictions between Jewish studies and secular studies are to be resolved in favor of Jewish studies since they contain the word of God.

Reconstructionist Approach to Moral Education

Mordecai Kaplan has been a foremost spokesman for liberal or Reconstructionist Judaism for half of this century. He espouses a naturalist theology and an evolutionary approach to Jewish theology and practice. Like Hirsch he is interested in the use of texts but he takes a different approach. His thought is rather close to Martin Buber's theology and educational philosophy. In my treatment of Kaplan I am also indebted to Dorff's (1980) comprehensive article.

Kaplan gives prominent place to the Bible and Jewish law but recognizes that the law does not provide correct moral instructions in many areas where either it does not legislate or where the law itself must be updated. In his overall perspective to Judaism Kaplan prefers putting specific issues within the broader contexts of working for the betterment of the Jewish people and of the world. Text study has as its purpose to fortify Jewish consciousness so that Jews might make a greater contribution to a better future for mankind. Jewish moral education should seek to transmit ultimate goals of morality as well as specific norms, while recognizing that in both areas the text needs updating and correction.

Kaplan sees text study as promoting the powers of judgment and reasoning. He is less interested than Hirsch in having students master the reasoning of the text's argument than he is in showing students how to approach the texts. Students, especially adult students, should be taught to re-interpret the texts so that this fallible tradition might shape their moral and spiritual values. Kaplan is thus interested in conveying a content and in promoting reasoning and debate. Reasoning power should be applied to texts so that students can learn a system of values and develop powers of moral judgment.

The study of texts has, for Kaplan, a strong motivational element. Kaplan closely connects the desire to be moral with fostering a feeling of peoplehood and group consciousness. Moral motivation comes from the fact that one is rooted in a tradition which has noble goals. Membership in a community gives a person personal ideals, ideals to teach children, a sense of self-worth, and a host of moral expectations about people whom one would not want to disappoint. Though Kaplan recognizes the dangers of excessive nationalism in stressing this collective purpose of Jewish education, he judges the force of religion as able to direct such feelings to good ends. Also, positive Jewish identity needs to be fostered because of the many negative portrayals of Jews in modern society. Like Hirsch, Kaplan recognizes the value of exposing students to exemplary and non-exemplary persons in Jewish history, though he does not want an apotheosis of past and present heroes. The role of teachers as motivating factors comes not from their transmission of eternal and immutable moral truths but from their example as persons involved in a common search with students, which includes challenges, questions, and even alternative solutions not found in the tradition. Kaplan values this tradition not because it is the authority of God but because obedience to Jewish moral rules is an act of identification with the Jewish people and a part of the effort to bring the divine into human life.

Kaplan does not see any particular moral value attached to the study of the text. He does not list study among the moral values in the Jewish religion. For him world betterment is the aim of education and this is achieved by making the Jewish heritage applicable to present problems. He does, however, advocate more study and less praying, arguing that prayer is for the betterment of peace of mind while the study of the Torah can influence character and indirectly help reshape society. Thus the aims of moral education are pragmatically described in terms of what they will do to reconstruct both individual and society. Texts are useful in so far as they foster feelings of peoplehood among the Jewish people and help to develop moral commitments. Teaching moral values entails some particular content provided by the sacred texts, but their study is not a moral value in itself. The text must be studied with an eye to re-interpreting the tradition in the light of present knowledge. Kaplan rejects the traditional approach which takes the text literally. He contends that people will be repelled by this approach and will judge the tradition as irrelevant. A reconstructionist attitude will be persuasive and inspiring since it entails full intellectual honesty.

Kaplan is clearly aware of the limitations of text study. He recognized that the teacher is more important than the text. Teachers select and interpret texts. Also teachers can be effective moral educators without the use of classical texts. Kaplan was also conscious of the importance of home and community in moral education. He points out the small number of hours students attend religious schools. Jewish educational efforts are better aimed at getting the home to instill in children Jewish ideals and religion. Also, a reconstituted Jewish community would be in a position to set, teach, and enforce, moral standards. He contends that a Jewish education restricted to Jewish schools will certainly fail unless this is done in the context of Jewish homes and a Jewish community where moral values are exemplified. Kaplan also saw value in the camp setting as a context for Jewish education. Furthermore, Kaplan sees the need for general education for Jews because he contends that Jewish moral reasoning must be done with full knowledge of secular culture, otherwise Jews will be out of touch with the real world. Finally, while Kaplan recognizes that a religious perspective is not necessary for being moral, he sees certain advantages in a religious perspective. Persons get a feeling of worthwhileness from religion, which makes individual effort and sacrifice reasonable, and which furnishes a sense of direction and meaning in life.

Assessment of Jewish Moral Education

The writings on Jewish moral education reveal important differences from Christian discussions on these issues. The method of teaching through the use of texts is not common among Christian educators, except for some evangelicals and fundamentalists. This system has many advantages. It grounds moral education in a specific tradition. Texts provide a valuable starting point for moral discussions. Continuous contact with the tradition also provides the sense of Jewish identity and community which Jewish educators wish to accomplish through their endeavors. The stories, laws, myths, and events within this tradition can form a powerful moral consciousness which may carry over into moral action. Finally, study of texts is a valuable aid to reasoning which no doubt shapes attitudes and behavior.

The value of text study for moral education, and for that matter, for all education has been forcibly argued by Bloom (1987). Not many who have discussed Bloom's book have commented on the strong argument he makes for both religious and moral education. With regard to text study he notes:

> I mean that a life based on the Book is closer to the truth, that it provides the material for deeper research in and access to the real nature of things. Without the great revelations, epics, and philosophies as part of our vision, there is nothing to see out there, and eventually little left inside. The Bible is not the only means to furnish a mind, but without a book of similar gravity, read with the gravity of the potential believer, it will remain unfurnished (p. 60).

The dangers and limitations of education through texts are well recognized by Jewish educators. Legalism, narrow interpretations, irrelevance to present problems, and intolerance may come from relying too heavily on texts written in historical and cultural contexts different from our own. The criticisms of Buber and Kaplan offer an approach to texts which relates them to contemporary issues. When texts are used to provide norms and an ethical spirit, they have great value. If, however, they are used as absolute and definitive rulings on all moral issues, there is a danger of closing students off from many considerations that should enter into decision making.

The connection between moral education and Jewish identity makes us realize the broader context of all moral education. Morality is not merely an individual matter, as Kohlberg and other theorists seem to make it. People do not stand but are rather situated within a people and a community which is in constant dialogue about what is moral or immoral. Individuals are influenced by this people and have a role in influencing them. This may be one of the particular advantages for a religious moral education over a secular one. The latter takes place in communities where there are competing moral traditions and values, making the task more difficult because an agreed upon moral ethos is lacking. While differences exist within a particular religious tradition, these differences are not greater than those in the wider society. This is the main point of the analysis of American individualism offered by Bellah et al. (1985). A grounding in the original traditions of this country, both the biblical and the republican traditions, is needed to counter this individualism.

What is an advantage, namely, the particularity of a tradition, should not be turned into a disadvantage. This may happen if the particular tradition cuts itself off from dialogue with the wider community, as has happened with certain forms of American individualism. The insights of Kaplan are particularly important here when he argues for a moral education which is both particular and universal. The method he proposes has as its purpose individual, community, and societal reconstruction. It is not always easy to balance these goals. Kaplan may be too optimistic on this point. Tensions will eventually develop between a particular religious tradition and morality and the ethos and values of a particular society. Differences exist on such issues as abortion, capital punishment, legalization of drugs, nuclear armaments, and others. It is important that there are individuals within religious tradition who can articulate the moral positions so that persons outside the community will come to understand and respect them.

Conclusion

In this chapter I have presented an important, but often neglected, partner in the dialogue on moral education in the United States. In the effort to develop a secular morality, some have succumbed to the danger of neglecting a valuable resource for moral education, religion and theology. Many Western countries have done better by including religious education within the school curriculum and by paying specific attention to moral issues. This option is not an open one to us in the United States on any wide scale.

The resources of religion can be used for moral education within homes, schools, faith communities, and organizations. In a limited way they may be made available to public school educators who can use them in certain curriculum areas such as the arts, humanities, and social studies. Religion has been ignored in the curriculum of American schools to the disadvantage of both students and society.

There is a responsibility for religious ethicians and educators to enter the current debate over the teaching of values. Their voices need to be added to the voices of politicians, parents, and educators who have in recent years called for more attention to the teaching of values. From this chapter it is clear that religion has much to offer. All religious traditions contain moral teachings. These traditions have dealt with many issues of a personal, interpersonal, and social nature. They also have extensive experience in socializing members, young and old, into the value of a tradition. These traditions include not only a personal ethic but also an ethic that urges or even obligates believers to work for a better society and a better world.

I began this chapter with the observation that theologians have not devoted as much attention to moral education as might be expected. I end the chapter on a more hopeful note when I consider the attention that moral education is beginning to receive from theologians, religious educators and philosophers of religion. This work needs to become part of the public discourse and debate on moral education.

CHAPTER 6

EDUCATIONAL APPROACHES

In previous chapters I have examined approaches to moral education directly connected with such academic disciplines as philosophy, psychology, social sciences, and theology. The theories studied in each of these disciplines all contain certain implications for educational practice. Only in a few instances did the theories include a fully developed educational practice and strategy. The emphasis was rather on the investigation of moral education or development from the perspective of a particular discipline.

In this chapter I will present and analyze approaches to moral education which have been developed primarily by educationalists. What distinguishes them from perspectives in earlier chapters is more explicit attention to methodology in educational practice. Although all of the theories to be presented have philosophical, psychological, and sociological foundations, what is of particular importance is the development of curricular theory and methodology for the practice of moral education.

These educational ideas have a particular bias for the classroom because they have been developed precisely for classroom programs. Some systems might also be useful in other settings such as in homes and churches. But usually in these settings more informal and less organized approaches are utilized.

This chapter will necessarily include some references to earlier theories. When this is done the emphasis will be more on the educational methodologies which spring from those theories. The repetition may be useful for this concluding chapter will bring many of the preceding discussions to a more practical discussion and application.

This chapter will also explore the possible role that religion might play in each of the approaches. Though these approaches have been developed by secular educators, all of them can also be adapted with some adjustments and additions to religious contexts.

There have been a number of attempts to classify approaches to moral or values education from an educational perspective. Hall (1979) offer a three-fold classification: 1) *hard line approach*: inculcation and indoctrination of moral values by direct teaching methods; 2) *soft line approach*: the nondirective, value-free teaching of moral values in which values are considered to be totally relative to situations; 3) *the middle way of creative tensions*. This method attempts to avoid the extremes of the first two and includes such strategies as awareness, debate, rational analysis, concept analysis, game strategies, modeling, and expanding the moral concepts.

Another attempt at classification is offered by Hersch, Miller, and Fielding (1980). This work presents six models: rationale building, consideration, values clarification, value analysis, cognitive moral development, and social action. Examples of each are offered with analysis of their possible effectiveness.

This chapter is organized into three main types: cognitive approaches, affective approaches, and action approaches. This classification is based on the perceived major thrust of each theory. This is not an attempt at narrow classification since it is clear that all approaches include attention to all three dimensions. But for the purposes of analysis and classification I believe the approaches do have these major foci.

COGNITIVE APPROACHES TO MORAL EDUCATION

Many of the approaches presented by educationists fit into the category of cognitive or rational. Education has a strong cognitive dimension in that one of its major purposes is to bring about knowledge and understanding. Thus it is no surprise that many systems have stressed that moral education, especially in school settings, should focus on knowledge and understanding.

Cognitive Moral Education

Michael Scriven (1975), a respected philosopher, stresses that the task of moral education is to teach students how to *do* moral analysis rather than to present them with the results of moral analysis or edicts from others. He recognizes that this is a difficult task in itself and an even more difficult one to accomplish in schools.

According to Scriven moral education has several components: 1) the legitimation of ethics; 2) the legitimation of moral education; 3) the cognitive structuring of moral education; 4) the teaching of the basic cognitive elements in ethics; 5) and the appeal to the affect of the student.

Cognitivists such as Scriven devote considerable attention to establishing the foundations of ethics and moral reasoning, viewing these as matters for reason to investigate and establish. Law and morality are considered sensible and reasonable institutions of a civilized society. Such a cognitive education takes many years to accomplish. Cognitive moral education has a sound basis because it is open to public and personal scrutiny. The cognitive approach is interested in action but sees this action as coming about only as a result of a curriculum which is cognitively oriented.

Scriven's cognitive curriculum usually includes three areas. First, the curriculum requires a knowledge about and understanding of the facts, including arguments and positions involved in moral issues. For example, a study of the morality of capital punishments entails a knowledge of the history of this punishment, the various justifications given for it, the arguments against it, and a scrutiny of social science studies on its effectiveness for its intended purposes. Affective techniques such as role playing may be used in this educational endeavor but the main purpose is to generate cognitive understanding.

Secondly, the cognitive curriculum involves the development of the cognitive skills of moral reasoning; these are developed to the point where they can be utilized in arguing reasonably about moral issues. Such moral reasoning is related to reasoning in scientific matters and legal matters. Students should be trained in principles of logical reasoning as applied to moral issues.

The third area of the cognitive curriculum concerns the nature, origins, and foundation of ethics. This involves a study of such questions as: what is morality, why should persons be moral, and what distinguishes morality from convention and self interest. It is clear that what Scriven proposes as moral education is actually a course in ethics.

Reflective Approach to Values Education

Clive Beck (1981) has developed an approach to values education which underlies the curriculum of the Values Series published by the Ontario Institute for Studies in Education (OISE). He prefers the broader term values to morals in order to include political, social, and cultural values. This approach attempts to identity the basic human values which should provide the reference point for reflecting on moral questions in public education. While this approach includes both cognitive and affective components—attitudes, desires, and interests—the cognitive dimension receives greater attention.

The philosophical roots of the reflective approach are found in the rationalist ethics of Aristotle, Hobbes, Bentham, Dewey and Morris Ginsberg. Dewey's influence is found in the emphasis which Beck gives to critical inquiry. Beck borrows from Dewey his idea of maintaining an openness to all possible values, reflection on consequences of actions, and the serious consideration of human nature as well as the critical evaluation of traditions. From Ginsberg, a twentieth century philosopher and sociologist, Beck derives the important concept of basic human needs which transcend cultural situations: needs of body, mind, and society.

Before presenting his reflective approach Beck criticizes other approaches to values education. He finds the reasoning skills approach to be lacking in content, the moral dilemma approach restrictive and educationally unsatisfying, the values clarification approach hopelessly relativistic, and the school climate and atmosphere approach as valuable but limited in its failure to challenge the critical powers of students. Beck's attempt is to integrate the strengths of these approaches into his theory, while avoiding the weaknesses which they possess.

Beck's reflective system includes three elements: 1) identification and refinement of basic human values; 2) an assessment and refinement of specific and intermediate values which are related to the basic values; 3) the development of emotions, attitudes, and behavior patterns that flow from the values which have been established through values inquiry. Beck has chosen the term reflective in an attempt to avoid the harshness of such terms as critical or questioning. Values education is to take place with a positive spirit and in a way in which sufficient attention is given to affective experiences.

A common set of values in public schools is identified:

> survival, happiness (enjoyment, pleasure, and so forth), health, fellowship, (friendship, love and so forth), helping others (to some extent), wisdom, fulfillment, freedom, self respect, respect from others, a sense of meaning in life, and so on (Beck 1981, p. 196).

Beck believes these values are shared by persons of different religious and philosophical perspectives. They are not in opposition to or an alternative to religious values; in fact they have developed out of religious and cultural traditions in interaction with elements which are natural to all persons.

While Beck recognizes that people esteem these common values differently, are self interested, and draw different conclusions, he does not think that these factors will prevent classroom inquiry because life in society is based on developing compromises among people who have different interests. As will be seen, this approach places great emphasis on dealing with the notion of compromise in values education.

Beck's curriculum in the reflective approach is organized around problems or topics. Units of study include such topics as friendship, children in the family, sharing television, bullying, trusting, getting even, differences in values, learning from parents, work and leisure, social conflict, and prejudice. Topics are examined through the use of key questions, principles, concepts, examples, and related activities. Though these elements provide the structure of the curriculum, sufficient time is permitted to give examples, disagree, and make responses. The approach is distinguished from the case study approach or the dilemma approach in that it deals with both principles and specific cases.

There are four ways in which the reflective approach found in the Values Series developed by the Ontario Institute for Education (OISE) can be used in a school. Firstly, the organization and atmosphere of the school should encourage reflection on values. Secondly, school rules should be made explicit and open to discussions. Reasons should be given for the rules and for the sanctions connected with them. Thirdly, values can be taught in courses such as literature or social studies. Finally, values can be taught in a separate course. Beck favors the concept of a separate course in order to furnish greater prominence to the importance of value analysis and inquiry.

Example from Values Series: Myself and Other People

KEY IDEA: *It is right to look after yourself a lot and others a lot.*

You should look after others and not care about yourself.
You should just look after yourself and not care about others. What do you say? Why?
Draw a picture of yourself looking after yourself a lot.
Draw a picture of yourself looking after someone else a lot.

It is right to look after yourself a lot and also to look after others a lot.

Think of times when people look after others too much.

Examples:

a) A boy gives away all his money to his friends and he has none left to buy toys for himself. What should he have done?
b) A wife spends all day cooking and cleaning for her family and she has no time left for sports or reading. What should she do?
c) A mother always puts her son's skates on for him and so he never learns how to do it for himself. Is this right?
d) A girl gives food to her pet dog whenever it wants some. Is this right?
Think of a time when you looked after others too much. Draw a picture about it and tell what you should have done instead.

It is right to look after yourself a lot and also to look after others a lot.

Think of times when people look after *themselves* too much:

Examples:

a) A girl keeps all her toys to herself. What might happen? What should she do?

b) A quick reader always calls out the answers before the other children in the class. Why is this not a good idea? What should he do?

c) A father just does what he likes to do on weekends. How could this hurt his family? What should he do?

Think of a time when you looked after *yourself* too much. Talk about what you should have done instead.

You have to look after both yourself and other people. This means you have to COMPROMISE.

What is a compromise?

Here are some examples:

a) The parents and children in a family *take turns* choosing TV shows.

b) A boy lets his baby brother play with his football *some of the time*.

c) A girl keeps her two favorite toys for herself but she *shares the rest* of her toys with her friends.

Why are compromises good? Think of times then you made a compromise. Why did you do it? (Ontario Institute for Education, n.d.)

This example of a unit in values education has been developed for primary school children. The cognitive approach is made clear in the key ideas which are at the heart of the curriculum. The student learns these but is also given opportunities to reason about these key concepts and their implications. Affective elements are included (drawing pictures, expressing one's feelings) in the unit but these are clearly subordinated to the learning of cognitive content and the development of moral reasoning.

The above example is designed for rather young children. As children move from grade to grade in the school they are presented with more complicated and disputable problems. This curriculum was the result of extensive philosophical and pedagogical research and has been widely used in Canadian schools.

Value Analysis

The value analysis approach was developed by a group of educators, philosophers, and psychologists (Jerrold Coombs, Milton Mieux, and James Chadwick) and is found in a yearbook of the Council for the Social Studies (Metcalf 1971). This model is concerned with helping students gather and weigh the facts involved in value judgments. The approach, though developed for social studies, can be applied in other areas.

The value analysis approach distinguishes between value criteria and value principles. *Value criteria* ascribe value to some set of conditions, e.g., cheating, stealing, lying, hurting others, keeping promises, paying debts. The criteria do not tell us about the exceptions in which they do not apply. Value criteria give a "balance" or a weight to certain facts. *Value principles* are more complex. They apply to the total situation; they are the qualified positions taken after facts have been assessed and value criteria are clear. An example of a value criterion would be that nations should not interfere in the internal affairs of other nations. In a concrete situation, however, a nation may act on the value principle that interference is necessary to preserve one's own safety given the buildup of arms in a hostile nation.

Proponents of value analysis have developed a strategy for teaching and for conflict resolution. These strategies are similar to the steps in the scientific method or reasoning. This approach has shown a particular sensitivity to pedagogical procedures.

Value Analysis Tasks (Metcalf 1971)

1. *Identifying and clarifying the value question.* Students and teachers share responsibility for clarifying value questions. This is a difficult matter, for such questions are often presented in vague or ambiguous terms. The question, Is it all right to use drugs? should be clarified in terms of which drugs, whether we are speaking of right in a moral or legal sense, and what is the age of persons involved? maturity of person, etc?

2. *Assembling purported facts.* Questions of fact need to be separated from questions of value. A question of fact is concerned with whether or not a person did a certain crime. A question of value relates to whether or not and to what degree should a person be punished for the crime. Facts need to be organized and assessed as to their relevance.

3. *Assessing the truth of purported facts.* Facts are of three kinds. *Particular* facts describe a single event or condition, e.g., the fact that it is raining today. *General* facts are generalizations that can be tested, e.g., it generally rains in April. *Conditional* facts depend on some other fact for their verification, e.g., if it rains, we will not play. It is suggested that factual questions be appraised according to the following criteria: How do you know this is true? What evidence is there to indicate this is the case? Who said this is the case? Why should we believe this person? Do other authorities agree with what this person says?

4. *Clarifying the relevance of facts.* Facts are relevant only if they have bearing on the moral judgment to be made. For example, the number of cases a judge has heard is not necessarily relevant for his appointment to the

Supreme Court. The fact that welfare clients receive money which they have not earned is not relevant to the morality of welfare, since many people inherit money and thus do not earn it.

5. *Arriving at a tentative value decision.* The tentative moral judgment is arrived at in light of the four previous operations in reasoning.

6. *Testing the value principle implied in the decision.* A value principle must be submitted to four tests to determine whether it is adequate. First, the principle should be able to cover new cases (*new cases test*). The principle that persons should not get unearned money cannot be readily applied to the case of inheritance. Thus it is not an adequate value principle. Secondly, the principle should be able to be subsumed (*subsumptive test*) under a more general value principle that a person generally accepts. For example, if I turn a person in to the police for using drugs, is this compatible with the values of friendship? Thirdly, the one making the value judgment should be able to accept the consequences if he or she is on the other end of the value judgment (*role exchange test*). If I make the judgment that capital punishment should be inflicted on a particular person, am I willing to have it inflicted on me if I were in that person's place? Fourthly, the value principle should be able to be applied universally (*universal consequences test*). For example, am I willing to extend to all persons the right not to pay income tax that I assume in my own case because of opposition to certain government policies? What would happen to lawful government in this case?

One of the strong points of this approach to value analysis is its explicit attention to the resolution of conflict. The theory recognizes that often there will be conflicts among persons in their discussion of values and offers a strategy for dealing with these classroom conflicts which parallels the steps in value analysis. The approach offers these six steps for conflict resolution.

1. *Reducing differences in interpretation of the value question.* This is to be done by finding common ground for an accepted interpretation of a value question. There should be common agreement on what values are, what morality is, etc.

2. *Reducing differences in the purported facts assembled.* Students should understand the difference between questions of fact and questions of value. Students can share data among themselves.

3. *Reducing differences in the assessed truth of purported facts.* Students should understand the difference between causation and correlation among events. Also there should be some agreement about the standards of evidence needed to establish facts.

4. *Reducing differences in the relevance of facts.* Often differences develop because of diverse standpoints. For example, environmental pollution may be examined from an economic, political, or health perspective.

5. *Reducing differences in tentative value decisions.* Disagreements occur because persons make value judgments prematurely or state them in very general terms. It is wise to separate the various elements in a value decision, focusing on those of agreement and disagreement.

6. *Reducing differences in the testing of the acceptability of value principles.* This is best done by encouraging students to consider new cases, new roles, and new consequences of their value principles.

These principles will certainly not remove all differences among students but they will point out where the differences lie and the reasons for them. People will come to their own conclusions as to what values they hold and why they hold them, while recognizing that others hold different values for different reasons. Students may also be led to challenge their own values.

Cognitive-Development Model

The work of Lawrence Kohlberg has given an impetus to strategies for moral education which are clearly cognitive in their orientation. In chapter three the work of Kohlberg was reviewed mainly in its psychological and philosophical aspects. Kohlberg has also advocated an approach to moral education which he feels will promote moral development through the stages of his theory. I do not intend to review the philosophical and psychological aspects of the theory in this chapter. But I will present the work of educationists who have developed a systematic approach to moral education which is inspired by his theories and those of Piaget (Hersh, Paolitto, and Reimer 1979).

The main dynamic of moral education is to produce in students a cognitive disequilibrium by exposing them to patterns of moral reasoning which are higher than their own. Exposure to a higher logic and a more comprehensive and consistent reasoning produces a cognitive unsettling and often a desire to move beyond one's present level of reasoning. This disequilibrium results because persons have the capacity to take the role of others.

To produce cognitive disequilibrium teachers should make use of moral dilemmas. These may be hypothetical such as the classic Heinz dilemma used by Kohlberg, content-based dilemmas such as a study of Truman's decision to use the atomic bomb against Japan, or real dilemmas from the lives of the students.

The teacher's role in this educational effort is to make skillful use of questioning strategies. Such questioning has as its purpose to invite students to explore their moral judgments and their reasons for them. The emphasis is not on right answers.

Two phases of questioning are proposed. Initial questions should introduce moral issues and develop moral awareness. The teacher attempts to ensure that the moral dilemma or problem is understood, that students attend to the moral aspects of the problem, that they give their reasons for their judgments, and that students with different responses and rationales interact with one another. The teacher should begin with questions which highlight the moral issue: Should Heinz steal the rare drug for his dying wife since he does not have the money which the druggist asks for it? Is it wrong to steal? Is it wrong to steal to save another's life. Then the teacher should move to "Why" questions such as: Why do you think your solution to the dilemma is correct? What is the main reason you decided in the way you did? The teacher may also probe further by adding circumstances that complicate the dilemma. The teacher might ask: What if Heinz' wife asked him not to steal the drug? Also, teachers might ask questions which prevent students from escaping the horns of the dilemma by introducing solutions which avoid the dilemma. In the famous case of deciding who should be put overboard on a sinking ship people come up with such suggestions as the use of ropes to tie people to the boat. The teacher would respond: Suppose there were no ropes on board.

Hersch et al. (1980) also propose in depth questioning strategies which teachers might use. Four general in-depth strategies are suggested:

1. *Refining questions.* Five types of refining questions are suggested:

a) a *clarifying probe* asks students to explain the terms they use: What do you mean by murder and how is it different from killing?

b) an *issue-specific probe* asks students to explain one moral issue which is related to the problem being discussed: What is the difference in moral obligation towards members of our family and strangers?

c) an *inter-issue probe* seeks to challenge students to resolve the conflict between two moral issues: What is more important, loyalty to one's country or obedience to one's conscience?

d) *a role-switch probe* suggests that students take up a different role from the one they have assumed: Put yourself in the place of the person who is awaiting capital punishment;

e) *a universal-consequence probe* asks students to apply their reasoning to all cases: What would happen in society if everyone decided to be a pacifist?

2. *Highlighting contiguous-stage arguments.* The cognitive-developmental approach stresses the importance of exposing students to reasoning at a higher stage than their own. There are at least two opportunities for doing this. When the teacher notices that the reason one student offers is at a higher level, he or she may point this out to other students and ask them what they

think of that reason and then ask them to explain how it differs from their own reasoning. A second way of doing this is for the teacher to present a response which is at a higher level of moral reasoning and then ask students to respond.

3. *Clarifying and summarizing.* It is important for the teacher at various points to clarify and summarize what the students are saying. In linking important elements of the discussion the teacher can make students aware of different patterns of reasoning and thus increase for some of them the effect of cognitive conflict and role taking. This also affords teachers the opportunity of adding missing dimensions or their personal views, though teachers should avoid making their answers appear to be the right answers.

4. *Role-taking questions and strategies.* These strategies are designed to challenge students to move from egocentric perspectives to perspectives that take into account the thoughts, feelings, and rights of others as well as those of lawful authorities. Various methods can be used to accomplish this purpose: role playing, debates, student-designed plays, films, slides, tapes, and short stories. The value of these activities is that they expose students to the thinking and behavior of others. Discussion of these experiences should focus on the reasons for the person's moral judgments. Especially in dealing with adolescents it is helpful to explore family relationships in order to facilitate the young person's ability to take the role of parents or siblings.

Those committed to the cognitive-developmental approach have recognized the limitations of a purely cognitive moral education. They have also recognized the effects of the hidden curriculum in schools and other institutions which shape moral attitudes and behaviors through peer pressure, praise, and the power of rules and authority. It is their view that moral education should take place within the larger context of an attempt to establish a just school or just community. This approach brings an affective and action dimension to what is otherwise an overly rational approach.

The *just school* was an attempt that Kohlberg and his colleagues attempted in Cambridge, Massachusetts. It involved about sixty students and six staff members. The major thrust was to develop democratic governance and opportunities for moral discussion about issues that arise in the life of the school.

Democratic governance was introduced whereby rules were made at a two hour community meeting held once a week. Students were responsible for enforcing decisions made at the community meetings. The experiment was a painful one for all persons involved. It took over two years for some of the conditions for a just community to become present. As time went on students became more active in the school, meetings improved, and students started to take responsibility for violations of school rules (Wasserman 1978).

Assessment of Cognitive Moral Education

Cognitive moral education has many strengths. Its focus on understanding and moral reasoning highlights an essential aspect of education. The most important components of education are knowledge, understanding, and criticism, all of which are stressed in these approaches. This rational approach is most appropriate for classrooms where understanding is a primary objective.

Cognitive moral development may be criticized for paying less attention to affective or action dimensions of moral education, though the programs presented do in various ways address these issues. A purely rational view may fail to recognize that moral behavior is the result of many factors, not only knowledge and understanding.

An examination of the four approaches presented indicates some differences among proponents. Scriven's approach amounts to a course in ethics and is suitable for older youths and adults. He recognizes that such an approach is beyond the capabilities of small children. Yet he contends that the education for small children should not be indoctrinatory but based on community consensus and standards.

Beck's reflective method has much to recommend it, especially its attempt to introduce affective elements within the cognitive approach. His ideas would give greater emphasis to agreed content or key ideas that would give important direction to the efforts of teachers and students. Although his approach has been developed within the context of the Canadian educational system, the themes presented appear general enough to be applied to other cultural contexts. The focus on core values is commendable, though the danger is that in order to avoid controversy these values will be defined in a rather abstract and general manner. Another question is whether or not the theory based on consensus values allows for criticism of values, especially in the social and political realms.

The particular strength of value analysis lies in its attention to methodology. It utilizes in a creative manner the elements of the scientific method. If the method is used in an imaginative and not in a rigorous manner, teachers would have a helpful series of steps by which to conduct investigation into issues which are value laden. The system, however, neglects two dimensions. The affective component is not strong and little attention is paid to action. There is no reason why these elements cannot be integrated within the various steps or serve as additional components.

In chapter three I have already offered some criticisms of Kohlberg's ideas. As to the methodology drawn from his theory, the main question concerns the validity of the stages as setting the goals for moral education. The use of dilemmas is a valuable tool, but exclusive dependence upon it will make education a boring enterprise. Dilemmas, however, are helpful in encouraging students to deal with complex issues open to a pluralism of views. Challenging the moral reasoning of students is a worthwhile goal, provided that it is not done in a threatening manner. Finally, teachers should be wary of the danger in defining one form of reasoning as higher or more adequate since this part of the theory is under serious criticism.

Cognitive Moral Education in Religious Contexts

Many religious educators have proposed forms of cognitive moral education for dealing with in the moral aspects of religious faiths. Forms of religious education which stress the use of reason and natural knowledge are especially drawn to these approaches.

A tension may exist between cognitive forms of moral education and religious education in morality. Cognitive approaches tend to be open ended and allow students the freedom to present their own responses to moral dilemmas, issues, and problems. Religious ethical systems that are largely based on authoritative teachings of the Bible or of the church do not usually allow this type of openness.

Scriven's approach would be accepted by religious educators committed to a rational religious ethics. Those who espouse a more authoritarian ethical system or one that is based on biblical or church authority would have difficulties with the emphasis on rationality and autonomy.

Beck's reflective approach has a feature which religious educators might find helpful. He presents key concepts emphasized in religious traditions and provides an opportunity to apply them. His approach would seem to allow for religious teachings but also to permit freedom in applying them to real life situations.

While value analysis has been developed for social studies, I believe that it can be adapted for purposes of moral education in religious contexts. Religious groups want students to consider as relevant facts and interpretation those which are found in the religious tradition. So long as religious teachings are not viewed in an absolutist manner, value analysis would appear to be an appropriate way of dealing with the moral dimensions of religious teachings.

In the last chapter I analyzed the debate among theologians and religious educators with regard to the use of Kohlberg's theory and practice for religious moral education. While many do not see the possibility of any reconciliation between the two, I have contended that his approach has much to recommend it.

The judgment of the usefulness of cognitive approaches in religious education comes down to how one views the religious ethical system that forms the basis for student's education. I believe that cognitive moral education is necessary for a sound religious education. It is not the only thing that is necessary and it may not be appropriate at all age levels. But from adolescence on people need the opportunity to use reason and to exercise autonomy in moral decision making. The teachings of the religious traditions are presented as wise counsel in these areas; but ultimately people have the choice to become moral decision makers. Enough differences exist in teachings among religious bodies and their leaders to make it obvious that no religious body can teach with absolute authority about morality. Given this reality, cognitive approaches which encourage students to think, argue, debate, and come to their own decisions should play a major role in moral education in religious bodies.

AFFECTIVE APPROACHES TO MORAL EDUCATION

In recent years a dissatisfaction among educators with cognitive approaches has led to the construction of theories which emphasize affective dimensions of persons. These approaches do not primarily engage students in moral reasoning or analysis but encourage them to explore their emotions, feelings, attitudes, and personal preferences. Since these approaches have been presented in the form of handbooks of exercises for teachers, they have been widely used, especially in the United States and Britain. I will examine two of the more popular approaches: values clarification and the consideration model.

Values Clarification

Values clarification came on the scene in the 1960s and has been at the center of controversy since that time. It is an attempt to deal with moral confusion in society by presenting not a set of values but a process which will enable persons to identify the values they profess and the reasons they hold them. Values clarification attempts to deal with real life situations by helping persons explain their values and by encouraging them to reflect more deeply on them with the hope that they will develop personal powers of judging. The proponents believe this approach is appropriate for schools and other educational settings.

The Theory and Its Criticisms

Values clarification emphasizes the personal nature of values. They are personal things, uniquely individual dimensions of human experience. Values are personal preferences, inclinations, and choices. Individuals determine values and not external forces as such religion, society, or tradition. Critics of values clarification have contended that this is unrealistic because external forces play a large role in the shaping of our values. The theory does not deal well with the tension between the individual and the social, but its emphasis on the personal dimension is an important one in countering the determinism of other approaches to the understanding of values.

Values clarification is not a theory of moral education as such but a theory and practice of values education. It deals with values, both moral and non-moral. It also deals with issues of right and wrong, moral issues. Also, many teachers of morality have utilized its exercises in the practice of moral education. Though its critics charge it with being value neutral, it does present a humanistic ethic of openness and acceptance, concern with others, self-awareness, and thoughtfulness.

Since the theory contends that there are no absolute values derived from any source, it focuses on the valuing process. With little attention given to the content of values or to value principles, the processes or skills of valuing become the heart of the approach. The process of valuing involves seven subprocesses:

Choosing: 1) freely, 2) from alternatives, and 3) after thoughtful consideration of the consequences of each alternative

Prizing: 4) cherishing, being happy with the choice; 5) willing to affirm the choice publicly.

Acting: 6) doing something with the choice; 7) repeatedly, in some pattern of life (Raths et al. 1978, pp. 27–28).

Under the impact of criticisms leveled against the theory, Kirschenbaum (1977) has added to the valuing process the subprocesses of *thinking* (thinking on various levels, critical thinking, moral reasoning at higher levels, and divergent or creative thinking) and *communicating* (the ability to send clear messages, empathy, listening, taking in another's frame of reference, and conflict resolution). These changes place more importance on the social context of the valuing process. Although these modifications give greater stress to thinking processes, the theory still maintains its emphasis on the person as a feeling and acting being. While the theory has been modified, it remains to be seen whether these changes carry over into actual practice.

Finally, the theory defines the role of the teacher. The teacher does not teach values or even attempt to be a role model. The teacher's role is to facilitate in students through appropriate questions the development of skills.

In some ways the teacher is more a therapist than an instructor. Critics of the theory have questioned the neutrality of teachers both as to its possibility and advisability. Experienced teachers know that sooner or later they will manifest their own values and preferences in educational situations. Also, the value stances of teachers can be helpful in the educational process in so far as their values are representative of community standards or are well reasoned dissents from them.

Values clarification, even with its modifications, places greatest emphasis on affective elements in education. The approach stresses the need to deepen awareness of the individual's feelings. An examination of the exercises in the manuals shows that the majority of them are concerned with prizing and feeling components. Students are encouraged to respond briefly to questions and for the most part are urged to avoid lengthy dialogues. The emphasis is on personal expression and less on critical thinking and action, though these elements are not entirely ignored.

The theory includes an action component that emphasizes not single actions but action skills and a pattern of actions by which persons establish their character. This component, however, is weakened because the theory seems to put all actions on a par and does not distinguish moral actions from actions which imply only personal preferences. The moral sphere is made to appear trivial when personal preferences about clothing, friends, and food seem to be treated with the same importance as questions about supporting parents, protesting government policies, or making decisions about abortion.

The Practice of Values Clarification

Many teachers believe values clarification is the system they can most easily learn and utilize in educational settings. The proponents have offered practical exercises and suggestions that can apply to many subjects. Values clarification as a method can be easily learned, is applicable to many areas, and generates interest among students. It is no wonder that thousands of copies of books on value clarification have been bought by teachers. A brief summary of the main components of the practice shows why the theory has found favor with many teachers.

1. *Value Indicators.* Value indicators are not values in themselves but entities from which values may eventually emerge. Teachers should be attentive to these indicators. Eight such indicators have been suggested. Some examples of these are also given (Raths et al. 1978).

    a. *goals and purposes* indicate values since they give general directions. Examples: We're thinking about doing. . . . I'd like to. . . . When I get this. . . . I'm going to do that. . . .

b. *aspirations* can indicate value commitments that persons might make. Examples: In the future. . . . When I grow up. . . .

c. *attitudes* indicate what we are for or against. Examples: I'm for. . . . I'm against. . . . The way I see it. . . .

d. *interests* represent a more casual attitude toward something. Examples: I love making. . . . I really enjoy. . . .

e. *feelings* are passing emotions that may or may not reflect deep value commitments. Examples: I'd feel bad about. . . .

f. *beliefs and convictions* are strongly held truths which may be values. Examples: I believe in God. . . . I believe in future life. . . .

g. *activities* which we engage in may be manifestations of our values. Examples: On Sundays I. . . . On my day off I. . . .

2. *Clarifying Response.* The teacher-facilitator is to make use of the clarifying response as a strategy for promoting a non-threatening dialogue in which students think about their own values. The teacher does not provide guidelines or evaluate responses but rather puts responsibility on the students to think for themselves. Students are free not to respond and responses are to be rather short. This question and answer style of teaching is designed to stimulate thinking. Some examples of clarifying responses related to *prizing and cherishing* are:

a. Are you glad you feel that way?

b. How long have you wanted it?

c. What good is it for? What purpose does it serve? Why is it important to you?

d. Should everyone do it your way? (Raths et al. 1978, 64–65).

Some examples of clarifying responses relating to *acting on choices* are:

a. I hear what you are for; now, is there anything you can do about it? Can I help?

b. What are your first steps, second steps, etc.?

c. Are you willing to put your money behind this idea?

d. Have you examined the consequences of your act?

e. Are there any organizations set up for the same purposes? Will you join? (Raths et al. 1978, 64–65).

3. *The Value Sheet.* A third strategy presented by value clarification educators is the value sheet on which students write their responses to value questions. The value sheet consists of a provocative or challenging statement and a series of questions which students should answer. Students write their personal reflections and then small groups of students may discuss their responses. These sheets can be used in many different subjects, which contain moral issues.

Simon (1973, pp. 238–239) has presented a values sheet which he has based on the New Testament story of Jesus' triumphant entry into Jerusalem as told in the Gospels. Two levels of teaching are presented: the Facts Level and the Values Level. I will only give the questions which he suggests for the clarification of values.

1. Would you have been able to turn over the tables of money changers in the temple? Wasn't this violent and destructive of private property? Is this anything like the cases of students who force deans out of their offices? . . . Have you ever participated in an action that destroyed property? Name a time when you feel you could do so.

2. The disciples seemed to have no embarrassment about demonstrating their beliefs in public. How easy is it for you to announce to anyone what you believe when it is unpopular or you might be punished for doing so? Have you ever participated in a demonstration for civil rights or to end the war in Vietnam? Why? What kind of demonstrations do you think are acceptable? When should people participate in a demonstration?

4. *Activities for Large-Group Discussions.* There are many exercises in values clarification manuals for group discussions which enable individuals to explain their values. Handbooks include such activities as scenes from plays or movies, provocative questions, humorous stories, etc. A four fold strategy for discussion is presented: 1) a topic is chosen and discussion is initiated through questions, a scene from a play, or a role playing exercise; 2) students think about their responses and at times write down what they think on the issue; 3) the class discusses the topic in small groups or as an entire group; 4) the students reflect on their experience by answering such questions as: what did I learn or discover? What surprised me was. . . .

A number of ways are suggested for increasing reflection and discussion on value issues. These few are only samples from literally hundreds of exercises which have been developed.

a. *values continuum strategy.* Students are encouraged to make a public affirmation of their values. The teacher places on the board a values continuum on the issue of government control of the economy:

complete control . . . . no control

Students are asked to place themselves along the continuum and give reasons for their choices. The exercise is to show that there are few black and white issues but many grey issues.

b. *values voting.* The teacher reads a question aloud and asks students to raise their hands in the affirmative or negative. Undecided persons can just fold their hands. Discussions can take place on such questions as: Do you think there are times when cheating is justified? Will you raise your children more strictly than you were raised?

c. *rank order.* Students are asked to put a number of alternatives in rank order. Example: Which would you give highest priority to today: space, poverty, defense, ecology.

d. *values focus game*. Students are asked to respond to a question such as, I feel most comfortable in a group that. . . . Groups of three are then formed and each student has the attention of the two others for five minutes. Eye contact is to be maintained. What a person says should be accepted; disagreement would be deferred till later in the process. Questions should be framed to draw out individual views or feelings.

Assessment of Values Clarification

It is hard not to be impressed by the imaginative efforts of the proponents of values clarification. Notwithstanding the many criticisms that have been leveled against the theory in the past two decades, it still remains an attractive approach to values education, mainly because of its many practical strategies. The heyday of values clarification seems to have passed but nothing has emerged to replace it in the current rekindling of interest in values and moral education. I think that the strategies presented are still workable and might be used in many contexts. However, teachers will have to go further than what the theory proposes to deal with moral values adequately in current situations. Clarification of values is one thing but it does not go far enough. Harder and deeper thinking and analysis needs to be done. A more thorough analysis of society, cultural systems, consensus of values, and moral relativism should be brought into any form of values education.

Efforts have been made to utilize values clarification in religious education (Simon 1973; Simon, Daitch, and Hartwell 1973). Religious educators have shown an interest in this approach since many of the strategies are adaptable to moral education in religious contexts. Religious educators, however, have offered similar criticisms to those generally made of the theory. The total openness espoused by values clarification is usually not acceptable to religious educators. Educators in religion are more concerned with tradition and authority than proponents of values clarification. I feel, however, that many of the strategies can be used in religious education so long as teachers bring into the discussion the values of the religious traditions as important sources for individuals and societies.

Consideration Model

Another example of an affective approach to moral education is found in Schools Moral Education Curriculum Project which has been used in Britain and North America. Peter McPhail and a group of associates have developed the Lifeline Series which presents an approach to moral education that stresses consideration and care (McPhail et al. 1975). In recent years McPhail has more often used the terminology of social education to describe his ideas.

Theory and Criticisms

Moral education is not a matter of analysis of rules and prohibitions but is rather a focus on a person's general style of relating to self and others. Moral education is to liberate persons from fear and distrust of self and others and to empower them to give and receive love. Moral education applies to the whole person and focuses on the development of attitudes of love, empathy, and active consideration of others.

The theory has a research base developed from a study of adolescent needs conducted in England from 1967 to 1971. Eight-hundred secondary school youths were asked critical incident questions. The sample recounted incidents where they were treated well or badly by adults. They also responded to questions about peer relations. McPhail concluded from the research that good treatment means the showing of consideration for one's needs, feelings, and interests. Bad treatment indicates the lack of such consideration. The fundamental human need emerging from the research was the need to get along with others, to love and be loved. McPhail concluded that it was the prime responsibility of organized education to help meet this need.

Another conclusion drawn from the research concerned the maturity of students to distinguish between freedom and license. Students seemed able to make distinctions between being firm and being stubborn, and between positions coming from dogmas and those coming from convictions. Adolescents were shown to be growing in maturity of social judgment and behavior in the years between twelve and eighteen. Maturity is the ability to help persons to be creative carers.

In developing his theory McPhail attempts to blend humanism and a moderate behaviorism. Moral values are learned by observing how significant persons act toward us and others. Moral values are learned from the example of others, including the example of teachers. Observational learning and social modeling are thus important in this theory. The ideal learning environment is one in which there is no wariness, hostility or suspicion. McPhail also relies on the principles of humanistic psychology in his emphasis on the need for personal maturity, authenticity, insight, and creativity.

These two diverse psychological views occasion some theoretical difficulties for this model. It is not easy to reconcile a theory of conditioning with a theory of personal choice. It is clear that both factors are involved in learning moral values and behavior. Conditioning is a fact of human learning but the crucial question is to what extent are individuals determined by conditioning and what is the power to overcome all the factors that make up our conditioning. McPhail tries to distance himself from Skinner's operant conditioning but does not clearly describe the form of conditioning he espouses. He contends that the rightness or wrongness of actions is determined by the feedback from others.

If one looks at the types of exercises used in this approach, it is clear that the humanistic view of the person is what predominates. Conditioning seems to play little role in these exercises. Thus there does not appear to be a neat fit between theory and the practice in the consideration model.

The Practice of Moral Education

McPhail is against highly cognitive approaches which ask students to grapple with tough issues of moral obligation. The moral life involves a personality style and not a mode of reasoning. The purpose of moral education is to develop a moral style—a way of behaving which is genuinely affiliative. To educate morally is not a matter of helping students balance conflicting claims but rather a matter of aiding them to fulfill their natural harmony with others. Effective moral education entails educating students to care and to develop a considerate style of life which will be rewarding and attractive in itself.

McPhail's *Lifeline Series* was developed for secondary school students. It could easily be used with older children; some of the material might also be applied to adults. The series is divided into three sections that present progressively more complicated social situations. The three sections are: 1) *In Other People's Shoes*; 2) *Proving the Rule*; 3) *What Would You Have Done?* An examination of the materials indicates that though affective elements predominate, there are ample suggestions for moral reasoning and action. *Section One: In Other People's Shoes* This section has three units: *Sensitivity, Consequences,* and *Points of View*. Students are asked to deal with interpersonal problems which they might experience at home, in school, or in their neighborhoods. The situations come from the survey research done for the project. Role playing and dramatic representation are suggested for dealing with these situations in order to promote emotional as well as cognitive involvement. The educational goal is to encourage students to form attitudes and behaviors which manifest care and consideration. Finally, students should choose which incidents they want to deal with.

1. *Sensitivity.* Forty-six situations are depicted on colorful sensitivity cards. Students are asked what they would do in the situation. They can make

statements, role play, mime, describe in writing, paint, or discuss what they would do in the situations.

Examples

You know that your best friend is doing something which is causing him or her to suffer? What would you do?

Your mother, who is tired and distracted by a younger child, is not listening to something important you are trying to tell her? What would you do?

An acquaintance of yours often butts in and tries to change the subject when you are talking? What would you do?

(McPhail et al. 1975, Section 1)

The series presents procedures teacher can use in dealing with the sensitivity situations: 1) read the situation or put it on the board; 2) ask students to write down what they would do; 3) ask for courses of action or choose one response to start with; 4) invite students who make a similar response to role play their response; 5) initiate discussion and criticism of the response or suggest alternative role plays; 6) continue discussion or role play as long as there is interest; 7) sum up the discussion by presenting pros and cons but let students make final judgment.

In the research which he did prior to developing the *Lifeline* approach, McPhail categorized the responses which students made to critical situations. He lists the following categories.

Situation. A boy or girl of your own age, with whom you are friendly, appears to be very upset for some reason unknown to you. You would:

Response	*Category*
1. Do nothing	passive
2. Feel disturbed but not know what to do	passive emotional
3. Point out the situation to some adult	adult-dependent
4. Talk to your friends about it	adult-dependent
5. Tell the person concerned to pull himself/ herself together	peer-dependent
6. Make fun of that boy or girl	very aggressive
7. Avoid him/her	avoidance
8. Try asking your friend what is the matter	experimental crude
9. Attempt to talk to him/her as if you have not noticed that anything is wrong	experimental sophisticated
10. Comfort your friend	mature conventional
11. Set about interesting the person concerned in something that is going on, at the same time being available to help if asked. (McPhail et al. 1975, section 1)	mature imaginative

McPhail supplies no detailed explanation of the categories. Although the goal is to guide students give more mature responses, the taxonomy is not presented as a hierarchy as is the case with Kohlberg stages. The taxonomy lists various types of maturity which can be manifested in student responses.

2. *Consequences* This unit consists of seventy-one situations which deal not with interpersonal issues but with issues that involve large groups of people. The purpose is to have participants take on a third party or more objective perspective on moral issues. The question posed in these situations is: What is likely to happen next? The same processes are suggested that were used in the *Sensitivity Unit*: mime, role play, creative writing etc.

Examples

Someone tries to get a friend to drink more than he or she wants to.

Someone buys a puppy without considering whether he can afford it.

Someone blames minority groups for everything that is wrong with the country (McPhail et al. 1975).

3. *Points of View* The purpose of this unit is to urge students to take the role of other persons before they give their opinions on how they would react. The sixty-three situations presented here raise issues about: sex attitudes; age conflicts; class attitudes; racial, cultural, religious, and political conflicts; and psychological conflicts. The following example from the section on sexual attitudes illustrates the type situation presented.

Situation.

The girl's position

I am the only daughter in the family and am trying to take care of the house while my mother is in the hospital. I think that my brother should accept his share of the household jobs, and I have asked him to help with the cleaning and dishes. He has refused because he does not think that these are jobs for a man.

Try to put yourself in the girl's position. What would you do, say, and feel about it? What might be a solution to this situation that would be acceptable to both the brother and the sister?

The boy's position

My sister is taking care of the house while our mother is in the hospital. She asked me to help with the cleaning and dishes, but I'm not going to because I think that these are a woman's job.

Try to put yourself in the boy's position. What would you do, say, and feel about it?

Section 2: Proving the Rule

This section of the *Lifeline* series presents participants with more complex issues which students face as they move toward adult status. These issues arise in the social settings of school, home, and job. The unit does not deal with controversial issues in public life, though it is concerned with skills and dispositions that are applicable to these issues. Five units are presented, each with a different focus. I will give examples from two units.

Rules and Individuals

The short situations in this unit deal with the importance of individuals acting morally according to rules. Rules are considered laws, regulations, and moral principles. Very often persons must face conflicts among rules. Rules in many cases are in opposition to individual inclinations. An example from the realm of the school is as follows:

Situation

Paul was helping with the school fund drive. It was Wednesday, and he had promised to take Liz to the movies. But he was broke. He was "borrowing" a few dollars from the fund when he was caught red-handed and sent to the principal. The principal called Paul's parents to tell them about the situation and to notify them that he was suspending Paul from school for a week.

Questions

1. Do you think that the principal behaved fairly or unfairly in this situation? What would you have done if you were the principal?
2. How do you think Paul's parents would react to this situation? Do you think they might punish him too? If so, how?
3. Think of some of the rules which people you know have broken, and then say: a) if you think the punishment they got was fair; b) if not, what you think a fair punishment might have been.
4. What about people who break rules and are not caught? Use the following situations: in schools, in a movie theater, at home.

Who Do You Think I Am

In a booklet that deals with issues of person-perception and self-definition such notions as stereotyping, scapegoating, idealization of public figures, and communication breakdown are examined. The assumption of the unit is the need for a secure and reality-based personal concept in order to face social issues with integrity. The goal of the unit is that students develop an image of themselves and others as significant, unique individuals who have an effect on situations and make real decisions. An example on identity is as follows.

Situation

John's friends think of him as a clever person because he is so good at mechanics. John likes to be thought of in this way. He doesn't like school very much, and as a result, doesn't get along with a group of bright kids in his class. He calls them bookworms. They say that he's a dummy. John and this group of students never really talked to each other, because neither admired nor respected the other for what each could do well.

John needed to be admired as a good mechanic because this is how he saw himself. The other group needed to be admired for their school work.

Many people seem to pigeonhole others into "types" or "kinds." Of course, people can't be easily labeled like this. If you selected one aspect of a person and used that as a label, it wouldn't tell you much about what kind of person he or she really is. Could anyone put you in a jar marked "teenager" and say what kind of person you are?

Questions

1. Write a list of labels you have used for other people.
2. Draw some jars, label them, and try to fit people you know into them (McPhail et al. 1975).

Section 3: What Would You Have Done

In this section events in history are used to provide impetus for moral reflection. This material can be integrated with study in history, social studies, and English. The events in the unit are: the birth of an African baby in South Africa, the confinement of a conscientious objector during the First World War, the arrest of Anne Frank, the riots in Watts, Los Angeles, the war in Vietnam, and a girl who suffers from drugs.

Assessment of the Consideration Approach

The Consideration Approach incorporated in the *Lifeline* series is a comprehensive treatment of moral education. A range of methods and strategies are used. The materials are excellent and apparently have had wide use among British students.

Questions raised concern the theoretical basis which does not appear firm enough to guide teachers and students adequately. McPhail discusses many factors of moral motivation without weighing the adequacy or the particular value of each. He seems to imply that pleasure is the most important principle of moral motivation.

I have indicated above the problem in the theory with the apparent acceptance of moral values as determined by conditioning and moral values as the object of human choice. Also, a number of important categories are left undefined, for example, the meaning of the various classification of adolescents into aggressive, passive, etc.

The Consideration Approach can be adapted to efforts in religious education. Religious ethics might establish a stronger theoretical basis by providing a consistent and comprehensive ethic. The values of religious traditions and authorities could be brought into the discussion of situations, problems, and issues. This should be done not in an authoritarian manner but by providing a moral context, a form of moral motivation, and authoritative teachings on particular moral issues.

Many of the values which the theory stresses are found in religious traditions. The teaching of these values in religious contexts could be fortified by the well thought out exercises and examples found in the practical exercises. Both the personal and social emphases in religious ethics find expression in this theory and in its application.

ACTION APPROACHES TO MORAL EDUCATION

All of the approaches discussed thus far give some attention to the dimension of action. Though cognitive approaches focus on understanding and judgment, they recognize that the ultimate goal of moral education is to influence the actions of students. Cognitive approaches are wary of concentrating too much on action because doing this may lead to manipulation or to action without sufficient reasoning. Affective approaches include an action dimension. Action is made an explicit part of the theory of values clarification. The consideration model also recognizes that classroom discussion should begin with the activities of students in their every day life and attempt to shape or influence future actions.

While all theories consider action to some degree, there are some which center primarily on the element of personal, social, and political action. I will present one method which pinpoints social and political action.

Social Action Approach

Fred Newmann (1975) has developed an approach to moral education which places its greatest emphasis on involving high school students in efforts to bring about social change. The approach includes the development of moral reasoning skills and the development of such affective dimensions as trust and commitment. But the ultimate goal is to teach students how to influence public policy as citizens in a democratic society.

It is Newmann's view that other systems usually produce passive citizens. He is concerned that moral education produce active citizens, citizens who have developed *environmental competence*. Environmental competency includes three types: 1) *physical competence*, the ability to have an impact on objects, e.g., painting a picture or building a house; 2) *interpersonal competence*, the ability to have an impact on persons through nurturing relationships (caring for a friend) or economic relationships (selling a car); 3) *civic competence*, the ability to have an impact on public affairs through the electoral process (helping a person get elected) or through interest groups (e.g., through a consumer protection group). The social action approach is mainly interested in the development of civic competence (Newmann 1975, p. 18).

The Theory and Its Criticisms

Newmann contends that it is through social action that we develop moral sensitivity and values. A moral agent is described as "someone who deliberates upon what he or she ought to do in situations that involve possible conflicts between self interest and the interests of others, or between the rights of parties in conflict" (Newmann 1975, p. 29). Moral agents must feel that they can act in the society and deal with injustices which they experience or see others experience. What prevents the development of moral values and sensibility is not lack of reasoning skills or affective attitudes but the failure to act socially and politically because of a belief that there is nothing one can do. One learns moral values by developing competencies in the physical, interpersonal, and civic realms of life.

The goal of social action is to teach students how to take part in the democratic process. This is accomplished by getting involved in social actions. These actions include:

telephone conversations, letter writing, participation in meetings, research and study, testifying before public bodies, door-to-door canvassing, fund raising media production, bargaining and negotiation; and also publicly visible activity associated with more militant forms. Social action can take place in or out of school, and if out of school, not necessarily in the streets, but in homes, offices, and work places (Newmann, 1975, p. 54–55).

These are social actions if they are part of a strategy to influence public policy on recreation, housing, environment, drug abuse, election of a public official, and other issues of public concern.

The social action model has three major components. The first step is the formulation of goals based on moral deliberation and social policy research. Moral deliberation is reasoned, open debate concerning policies and principles. Deliberation is necessary because often there are conflicting values on particular issues. Social policy research is necessary to determine what the consequences of certain policies will be. The findings will not always be convincing, e.g., the effect of busing on educational achievement.

The second step is working to support the goals. The moral activist should become familiar with the political and legal processes, both formal and informal. Formal processes include the making of a law. An informal process is a knowledge of who has particular influence in a town or corporation. Advocacy skills are needed so that activists can make the best possible case for their positions. Group process knowledge and skills help people determine whether they should join an existing group or form a new one. Finally, a knowledge of organization and management skills helps moral activists be more efficient in their use of time and effort.

The third step is the resolving of psycho-philosophic concerns or dilemmas. The effective citizen must resolve several issues. The person must balance commitment to a cause and openness to criticisms of this cause. The extremes of over-commitment and total openness should be avoided. A second dilemma revolves around a consideration of persons versus a commitment to causes or institutions. People may become so committed to causes or institutions that they treat opponents as enemies. Related to this problem is the issue of maintaining integrity but still being able to work out compromises. A third dilemma concerns the use of power, i.e., the avoidance of using power to hurt others or to ignore their views and needs. Finally, activists should probe their own motivations. Are they acting for personal gain or are there true social justifications for their actions?

The value of this model is that it clearly recognizes that moral reasoning and affective education are not equal to the task of moral education. The serious attention to the action element most recommends the theory. Since the approach has been developed as a social studies curriculum, action in the social and political contexts is emphasized. I will offer a fuller assessment of the theory after presenting its practice. The theoretical basis has not been sufficiently developed. The curriculum developed because of Newmann's dissatisfaction with Kohlberg and others who used case studies. Newmann came to the conclusion that moral reasoning was not enough, even when it concerned public issues. In preliminary testing of these other approaches there appeared to be little transfer of classroom learning to out of class situations. Thus he moved to the present theory which changed the focus to action in society.

The Practice

Newmann's program, *Education for Citizen Action*, is an ambitious program for high school students. The competencies to be developed through
the course include:

1. Communicate effectively in spoken and written language.
2. Collect and logically interpret information on problems of public
concern.
3. Describe political-legal decision-making processes.
4. Rationally justify personal decisions on controversial public issues and
strategies for action with reference to principles of justice and constitutional democracy.
5. Work cooperatively with others.
6. Discuss concrete personal experiences of self and others in ways that
contribute to resolution of personal dilemmas encountered in civic action
and that relate these experiences to more general human issues.
7. Use selected technical skills as they are required for exercise of influence on specific issues (Newmann 1975, p. 6).

The course is recommended for an entire year and students would spend
almost full time in it. Newmann recommends that only students in grades
eleven and twelve be invited to participate in the course. They would receive
credits in English and Social Studies from taking the course and still have
some time for an additional course in math, science, or a foreign language. I
seriously doubt if many schools would give this much attention to the course.
But the course could be adapted, with certain units treated and others left to
the discretion of students. It involves six courses.

1. *Political-legal process course.* The realities of the political system are
studied, both formal structures such as the process of legislation and informal structures of lobbying and bargaining. Students would observe these
operations first hand by attending meetings and conducting interviews.
Moral deliberation skills would be treated and the students would have to
develop position papers on controversial public issues.

2. *Communication course.* The students would develop skills in written,
spoken, and nonverbal communications. These skills would be applied in
these contexts: intrapersonal, interpersonal, group, and public. Focus would
be on such skills as empathy and problem identification.

3. *Community service internship.* For two mornings a week in the first
semester the students would do volunteer work in social agencies, government bodies, and groups promoting public interest. The students might serve
as aides to reporters, tutor young children, assist the elderly, or work with a
public interest group. This internship is not passive but should comprise

action by the students. On one afternoon a week the students would discuss their experiences, sharing insights and problems with teachers and each other.

4. *Citizen action project.*   On four mornings a week in the second semester students would work in some way to affect public policy. They might work or political campaigns, lobby for legislation with the school, community or nation. In conjunction with this course students would participate in skill clinics on such topics as canvassing, negotiating, fund raising, and running a meeting. Some group counseling sessions would also take place to give students psychological support and aid in their projects.

5. *Action in literature project.*   This course focuses in a general way on how individuals can make a difference in social change. This is explored through works of fiction, biography, poetry, and drama. Among the suggestions are biographies of Gandhi and Martin Luther King, Thoreau's essay on civil disobedience, and the works of the black novelist James Baldwin.

6. *Public message.*   Each group in the class develops a final message to be shared with other members of the class and with the public at large. A report on the media could be prepared. The emphasis is on what happened in the project and on how the students interpreted these happenings.

The course places an emphasis on three types of student projects. The students would do an exploratory research project to study the community and gather information through field trips, interviews, guest speakers, and observation. The second project, volunteer service, has the purpose of placing students in helping relationships, with the elderly, young children, and peers. Finally, social action projects require students to take advocacy positions. Among the three projects there is a developmental pattern of moving from self, to others, and to the broader community. Criteria are given for evaluating the projects in terms of mastery of knowledge and skills related to citizen action, the successful completion of the project, persistence in taking the projects seriously, and the pleasure or enjoyment which students derive from the projects.

It is clear from a description of the program that great demands are made on teachers. They are to serve as resource persons who supply information about what is available in libraries and in the community. They counsel the students by helping them deal with personal problems and dilemmas which they may face. Thirdly, they may be expert resources in particular areas of competence by reason of their knowledge. Finally, teachers are urged to become activists themselves to provide models and motivation to their students.

A number of additional items are suggested for the administration of the program. A well equipped resource center with books, maps, tape recorders, newspapers, etc. would make it easy for students to carry out their projects.

A citizen advisory committee made up of parents, community leaders and students could offer guidance and available contacts in the community. Students should be involved in decision making with regard to all aspects of the program.

Assessment of Social Action Model

Anyone who has taught courses in morals or values education has to be impressed with the basic assumption of the social action model: moral education should include a strong action component since moral action is the only true test of moral education. Newmann's approach pays attention to the various components of moral education: thinking, caring, and acting. But it is the action component that most recommends the approach to educators.

There is an intuitive sense that such a program would increase moral understanding, caring, and moral habits. But it should be bolstered by research which tests the results. Newmann has recognized this but little research has been produced.

Practical questions can be raised about the approach. It is rather ambitious and demands a great deal of time on the part of students and teachers. I question whether this much time can be spent on any program, given the other academic demands on high school students. Parts of the program may be used when the full program cannot be implemented.

Problems can be anticipated because one of the results might be a politicization of young peoples in values, attitudes, and actions which may be different from their parents. Teachers of social studies and literature have often faced these disputes. When these teachers use an approach which focuses on action, there will be even more danger of opposition and criticism by parents and members of the community. The implementation of a citizens advisory group is a helpful way of preventing and dealing with problems arising from politicization.

The program is certainly consonant with the demands of moral education in religious contexts. Religious sources can provide additional understandings of our historical and cultural traditions. The examples of many people who have dedicated themselves to social causes out of religious beliefs and motivations can be additional elements in the curriculum. Religious ethics can provide a system and context in which moral deliberation, affective caring, and social action can take place. This approach is similar to courses in peace and justice which many religious groups have stressed in recent years (Fenton 1975).

The model may be valuable in working with church or synagogue youth groups. In recent years the preparation for confirmation in some Christian churches has included a component of service to the church and community. This model gives a full rationale and program that might be utilized in initiating those to be confirmed into the action dimension of religious faith.

Conclusion

In this chapter I have presented a number of approaches to moral education which have been developed by educationists. I have grouped them according to their primary orientation to moral reasoning, caring or empathy, and action. I believe that while all the theories are valuable, none is adequate to the task of moral education at all levels. It would appear that affective approaches might best be initiated with young children by parents and teachers. They can be used with persons of all ages in all educational contexts. Moral reasoning can be introduced to older children and used more extensively with youth and adults. Action approaches would appear best begun in later years of high school and used in all moral education programs for adults.

All three approaches can be use in religious contexts with the provisos I have indicated. There are certain religious traditions which place particular emphasis on cognitive, affective, or action approaches. But within all the religious traditions each of these elements are found. Religious approaches can both contribute something to them and benefit from them. They can bring a sense of community, tradition, and authority which if properly exercised may aid in the task of moral education. They may learn that moral education is not merely a matter of socializing members into the ethical traditions but of using creative methods for the continuing moral education of its members.

EPILOGUE:
ARTISTRY IN CONDUCT

In reviewing the enterprise of moral education as I have done in the various chapters of this book one particular issue rises to the surface: the tension between the classical Greek view of education as a means of forming moral character and good citizens and the more modern view of education as essential to promote individual advancement and the service of various systems of society. Education in the United States, at least until this century, has focused on the Greek ideal. Ever since the progressive era, however, the second purpose has predominated. Great attention has been given to this purpose because many assumed that families, schools, churches and other institutions were successful in producing citizens of good moral character. This assumption has been challenged in recent years by the realization that educational processes, especially those in the schools, are no longer adequate to form moral character. Thus we are witnessing the contemporary rekindling of interest in the task of moral education which in previous centuries played a large part in the ideology of American education.

It is clear to me that the moral education for our times must be based on the sound inquiries and research found in the various academic disciplines which have formed the basis of this book. This moral education must be rooted in one or more of the philosophical traditions I have presented. It must take account of what we have learned from psychology and the social sciences about individuals and about the influence of groups and institutions on personal moral conduct. For all forms of moral education, but especially those in religious contexts, particular theological traditions offer perspectives grounded in religious faith and thus provide rich sources of motivation. Finally, a contemporary moral education must look to the curriculum development and methodology which scholars and practitioners have provided.

I am convinced that a wise and selective use of these components can form the basis for a moral education in the many agencies and institutions of society. Yet having reached the end of this study of the theories and research of the academic disciplines, I feel that one additional perspective is needed for the enterprise. It needs to include a sensitivity to the artistic dimension of life. The moral life is one that is lived beautifully. It is a life in which we express our deepest feelings and intuitions. From this perspective the moral educator is an artist in both the conduct of life and in the teaching of students.

I use the term artist to indicate one who has a skill or proficiency in producing something which is beautiful. There is a special beauty in the morally good person. This beauty comes from a harmonizing of diverse and conflicting parts. From the ancient Greeks we have received the notion that the moral person is the good and beautiful person who has made best use of natural endowments and virtue. In Judaism the good and learned person is called a beautiful person, a person of love and justice. Christians call their moral and beautiful persons saints and holy ones.

The moral person is an artist and has artistry in conduct because what he or she fashions is a beautiful thing to behold. Human lives are to be ultimately judged as works of art, by their power to express what is deepest within them. All cultures hold before their young certain heroes who are to be imitated for the expressiveness of their moral traits and actions. All religious groups hold up certain persons as saints who possess a unique moral beauty which is unusually pleasing and attractive to members of that group. The lives of heroes and saints are read because they are lives of beauty whose rich texture draws both to contemplation and to imitation. The gift of the artist is to able to grasp what is essential, appropriate, and fitting and to present it in such a way that we are attracted to it, admire it, embrace it and imitate it in our actions.

Moral persons are artistic creations because in their uniqueness they are not bound by the conventions of their culture. They incorporate the best of what is in the culture but go beyond it. As artists they cannot be dictated to by what is external to them but rather follow an inner voice or power. These persons often travel different roads from their contemporaries. Such persons are not always recognized in their own times because of their freedom from the compulsions and conventions of society. Contemporaries of Joan of Arc and Thomas More did not see them as saints. Yet through the works of George Bernard Shaw and Robert Bolt we are privileged to see the artistic beauty of their lives.

Moral persons have a certain moral style that others find compelling. We are moved by the particular moral styles of Jesus, Gandhi, Martin Luther King, and in our time the styles of Elie Wiesel and Mother Theresa of Calcutta. To lack moral style is to lack imagination. The moral person is interesting, imaginative, and distinctive as are works of art. The conventionally pious do-gooder lacks style and is uninteresting. Style refers not only to what is done but also to how it is done. Just as painters and novelists have a distinctive style which presents the beautiful to us, so persons through their moral behavior reveal a distinctive style. I have been taught by teachers, treated by nurses and doctors, some of whom performed their tasks adequately, efficiently and mechanically. Others revealed a moral beauty of personality in the way they related to me and to others.

The beauty of the moral person has a fulness of life which enables this person to tower over others. Though it takes great effort to be moral, the moral person, like the artist, appears to work effortlessly. Such persons have subtle perceptions, flexible attitudes, open minds, and wider perspectives. Like all works of art, every time we encounter them we are moved, we discover new facets. Such persons appear to deal well with the ordinary but they deal with it in a distinctively graceful manner. As works of art moral persons do not have to draw attention to themselves, but are rather recognized by others for the beauty of their lives and its expression.

All who would want to be moral educators must labor to become works of moral beauty themselves. The difficulty of this task may be one reason why many prefer to avoid it and prefer to educate for self fulfillment and for work in the world. To be a moral educator implies both being a moral person and educating in a moral manner. Moral artistry in teaching means more than demanding obedience. It requires an education that takes great account of individual temperaments and endowments. The teacher as artist puts greater emphasis on self-knowledge, self-discipline, and personal style in the moral life. This entails making fuller assumptions about the openness of persons to imagination, reflection, and receptivity to new experiences.

The teacher's task in moral education from an artistic perspective is to be a good model of artistry in moral conduct, to expose students to models in life and in the arts, and to encourage persons in their own artistic endeavors. The humanities and the fine arts can be a source of inspiration and criticism for such an endeavor. Works of art prevent us from missing the beauty in life by opening us to the deepest expressions of the human spirit. Storytelling, writing and reading poetry, and painting are to be encouraged not only for their powers of expression but also for their power to inspire persons to greater moral heights.

REFERENCES

Abbott, Walter, ed. *Documents of Vatican II*. New York: America Press, 1965.

Adler, Mortimer. *How to Read a Book: The Art of Getting a Liberal Education*. New York: Simon and Schuster, 1940.

Adler, Mortimer. *Paideia*. New York: Macmillan, 1982

Allport, Gordon. *Becoming; Basic Considerations for a Psychology of Personality*. New Haven: Yale University Press, 1955.

Allport, Gordon. "The Religious Context of Prejudice." *Journal for the Scientific Study of Religion*, 1966, 4, 447–457.

Alpert, J. L., and Richardson, M. S. "Parenting." In L. W. Poon, ed. *Aging in the 1980's*. American Psychological Association, 1980.

Anyon, Jean. "Social Class and the Hidden Curriculum of Work." In Henry Giroux and David Purpel, eds. *The Hidden Curriculum and Moral Education*. Berkeley: McCutchan, 1983.

Apple, Michael. *Ideology and Curriculum*. Boston: Routledge and Kegan Paul, 1979.

Aronfreed, Justin. *Conduct and Conscience: The Socialization of Internalized Control over Behavior*. New York: Academic Press, 1968.

✓ Aronfreed, Justin. "Some Problems for a Theory of the Acquisition of Conscience." In C. Beck et al., eds. *Moral Education: Interdisciplinary Approaches*. New York: Paulist, 1971.

Aronfreed, Justin. "Moral Development from the Standpoint of General Psychological Theory." In Thomas Lickona, ed. *Moral Development and Behavior*. New York: Holt, Rinehart and Winston, 1976.

Asham, Roger. *The Scholemaster*. London: Cassell, 1900.

Baltes, P. B., and Schaie, K. W. "On the Plasticity of Intelligence in Adulthood and Old Age: Where Horn and Donaldson Fail." *American Psychologist*, 1976, 31, 720–725.

Bandura, Albert. *Social Learning*. Englewood Cliffs, N. J.: Prentice Hall, 1977.

Baumrind, D. "Current Patterns of Parental Authority." *Developmental Psychology Monographs*, 1971, 4. 21–31

✓ Beck, Clive, et al. *The Moral Education Project, Year 3*. Toronto: Ontario Ministry of Education, 1976.

Beck, Clive, et al. *The Moral Education Project, Year 5*. Toronto: Ontario Ministry of Education, 1978.

Beck, Clive. "The Reflective Approach to Values Education." In Jonas Soltis, ed. *Philosophy of Education*. Eightieth Yearbook of the National Society for the Study of Education. Chicago: University of Chicago, 1981.

Beck, Clive, Crittenden, Brian, and Sullivan, Edward, eds. *Moral Education: Interdisciplinary Approaches*. New York: Paulist, 1971.

Beck, George. "Aims in Education: Neo-Thomism." In T. H. B. Hollins, ed., *Aims in Education*. Manchester, Eng.: Manchester University Press, 1964.

✓ Bellah, Robert et al. *Habits of the Heart: Individualism and Commitment in American Life*. Berkeley: University of California, 1985.

Benedict, Ruth. *Patterns of Culture*. Boston: Houghton-Mifflin, 1956 (1934).

Berger, Peter, and Luckmann, Thomas. *The Social Construction of Reality*. New York: Doubleday, 1966.

Bloom, Allan. *The Closing of the American Mind.* New York: Simon and Schuster, 1987.

Bowles, Samuel, and Gintis, Herbert. *Schooling in a Capitalist Society.* New York: Basic Books, 1976.

Brim, Orville. "Socialization through the Life Span." In O. Brim and S. Wheeler, eds., *Socialization after Childhood: Two Essays.* New York: Wiley, 1966.

Brittain, Clay. "An Exploration of the Bases of Peer-Compliance and Parent-Compliance in Adolescence." *Adolescence,* 1967–8, 12, 24–32.

Brittain, Clay. "Adolescent Choices and Parent-Peer Cross-Pressures," in R. Muuss, ed., *Adolescent Behavior and Society.* New York: Random House, 1971.

Browning, Don, ed. *Practical Theology: The Emerging Field in Theology, Church, and World.* New York: Harper and Row, 1983.

Broudy, Harry, and Palmer, John. *Exemplars of Teaching Method.* Chicago: Rand McNally, 1965.

Buber, Martin. *The Eclipse of God: Studies in the Relation between Religion and Philosophy.* New York: Harper and Row, 1957.

Buber, Martin. *I and Thou.* New York: Scribner, 1958.

Buber, Martin. *Between Man and Man.* New York: MacMillan 1965 (1947).

Burgess, Harold. *An Invitation to Religious Education.* Birmingham, Ala.: Religious Education Press, 1975.

Burnett, Joe. "Whatever Happened to John Dewey." *Teachers College Record,* Winter 1979, 81, 2, 192–210.

Burns, James M. *Leadership.* New York: Harper, 1978.

Byrnes, Lawrence. *Religion and Public Education.* New York: Harper and Row, 1975.

Callahan, Daniel, and Bok, Sisela, eds. *Ethics Teaching in Higher Education.* New York: Plenum Press, 1980.

Camus, Albert. *The Myth of Sisyphus.* New York: Knopf, 1955.

Chapman, William. *Roots of Character Education: An Exploration of the American Heritage from the Decade of the 1920's.* Schenectady, New York: Character Research Press, 1977.

Castle, Edgar Bradshaw. *Educating the Good Man: Moral Education in Christian Times.* New York: Macmillan, 1958.

Chazan, Barry. "Who is Moral Man?" *Religious Education,* 1976, 71, 1, 27–39.

Chazan, Barry. "Jewish Education and Moral Development." In B. Munsey, ed. *Moral Development, Moral Education, and Kohlberg.* Birmingham, Ala.: Religious Education Press, 1980.

Chazan, Barry. *Contemporary Approaches to Moral Education.* New York: Teachers College Press, 1985.

Chazan, Barry, and Soltis, Jonas, eds. *Moral Education.* New York: Teachers College Press, 1973.

Cochrane, D. B., Hamm, C. M., Kazepides, A. C., eds. *The Domain of Moral Education.* New York: Paulist, 1979.

Coe, George. *Education in Religion and Morals.* New York: Fleming Revell Co., 1904

Coe, George, *A Social Theory of Religious Education.* New York: Scribner, 1917.

Cohen, Adir. "The Question of Values and Value Education in the Philosophy of Martin Buber." *Teachers College Record,* 1979, 80, 4, 743–770.

Coleman, James, ed. *Youth: Transition to Adulthood.* Chicago: University of Chicago, 1974.

Comenius, John. *The Great Didactic.* Translated by M. W. Keatinge. London: Adam and Charles Black, 1896 (1632).

Comstock, George et al. *Television and Human Behavior.* New York: Columbia University Press, 1978.

Conger, J. J. *Adolescence and Youth.* 2nd ed. New York: Harper and Row, 1977.

Craib, Ian. *Modern Social Theory: From Parsons to Habermas.* New York: St. Martin's Press, 1984.

Cremin, Lawrence. *The Transformation of the School: Progressivism in American Education, 1876–1957.* New York: Random House, 1961.

Cremin, Lawrence. *American Education: The Colonial Experience 1607–1783.* New York: Harper and Row, 1970.

Curran, Charles. *Themes in Fundamental Theology.* Notre Dame: Notre Dame Press, 1977.

Curti, Merle. *The Social Ideas of American Educators.* Paterson, N. J.: Littlefield, Adams and Co., 1959 (1935).

Curtis, Russell. "Adolescent Orientations toward Parents and Peers: Variations by Sex, Age, and Socioeconomic Status." *Adolescence.* 1975, 10, 4, 45–53.

Dewey, John. *John Dewey on Education.* New York: Macmillan, 1916.

Dewey, John. *Democracy in Education.* Ed. and Introd. by Reginald Archambault. Chicago: University of Chicago, 1964.

Dewey, John. *Experience and Education.* New York: MacMillan, 1938.

Dewey, John, and Tufts, James. *Ethics.* Jo Ann Boydston, ed. Southern Illinois University Press, 1978.

Dittes, James. "Religion, Prejudice, and Personality." In Merton Strommen, ed., *Research on Religious Development.* New York: Hawthorn, 1971.

Dorff, Elliot. "Study Leads to Action." *Religious Education*, 1980, 75, 2, 171–192.

Dreeben, Robert. *On What is Learned in Schools.* Reading, Mass.: Addison-Wesley, 1968.

Dujarier, Michael. *A History of the Catechumenate.* New York: Sadlier, 1979.

Durkheim, Emile. *Moral Education: A Study in the Theory and Application of the Sociology of Education.* New York: Free Press, 1961 (1925).

Dykstra, Craig. *Vision and Character: A Christian Educator's Alternative to Kohlberg.* New York: Paulist, 1981.

Easton, David, and Hess, Robert. "The Child's Political World." *Midwest Journal of Political Science*, 1962, 6, 229–246

Elias, John. *Psychology and Religious Education,* Melbourne, Fla.: Krieger Publishing Co., 1983.

Elias, John. *Studies in Theology and Education.* Melbourne, Fla.: Krieger Publishing Co., 1986.

Elliot, Harrison. *Can Religious Education be Christian?* New York: Macmillan, 1940.

Engel, David, ed. *Religion and Public Education.* New York: Paulist, 1974.

Erasmus, Desiderius. *The Education of a Christian Prince.* Translated by Lester Bor. New York: Columbia University Press, 1936.

Erikson, Erik. *Young Man Luther,* New York: Norton, 1958.

Erikson, Erik. *Childhood and Society.* New York: Norton, 1962.

Erikson, Erik. *Insight and Responsibility.* New York: Norton, 1964.

Erikson, Erik. *Life History and the Historical Movement.* New York: Norton, 1975.

Ernsberger, D. J., and Manaster, G. J. "Moral Development, Intrinsic/Extrinsic Religious Orientation and Denominational Teachings." *Genetic Psychology Monographs*, 1981, 104, pp. 23–41.

Eysenck, H. J. *Crime and Punishment.* Third Edition. St. Alban, Hertsforshire: Granada Publishing, 1977.

Fahs, Sylvia. *Today's Children and Yesterday's Heritage.* Boston: Beacon, 1952.

Fee, Joan, Greeley, Andrew, McCready, William, and Sullivan, Theresa. *Young Catholics: A Report to the Knights of Columbus.* New York Sadlier, 1981.

Felder, Avraham. "Kohlberg's Theory and the Religious Jew." *Religious Education*, 1984, 79, 2, 163–183.

Feldman, Kenneth, and Newcomb, Theodore. *The Impact of College on Students.* San Francisco: Jossey-Bass, 1969.

Fenelon, François. *The Education of Girls.* Paris: A. Chevel, 1920 (1601).

Fenton, Thomas P., ed. *Education for Justice: A Resource Manual.* New York: Orbis, 1975.

Frankena, William. "A Model for Analyzing a Philosophy of Education." In Jane Martin, ed. *Readings in the Philosophy of Education.* Boston: Allyn and Bacon, 1970.

Freire, Paulo. *Pedagogy of the Oppressed.* New York: Seabury, 1970.

Freire, Paulo. *Education for Critical Consciousness.* New York: Seabury, 1973.

Freud, Sigmund. *New Introductory Lectures on Psychoanalysis.* New York: Norton, 1933.

Friedenberg, Edgar. *The Vanishing Adolescent.* Boston: Beacon Press, 1959.

Froebel, Friedrich. *The Education of Man.* New York: Appleton, 1911.

Gans, Herbert. *The Urban Villagers.* New York: The Free Press, 1962.

Geertz, Clifford. *The Interpretation of Cultures.* New York: Harper and Row, 1973.

Gibbs, John. "Kohlberg's Stages of Moral Development: A Constructive Criticism." *Harvard Educational Review*, 1977, 44, 43–61.

Gilligan, Carol. *In Another Voice.* Cambridge, Mass.: Harvard University Press, 1982.

Giroux Henry. *Ideology, Culture, and the Process of Schooling.* Phila.: Temple University Press, 1981.

Giroux, Henry, and Purpel, David, eds. *The Hidden Curriculum and Moral Education.* Berkeley, California: McCutchan, 1983.

Goodman, Norma. "Adolescent Norms and Behavior: Organization and Conformity." *Merrill Palmer Quarterly*, 1969, 15, 2.

Goodman, Ruth. "Dialogue and Hasidism: Elements in Buber's Philosophy of Education." *Religious Education*, 1978, 73, 1, 69–79.

Gordon, Haim. "The Hasidic Stories of Martin Buber." *Religious Education,* 1977, 72, 1, 61–73. (a)

Gordon, Haim. "Martin Buber's Impact on Religious Education: Reflection on the Centennial of his Birth." *Religious Education*, 1977, 72, 6, 580–594. (b)

Greeley, Andrew. *Catholic Schools in a Declining Church.* Kansas City: Sheed and Ward, 1976.

Greenberg, Bradley et al. *Life on Television: Content Analysis of US TV Dramas.* Norwood, New Jersey, Albex, 1980.

Griswold, A. Whitney. *Liberal Education and the Democratic Ideal.* New Haven: Yale University Press, 1959.

Grusec, John et al. "Learning Resistance to Temptation through Observation." *Developmental Psychology*, 1979, 15, 133–240.

Gustafson, James. "Education for Moral Responsibility." In Nancy and Theodore Sizer, eds. *Moral Education.* Cambridge, Mass.: Harvard University Press, 1970.

Gustafson, James. *Protestant and Roman Catholic Ethics.* Chicago: University of Chicago, 1978.

Guthrie, W. K. C. (Trans.) *Plato: Protagoras and Meno.* Baltimore: Penguin, 1956.

Hale, Nathan. "Freud's Reflections on Work and Love." In Erik Erikson and Neil Smelser, eds. *Themes of Work and Love in Adulthood.* Cambridge, Mass.: Harvard University Press, 1980.

Hall, Robert T. *Moral Education: A Handbook for Teachers.* Minneapolis: Winston, 1979.

Hamm, Cornel. "Moral Education without Religion." In D. B. Cochrane, C. M. Hamm, and A. C. Kazepides. eds. *The Domain of Moral Education.* New York: Paulist, 1979.

Hardie, C. D. *Truth and Fallacy in Educational Theory.* Cambridge, Eng., 1942.

Haring, Bernard. *The Law of Christ.* 3 vols. Westminster, Md.: Newman Press, 1961–66.

Hartshorne, Hugh. *Manual for Training in Worship.* New York: Scribner, 1915

Hartshorne, Hugh, and May, Mark. *Studies in the Nature of Character.* Volume I, II, III. 1926, 1929, 1930.

Hauerwas, Stanley. "Character, Narrative, and Growth in the Christian Life." In C. Brussels-man (Convener), *Towards Moral and Religious Maturity.* Morristown, N. J.: Silver Burdett, 1980.

Henle, Robert. "A Roman Catholic View of Education." In P. Phenix, ed. *Philosophies of Education.* New York: Wiley. 1965.

Herbert, Johann Freidrich. *The Science of Education.* Boston: Heath, 1893.

Hersch, Richard, Paolitto, Diana, and Reimer, Joseph. *Promoting Moral Growth: From Piaget to Kohlberg.* New York: Longman, 1979.

Hersch, Richard, Miller, John, and Fielding, Glen. *Models of Moral Education: An Appraisal.* New York: Longman, 1980.

Hess, Robert, and Torney, Judith. *The Development of Political Attitudes in Children.* Chicago: Aldine, 1967.

Hill, Brian. *Education and the Endangered Individual.* New York: Dell Publishing Co., 1973.

Hirst, Paul. *Moral Education in a Secular Society.* London: University of London, 1974.

Hoffman, Martin. "Development of Internal Moral Standards in Children." In Merton Strommen, ed. *Research on Religious Development.* New York: Hawthorn, 1971.

Hofmann, Justin. "Religion, Ethics, and Moral Education in Judaism." *Religious Education,* 1982, 77, 1, 57–68.

Hoge, Dean. *Commitment on Campus: Changes in Religion and Values over Five Decades.* Phila.: Westminster Press, 1974.

Hollins, T. H. B. "The Problem of Values and John Dewey." In T. H. B. Hollins, ed. *Aims in Education: The Philosophic Approach.* Manchester: Manchester University Press, 1964.

Howe, Reuel. *Miracle of Dialogue.* New York: Seabury, 1963

Hurn, Christopher. *The Limits and Possibilities of Schooling.* Boston: Allyn and Bacon, 1978.

Husserl, Edmund. *Being and Time.* 1927.

Hutchins, Robert. *The Learning Society.* New York: Praeger, 1968.

Hyman, Herbert. *Political Socialization: A Study in the Psychology of Political Behavior.* New York: Free Press, 1959.

Iacovetta, R. G. "Adolescent-Adult Interaction and Peer-Group Involvement." *Adolescence,* 1975, 10, 38.

Ignatius Loyola. *Ignatius Loyola and the Ratio Studiorum.* by E. A. Fitzpatrick. New York: McGraw Hill, 1933.

Jackson, Philip. *Life in Classrooms.* New York: Holt, Rinehart, and Winston, 1968.

James, William. *Talks to Teachers: On Psychology.* New York: Norton, 1958 (1892).

Kaestle, Carl. *The Evolution of an Urban School System, New York City, 1750–1850.* Cambridge: Harvard University Press, 1973.

Kant, Immanuel. *Education.* Ann Arbor: University of Michigan Press, 1960.

Kanter, Rosabeth Moss. *Men and Women of the Corporation.* New York: Basic Books, 1977.

Kaufman, Walter. *Critique of Religion and Philosophy.* Garden City, New York: Doubleday, 1961.

Keane, Philip. *Christian Ethics and the Imagination.* New York: Paulist, 1984.

Keniston, Kenneth. *Youth and Dissent: The Rise of a New Opposition.* New York: Harcourt, Brace and World, 1970.

Kierkegaard, Soren. *Fear and Trembling.* Princeton: Princeton University Press, 1941.

Kinsey, A. C. et al. *Sexual Behavior in the Human Male.* Phila.: Saunders, 1948.

Kinsey, A. C. et al. *Sexual Behavior in the Human Female.* New York: Pocket Books, 1963.

Kirschenbaum, Howard. *Advanced Values Clarification.* La Jolla, Calif.: University Associates, 1977.

Kluckholn, Clyde. *Culture and Behavior.* New York: Free Press, 1962.

Kohlberg, Lawrence. "Moral Education, Religious Education, and the Public Schools: A

Developmental View." In Theodore Sizer, ed. *Religion and Public Education*. Boston: Houghton Mifflin, 1967.

Kohlberg, Lawrence. "Stages of Moral Develpment as a Basis for Moral Education." In C. Beck et al., eds. *Moral Education: Interdisciplinary Approaches*. New York: Paulist, 1971.

Kohlberg, Lawrence. "The Implications of Moral Stages for Adult Education." *Religious Education*, 1977, 72, 6, 183–201.

Kohlberg, Lawrence. "Educating for a Just Society: An Updated and Revised Version." In Brenda Munsey, ed., *Moral Development, Moral Education, and Kohlberg*. Birmingham, Ala.: Religious Education Press, 1980.

Kohlberg, Lawrence. *Essays on Moral Development: Volume I: The Philosophy of Moral Development*. N. Y.: Harper and Row, 1981.

Kohlberg, Lawrence. "A Reply to Owen Flanagan and Some Comments on the Puka-Goodpaster Exchange." *Ethics*, 1982, 92, 3, 513–528.

Kohlberg, Lawrence. *Essays on Moral Development: Volume II: The Psychology of Moral Development*. San Francisco: Harper and Row, 1984.

Kohlberg, Lawrence, and Kramer, Robert. "Continuities and Discontinuities in Childhood and Adult Moral Development." *Human Development*, 1969, 12, 93–120.

Kohn, Melvin. "Job Complexity and Adult Personality." In Neil Smelser and Eric Erikson, eds. *Themes of Work and Love in Adulthood*. Cambridge, Mass.: Harvard University Press, 1980.

Kon, Igor, and Losenkov, Vladunur. "Friendship in Adolescence: Values and Behavior." *Journal of Marriage and the Family*, 1978, 40, 1.

Kurines, W., and Grief, E. "The Development of Moral Thought: Review and Evaluation of Kohlberg's Approach." *Psychological Bulletin*, 1974, 81, 453–470.

LaBelle, Thomas. "An Anthropological Study of Education." *Teachers College Record*, 1972, 73, 4, 519–538.

Lasseigne, Mary. "A Study of Peer and Adult Influence on Moral Beliefs of Adolescents." *Adolescence*, 1975, 10, 38.

Lebacqx, Karen. *Professional Ethics: Power and Paradox*. Nashville: Abingdon Press, 1985.

Lee, James M. *The Shape of Religious Instruction*. Birmingham, Ala.: Religious Education Press, 1971.

Lee, James M. *The Flow of Religious Instruction*. Birmingham, Ala.: Religious Education Press, 1973.

Lee, James M. *The Content of Religious Instruction*. Birmingham, Ala.: Religious Education Press, 1984.

Lefurgy, William, and Woloshin, Gerald. "Immediate and Long-term Effects of Experimentally Induced Social Influence in the Modification of Adolescents' Moral Judgments." *Journal of Personality and Social Psychology*, 1969, 12, 2.

Leichter, Hope Jensen. "Some Perspectives on the Family as Educator." *Teachers College Record*, 1974, 76, 2, 175–217.

Locke, John. *The Educational Writings of John Locke*. Edited by James Axtell. Cambridge: Cambridge University Press, 1968.

Lowenthal, M. F., Thurnber, M., and Chiriboga, D. *Four Stages of Life*. San Francisco: Jossey-Bass, 1975.

MacIntyre, Alistair. *After Virtue*. Notre Dame, Ind.: Notre Dame Press, 1977.

MacKenzie, Michael. *Hegel's Educational Theory and Practice*. 1909.

McClellan, James. *Philosophy of Education*. Englewood Cliffs, N. J.: Prentice Hall, 1976.

McDonagh, Enda. "Moral Theology and Moral Development." In C. Brusselsman, Convener, *Toward Moral and Religious Maturity*. Morristown, N. J.: Silver Burdett, 1980.

McGucken, William. "The Philosophy of Catholic Education." In *Philosophies of Education*, National Society for the Study of Education. University of Chicago Press, 1942.

McPhail, Peter, Ungoed-Thomas, John, and Chapman, Hilary. *Lifeline*. Niles, Ill.: Argus Communications, 1975.

Maitland, Karen, and Goldman, Jacquelin. "Moral Judgment as a Function of Peer Group Interaction." *Journal of Personality and Social Psychology*, 1974, 30, 5.

Marcel, Gabriel. *Problematic Man*. New York: Herder and Herder, 1967.

Maritain, Jacques. *Education at the Crossroads*. New Haven: Yale University Press, 1943.

Maritain, Jacques. *The Education of Man*. Edited and with an Introduction by Donald and Idella Gallagher. Notre Dame, Ind.: Notre Dame Press, 1962.

Marthaler, Berard. "Socialization as a Model for Catechesis." In P. O'Hare, ed. *Foundations of Religious Education*. New York: Paulist, 1978.

Maslow, Abraham. *Religions, Values, and Peak Experiences*. N.Y.: Viking, 1964.

Maslow, Abraham. *Toward a Psychology of Being*. N.Y.: Nostrand, 1968.

Mead, Margaret. *Culture and Commitment*. N.Y.: Doubleday, 1970.

Media Action Research Center. *Media and Values*. Los Angeles: 1962 South Shenandoah, 90034, 1980.

Metcalf, Lawrence, ed. *Values Education: Rationale, Strategies, and Procedures*. Washington, D.C.: National Council for the Social Studies, 1971.

Milgram, Stanley. *Obedience to Authority*. New York: Harper and Row, 1974.

Milhaven, Giles. *Toward a New Catholic Morality*. New York: Doubleday, 1970.

Miller, Donald E. *The Wing-Footed Wanderer: Conscience and Transcendence*. Nashville, Tenn.: Abingdon, 1977.

Miller, N. E., and Dollard, J. *Social Learning Theory and Imitation*. New Haven: Yale University Press, 1941.

Neil, A. S. *The Free Child*. London: Jenkins Ltd., 1953.

Neil, A. S. *Summerhill: A Radical Approach to Child Rearing*. New York: Hart Publishing Co., 1960.

Nelson, C. Ellis. *Where Faith Begins*. Atlanta: Knox, 1967.

√ √Nelson, C. Ellis. "What has Religion to do with Morality." *The Living Light*, 1973, 10, 3.

Neusner, Jacob. *Invitation to the Talmud*. New York: Harper and Row, 1973.

Newmann, Fred. *Education for Citizen Action: Challenge for Secondary Curriculum*. Berkeley, Calif.: McCutchan, 1975.

Newnham, William. *The Principles of Physical, Intellectual, Moral and Religious Education*. England, 1827.

Nietzsche, Frederich. *Thus Spake Zarathustra*. Walter Kaufmann, ed. and trans. New York: Viking, 1966.

Noddings, Nel. *Caring: A Feminine Approach to Ethics and Moral Education*. Berkeley, Cal.: University of California Press, 1984.

Nozich, Robert. *State, Anarchy, and Utopia*. Cambridge, Mass.: Harvard University Press, 1974.

O'Connell, Timothy. *Principles for a Catholic Morality*. New York: Seabury, 1976.

O'Connor, D. J. *An Introduction to the Philosophy of Education*. London: Routledge and Kegan Paul, 1957.

√ √ O'Donohoe, James. "Moral and Faith Development Theory." In C. Brusselsman, Convener, *Toward Moral and Religious Maturity*. Morristown, N. J.: Silver Burdett, 1980.

OISE. "Myself and Other People: Values Series, Year 1, Unit 6." Ontario: Ontario Institute for Studies in Education, n. d.

Oliver, Donald, and Bane Mary Jane. "Moral Education: Is Reasoning Enough." In C. Beck et al. *Moral Education: Interdisciplinary Approaches*. Baltimore: Newman Press, 1971.

Parks, Sharon. *The Critical Tears: The Young Adult Search for a Faith to Live By*. San Francisco: Harper and Row, 1986.

Parsons, Talcott, "The School as a Social System: Some of its Functions in American Society." *Harvard Educational Review*, 1959, 29, 4, 297–318.

Parsons, Talcott, and Bales, Robert. *Family Socialization and the Interaction Process*. New York: The Free Press, 1955.

Perkinson, Henry. *The Imperfect Panacea: American Faith in Education, 1865–1976*. Second edition. New York: Random House, 1977.

Pestalozzi, Johann Heinrich. *How Gertrude Teaches her Children*. Syracuse: Bardeen, 1894.

Peters, Richard S. *Ethics and Education*. Chicago: Scott Foresman, 1966.

Peters, Richard S. "Moral Principles and Moral Education." In D. Cochrane et al., eds. *The Moral Domain*. New York: Paulist, 1979.

Peters, Richard S. "Democratic Values and Educational Aims." *Teachers College Record*, 1979, 80, 3, 463–482.

Peters, Richard S. *Moral Development and Moral Education*. London: George Allen and Unwin, 1981.

Piaget, Jean. *The Moral Judgment of the Child*. New York: Free Press, 1965 (1922).

Pius XI. *Sixteen Encyclicals of His Holiness Pius XI*. Washington, D.C.: National Catholic Welfare Conference, 1936 (1929).

Postman, Neil. *Teaching as a Conservative Activity*. Delacorte, 1979.

Raths, Louis, Harmin, Merrill, and Simon, Sidney. *Values and Teaching*. Columbus, Ohio: Merrill, 1966.

Raths, Louis, Harmin, Merrill, and Simon, Sidney. *Values and Teaching*. Second edition. Columbus, Ohio: Merrill, 1978.

Rawls, John. *A Theory of Justice*. Cambridge, Mass.: Harvard University Press, 1971.

Rizzutto, Ana Maria. *The Birth of the Living God*. Chicago: University of Chicago Press, 1979.

Rogers, Carl. *Freedom to Learn*. Columbus, Ohio: Merrill, 1969.

Rokeach, Milton. *The Nature of Human Values*. New York: Free Press, 1975.

Rood, Wayne. *Understanding Christian Education*. Nashville: Abingdon, 1970.

Rosenthal, T. L., and Zimmerman, B. J. *Social Learning and Cognition*. New York: Academic Press, 1977.

Rousseau, Jean Jacques. *Emile*. New York: Teachers College Press, 1956.

Rushton, J. Philippe. "Socialization and the Altruistic Behavior of Children." *Psychological Bulletin*, 1976, 83, 898–913.

Rushton, J. Philippe. *Altruism, Socialization, and Society*. Englewood Cliffs, N. J.: Prentice Hall, 1980.

Rushton, J. Philippe, and Campbell, A. C. "Modeling, Vicarious Reinforcement and Extraversion on Blood Donating in Adults." *European Journal of Social Psychology*, 1977, 7, 297–306.

Rushton, J. Philippe, and Teachmen, G. "The Effects of Positive Reinforcement, Attribution, and Punishment on Model induced Altruism in Children." *Personality and Social Psychology Bulletin*, 1978, 4, 322–25.

Rushton, J. Philippe. "Altruism and Society. A Social Learning Perspective. *Ethics*, 1982, 92, 3, 425–446.

Ryle, Gilbert. *The Concept of Mind*. New York: Barnes and Noble, 1949.

Sapp, Gary L. "Moral Judgment and Religious Orientation." In Gary L. Sapp, ed., *Handbook of Moral Development*. Birmingham, Ala.: Religious Education Press, 1986.

Sapp, Gary L., ed. *Handbook of Moral Development*. Birmingham, Ala.: Religious Education Press, 1986.

Sartre, Jean-Paul. *Nausea*. London: Purnell and Sons. 1949.

Sartre, Jean-Paul. *Being and Nothingness*. New York: Philosophical Library, 1956.

Sartre, Jean-Paul. *No Exit*. New York: Knopf, 1948.

Scheffler, Israel. *The Language of Education*. Springfield, Ill.: Charles C. Thomas, 1960.

Scriven, Michael. "Cognitive Moral Education." *Kappan*, 1975, 56, 10, 689–694.

Sears, Robert, Maccoby, Eleanor, and Levin, Harry. *Patterns of Child Rearing*. Chicago: Row, Pearson, and Co., 1957.

Shorter, Edward. *The Making of the Modern Family*. New York: Basic Books, 1975.

Silberman, Charles. *Crisis in the Classroom*. New York: Random House, 1970.

Siman, Michael. "Application of a New Model of Peer Group Influence to Naturally Existing Adolescent Friendship Groups." *Child Development*, 1977, 48, 1.

Simon, Sidney. "Three Ways to Teach Church School." In Howard Kirschenbaum and Sidney Simon, eds. *Readings in Values Clarification*. Minneapolis: Winston, 1973.

Simon, Sidney, Daitch, Patricia, and Hartwell, Marie. "Value Clarification: New Mission for Religious Education." In Howard Kirschenbaum and Sidney Simon, eds. *Readings in Values Clarification*. Minneapolis: Winston, 1973.

Skinner, B. F. *Beyond Freedom and Dignity*. New York: Knopf, 1971.

Sloan, Douglas. "The Teaching of Ethics in the American Undergraduate Curriculum, 1876–1975." In Daniel Callahan and Sisela Bok, eds. *Ethics Teaching in Higher Education*. New York: Plenum Press, 1980.

Sloan, Ted, and Hogan, Robert. "Moral Development in Adulthood: Lifestyle Processes." In Gary L. Sapp, ed., *Handbook of Moral Development*. Birmingham, Ala.: Religious Education Press, 1986.

Spencer, Herbert. *Education: Intellectual, Moral and Physical*. Paterson, N. J.: Littlefield, Adams and Co., 1963 (1884).

Spilka, Bernard, Hood, Ralph, and Gorsuch, Richard. *The Psychology of Religion: An Empirical Approach*. Englewood Cliffs, N. J.: Prentice Hall, 1985.

Standing, E. M. *Maria Montessori: Her Life and Work*. New York: New American Library, 1957.

Strickland, Charles, and Burgess, Charles, eds. *Health, Growth and Heredity: G. Stanley Hall on Natural Education*. New York: Teachers College Press, 1965.

Sullivan, Edmund and Beck, Clive. "Moral Education in a Canadian Setting." *Kappan* 1975, 61(10), pp. 697–701.

Sullivan, Edmund. "A Study of Kohlberg's Structural Theory of Moral Development: A Critique of Liberal Social Science Ideology." *Human Development*, 1977, 20, 352–376.

Sullivan, Edmund. "The Scandalized Child: Children, Media, and Commodity Culture." In C. Brusselsman, Convener, *Toward Moral and Religious Maturity*. Morristown, N. J.: Silver Burdett, 1980.

Taylor, Monica, ed. *Progress and Problems in Moral Education*. Slough, England: National Foundation for Educational Research in England and Wales, 1975.

Tillich, Paul. *Systematic Theology, Vol. 1*. Chicago: University of Chicago, 1951.

Tolstoy, Leo. *Tolstoy on Education*. Translated by Leo Wiener. Chicago: University of Chicago Press, 1967 (1862).

Vanderberg, Donald. *Being and Education: An Essay in Existential Phenomenology*. Englewood Cliffs, N. J.: Prentice Hall, 1971.

Vandenberg, Donald. "Existential and Phenomenological Influences in Educational Philosophy." *Teachers College Record*, Winter 1979, 81, 2, 166–191.

Van Doren, Mark. *Liberal Education*. Boston: Beacon, 1959.

Velasquez, Manuel G. *Business Ethics: Concepts and Cases*. Englewood Cliffs, N. J.: Prentice Hall, 1982.

Wallwork, Ernest. "Morality, Religion, and Kohlberg's Theory." In B. Munsey, ed. *Moral Development, Moral Education, and Kohlberg*. Birmingham, Ala.: Religious Education Press, 1980.

Wasserman, Elsa. "Implementing Kohlberg's Just Community Concept." In Peter Scharf, ed.,

Readings in Moral Education. Minneapolis: Winston, 1980.

Weigert, Andrew, and Thomas, Darwin. "Parental Support, Control and Adolescent Religiosity." *Journal for the Scientific Study of Religion,* 1972, 11, 4.

√ Westerhoff, John. *Will Our Children Have Faith.* New York: Seabury, 1976.

✓ Westerhoff, John, and Neville, Gwen. *Generation to Generation.* Phila.: Pilgrim Press, 1974.

Whyte, William. *Men at Work.* Homewood, Ill.: Dorsey Press, 1961.

Wilson, John, Williams, Norman, and Sugarman, Barry. *Introduction to Moral Education.* Baltimore: Penguin, 1967.

Wilson, John. "Approach to Moral Education." *Religious Education,* 1970, 65, 6, 467–473.

Wong, David. *Moral Relativity.* Berkeley: University of California Press, 1984.

Wright, Derek. *The Psychology of Moral Behavior.* Baltimore: Penguin, 1971.

Wyse, Thomas. *Education Reform.* England, 1936.

Yankelovich, Daniel. *The Changing Values on Campus: Political and Personal Attitudes of Today's College Students.* New York: Washington Square Press, 1972.

Yankelovich, Daniel. *The New Morality: A Profile of American Youth in the 1970's.* New York: McGraw-Hill, 1974.

√√Yaron, Zvi. "Religion and Morality in Israel and the Diaspora." In M. Fox, ed. *Modern Jewish Ethics.* Columbus, Ohio: Ohio State University, 1975.

INDEX OF PRINCIPAL NAMES

INDEX OF PRINCIPAL SUBJECTS

VITA

John Elias, Ed. D., is a Professor in two Graduate Schools at Fordham University, New York City: the School of Religion and Religious Education and the School of Education. He is the author of *Philosophical Foundations of Adult Education, Foundations and Practice of Adult Religious Education, Psychology and Religious Education*, and *Studies in Theology and Education*. Dr. Elias has written and lectured extensively in the United States and Britain on ethics and moral education as well as on related topics.

See Review in Religious Education
Vol. 84, No 4, Fall 89, pp 633-34.